BEAMS OF LIGHT

EARLY METHODISM

IN AMERICA.

CHIEFLY DRAWN FROM THE DIARY, LETTERS, MANUSCRIPTS,
DOCUMENTS, AND ORIGINAL TRACTS OF THE
REV. EZEKIEL COOPER.

COMPILED BY

GEO. A. PHOEBUS, D.D.

NEW YORK:
PHILLIPS & HUNT.
CINCINNATI:
CRANSTON & STOWE.
1887.

Printing Statement:

Due to the very old age and scarcity of this book, many of the pages may be hard to read due to the blurring of the original text, possible missing pages, missing text and other issues beyond our control.

Because this is such an important and rare work, we believe it is best to reproduce this book regardless of its original condition.

Thank you for your understanding.

PREFACE.

THIS work was written for the purpose of giving the student of the history of the Methodist Episcopal Church facts concerning her early years that are essential to a clear understanding of them. These facts have been gathered from the documents, letters, tracts, and diary of that venerable man of God, Rev. Ezekiel Cooper, and after his decease transmitted to his nephew and heir-at-law, the honored Rev. Ignatius T. Cooper, D.D., late of Camden, Delaware, who held them until April, 1884, when he was called to join his uncle in the courts above, leaving the papers hereof spoken in the hands of his son, Ezekiel W. Cooper, M.D., also of Camden, who now holds them in possession.

Desiring to furnish the reader with such state-

ments as are vested with full authority, the character
and standing of these Christian ministers should be
acknowledged and recorded.

Of the uncle, Rev. Ezekiel Cooper, Rev. Daniel
Curry, D.D., LL.D., has spoken in the Introduction,
and frequent allusion is made to him in the volume
now submitted to the public. Of Rev. Ignatius T.
Cooper, D.D., by whose kindness the writer received
and held the documents for several years, it may be
said: He was a man of God; for fifty-five years led
the life of a pure and devoted Christian; for twenty-
five years served the Methodist Episcopal Church in
the effective work of the itinerancy, was an able and
impressive preacher, a wise counsellor, to whom was
intrusted the responsibility of legislation in the
Church of his choice, and was, as his biographer
truthfully remarked, " A man of unbending principle, of positive convictions, and uttered his sentiments fearlessly, but with a dignity becoming the
lofty character which he sustained. A warm advocate of temperance, and every progressive movement
in moral reform, he was unswerving in his devotion

to the cause he espoused." He fell asleep in Jesus
on the 12th of April, 1884, in the seventy-ninth year
of his age.

These papers, falling into his hands, were religiously preserved, and were loaned to the compiler of
this volume, who in order to obtain them was led to
give a written obligation to preserve them undefiled,
and to return them without loss of any one of them
when called upon to do so.

Among the facts drawn from these papers are
some that give proof to the Methodist of the
present day that the early days of our Church were
not altogether free from care and anxiety in relation to the harmony of the preachers and laymen.
This is illustrated in the disunion in Philadelphia,
which caused the removal of the Book Concern from
that city; the disharmony at Lynn, Mass., which led
to the stationing of one of the preachers in a field of
labor unheard of in the annals of the Church before
or since—Rev. Jesse Lee being appointed to the
Province of Maine, and Lynn, Mass. Other instances are also recited, but none without reliable

testimony to account for the causes producing the disorder.

The reader will also find valuable letters, from our Church Fathers, that have not hitherto been published, and in their perusal will gain knowledge of the various interests of the Church, her cares, sacrifices, triumphs, and prospects in those early days. Among them he will find letters from Bishops Asbury and Coke, and others; and by them all may be edified and instructed. G. A. P.

CONTENTS.

CHAPTER I.

EARLY LIFE AND EXPERIENCE OF EZEKIEL COOPER.

CHAPTER II.

CAROLINE, KENT, AND LONG ISLAND CIRCUITS, 1784–1786.

CHAPTER III.

EAST JERSEY CIRCUIT, 1786.

CHAPTER IV.

TRENTON CIRCUIT, 1787.

CHAPTER V.

METHODISM IN BALTIMORE, MD., 1788, 1789.

CHAPTER VI.

METHODISM IN ANNAPOLIS, MD., 1789, 1790.

CHAPTER VII.

METHODISM IN ALEXANDRIA, VA., 1791, 1792.

CHAPTER VIII.

THE METHODIST EPISCOPAL CHURCH IN CHARLESTON, S. C., AND IN NEW ENGLAND, 1792, 1793.

CHAPTER IX.

THE METHODIST EPISCOPAL CHURCH IN NEW ENGLAND, CONTINUED, 1793, 1794.

CHAPTER X.

METHODISM IN NEW YORK AND VICINITY, 1794, 1795.

CHAPTER XI.

METHODISM IN PHILADELPHIA AND VICINITY, 1796.

CHAPTER XII.

THE METHODIST EPISCOPAL CHURCH IN WILMINGTON, DEL., AND VICINITY, 1797, 1798.

CHAPTER XIII.

THE METHODIST BOOK CONCERN.

CHAPTER XIV.

THE METHODIST EPISCOPAL CHURCH IN PHILADELPHIA,
1799-1804.

CHAPTER XV.

PRESIDING ELDERSHIP IN THE METHODIST EPISCOPAL CHURCH.

ADDENDA.

INTRODUCTION.

THE history of the rise and early growth of Methodism in America is still very largely unwritten. Materials from which to construct such a history are as yet sufficiently abundant, though, no doubt, very much that once existed and might have been made available has perished beyond recovery, and what still remains of original information, whether in the form of personal reminiscences or of written documents, letters, memoirs, and crude semi-official papers, is rapidly perishing. The time for enriching that history from the recollections of individuals has very nearly passed away, with the generation that lived among its events and participated in its acts; but there are still living those who were, in their early lifetimes, the contemporaries and associates of those who made that history, and these heard from their own lips the stories of their labors and successes, their trials and their victories. From that resource, no doubt, valuable contributions of original historical information might be obtained were the proper efforts made for obtaining it; and here, too, there is no time for delay, for the few survivors of the second generation of American Methodists are rapidly passing away. The dew of its youth is being rapidly exhaled by the strong light and heat of the midday of that wonderful something called Methodism, and there is need that what still remains shall be seized and secured while it is yet practicable.

Happily for the interest of our historical inquiries, there still remain in existence and within easy reach valuable collections of private papers, letters, diaries, and records of personal observations and experiences, which contain an untold amount of the best kind of historical data. The art of letter-writing was in vogue, down to the earlier years of the present century, to an extent that is now but faintly appreciated. People were then accustomed to put their thoughts and feelings into their private epistolary correspondence in a manner that has since passed quite out of fashion; and the letters so written and received were usually carefully filed away, and kept as choice treasures. Many of these collections of old letters written by the Methodist fathers are still in existence, awaiting the examination of the real students of original Methodist annals. The keeping of personal journals was also a prevalent practice, in which, scattered through masses of introspective self-confessions, may be found nuggets of historical facts, which, if wrought into the history of those times, would explain many a hitherto inexplicable puzzle, and illuminate many an obscure historical entanglement, and correct not a few misconceptions. Very much of this kind of material that once existed has, no doubt, perished beyond recovery; but still very much remains, and it may be hoped that by the efforts of associations, and of individual collectors, most that still remains will be saved from destruction, and that all further compilers of Methodist histories will make free use of these original witnesses.

The volume to which this Introduction is prefixed is the result of an exploration, by a competent student of Methodist *oriʒinese*, among the papers of one of the ablest and best of the first generation of the American Methodist preachers; one who, without ostentation or design, has left on record for the use of later generations a record of the things which he certainly knew, and in which he was himself a not inconsiderable actor. Ezekiel Cooper was a great man in early Methodism, and his greatness, under God's grace, was all his own, and not the accidental outgrowth of official position. As soon as the Methodist body took organic form, he became one of its itinerant preachers, and after its incipient organization by the "Christmas Conference" he became both an active co-operator in its evangelistic propagandism and an effective directing agent in shaping its economy. In both these directions his influence was clearly manifest from the beginning, and the expressions which he helped to give to both the spirit and the form of the then infant Church have, no doubt, been perpetuated, and American Methodism is now, in its best features, what it is because such hands and hearts as his were upon it during its formative stages. Without a trace of fanaticism in his nature, he united the devotedness of a saint with the zeal of an apostle; and while in the presence of rightful authority he was obedient as a son in the Gospel, he never failed to assert his own manhood, nor consented to sink the rights of the individual in deference to the demands of official greatness.

Students of ecclesiastical history have found out

that in the conflicts of the early Church the right
was not always the exclusive possession of either
party, and some have come to believe that the sig-
natures of "orthodoxy" and "catholicity," in the
times of the Fathers and the early councils, were simply the records of the greater number of votes in a
nonrepresentative body, or the personal preferences
of certain individuals of commanding places or per-
sonalities. So, too, it is becoming more and more evi-
dent, as the oldest Methodist authorities are brought
to the light, that many things in our Church's economy now claimed to belong to the essence of the system, so that to call them in question is stigmatized
as disloyalty, and to fail to sustain them must be
accounted as infidelity to the system, were not
originally favored by many—apparently the most—
of the best men of the golden age of primitive Methodism.   As there were divisions and contentions
among the apostles, and factions in the apostolic
Churches, so the first Methodist bishops were not
always of one mind, and each had his friends and
supporters among those who served under them.
But they were good men, and could yield their own
preferences for the sake of the common interest, or
else they could win forbearance, with even unwarrantable self-assumption, by greater zeal and more abundant labors and sacrifices.

These pages, and especially Mr. Cooper's accounts
of his own methods as an evangelist and the success
that attended his labors, are full of suggestions in respect to the great questions of bringing the Gospel, in
its saving efficacy, to those that are farthest from these
things. It is seen in these accounts that, first of all,

he went to the people, wherever they were found, and delivered to them the message of the Gospel. The available appliances for prosecuting evangelistic work were the most meager that can be conceived. There were very few houses of worship of any kind, and these were usually closed to the Methodist itinerants; nor were there other places in which considerably large congregations could be accommodated. In warm weather their services were sometimes held in the open air; but in most cases private dwellings were utilized as preaching-places, and for all other forms of their religious exercises. The disadvantages of this condition of things were perhaps not so serious as they may seem, for the companies so gathered were usually small, and the people were not accustomed to better accommodations. The coming of the preacher broke in upon the monotony of the rural hamlet or neighborhood, and the novelty of a "preaching" sufficed to bring the people together. But the preacher had to contribute every thing to the service, and the reading and singing, not less than the praying and the preaching, devolved on him alone. It appears, also, that, as to its matter, the preaching was of the plainest character, without any labored expositions, or arguments to prove the truth of Christianity, or even an intimation that there could be any possible doubts or questionings respecting the things declared; the simple verities of the Gospel were stated; men were told that they were sinners, and that the wages of sin was death; that Christ came into the world to save them from sin and death, and that all who would might come to him and be saved; while in the back-ground rose to view the fearful menace of eternal death for all who should neglect this great salvation. And these things were told not as a formal message, but rather as an earnest plea, with urgent exhortations, made all the more persuasive by the abiding expectation in the heart of the preacher that the word would not fail of its proper results. They expected to succeed, and spake and acted accordingly, and they were not often entirely disappointed. In the present widely changed condition of things it may not be possible to reproduce these proceedings, and so to achieve like results; and yet it may be questioned whether the prevailing methods of preaching are any improvement upon those of earlier times, and the want of the expectation of speedy results is itself an occasion of unsuccess.

Another thing, quite remarkable, seen in these memoranda, is the action of these preachers in respect to slave-holding. The standing declaration of the Discipline committed the Church to "the extirpation of the great evil of slavery;" and among its practical regulations was a scheme looking to the emancipation of all slaves owned by the members of the Church. The preachers, acting in harmony with the law of the Church, set themselves actively to denounce slave-holding as contrary to the spirit of Christianity, and entirely incompatible with the religious life to which all Methodists were, by their profession, consecrated. Their testimony was, in most cases, accepted by the people as just and right, and not a few in Maryland and some in Virginia emancipated their slaves— some at once and others gradually. The Fourth of July, 1790, fell on Sunday; and the occasion was used for the public expression of the sentiment of the Church against slavery, as at once opposed to the Gospel and to the spirit of American liberty. Of course some opposed, but the prevailing sentiment of the people in and out of the Church was favorable. Mr. Cooper tells of the responses made to the declaration of the preachers, which were such as to show that the convictions of the people were at first with them. But with the abatement of the public zeal in favor of freedom and equality for all men, and the growth of cupidity and worldliness among professed Christians, the testimony against "the great evil" became fainter, and the law of the Church was suspended, or made practically inoperative, till at length the Church was rent asunder by it, and at last deliverance came at once to the Church and the country in the throes of civil war, and with a terrible baptism of blood—a fearful lesson concerning the folly of tampering with wrong for the sake of temporary advantages.

It is well known to all who have examined the early history of the Methodist Episcopal Church found in original records, instead of trusting wholly to its prepared histories, that there were not infrequently wide differences of view among its great leaders, which sometimes occasioned earnest conflicts, and in more than a single case resulted in disastrous divisions and permanent alienations. And of all such disturbing causes, those relating to the power of making the appointments of the preachers to their several fields of labor has, no doubt, been the most active and persistent, for it continues to the present time. Mr. Wesley claimed and exercised absolute authority in the assignment of their fields to his "helpers," as he had the *legal* right to do, since he had himself created the system, and each preacher had accepted his place with a clear understanding of its condition. The *expediency* of such a method would be a proper subject of inquiry in the proper place, and it may be said, in passing, that perhaps no other method could have been successfully used, in the then existing conditions. It can scarcely be doubted, however, that in his later years, when the number of the preachers had become large—and among them were found not a few able and judicious men, whose counsels, if called for, could not have failed to be reliable—he might have lightened his own burdens and greatly strengthened his "connection," by sharing his autocratic powers with them. Mr. Asbury, both from his admiration for Mr. Wesley's wisdom, which seemed to him to be worthy of the closest following, and no doubt from his own instincts, wished to hold the appointing power in his own hands exclusively, and this he did, consenting to share it only with those whom the General Conference placed by his side with equal authority with himself. Perhaps even here he would have preferred that his associates in the superintendency should have been constituted his suffragans, rather than his equals and co-ordinates. These high claims were not always quietly acceded to ; they are still submitted to only under protest by thousands of earnest and loyal Methodist ministers, who prefer to submit their own preference, and if needful, to forego their natural rights, rather than disturb the peace of the Church, and so hinder the work of saving souls and edifying the body of Christ.

Mr. Asbury's authority as a leader was also very much strengthened by the fact that he used it, not for his own ease or emolument, but solely for the promotion of his great work, and that while he laid heavy burdens upon the preachers, he did not spare himself, but labored and suffered beyond almost any others.

But from the beginning there were complaints, and widespread dissatisfactions, and efforts toward some modification of the power of the episcopacy in making the appointments, which was certainly favored by some of the ablest and truest fathers of the Church, including Dr. Coke and others of the early bishops. But the superintendency, at an early day, fell almost exclusively into Mr. Asbury's hands; the preachers were fully occupied with their evangelistic work, and there was at first no General Conference, and later, none well-organized and constituted, and administrative affairs were left to drift on, and to become solidified in their form by usage and common consent. This tendency also became intensified and its assumptions confirmed by the very opposition made to it; as in the case of O'Kelly, who, finding his not unreasonable demands denied, separated himself and his adherents from the body, and of course their cause was sacrificed by their violence and impatience. The readers of the following pages will see what were Mr. Cooper's views of this and other questions of Church polity and administration; and they will see in his conduct a noble example of fidelity to the Church, even when his own preferences were held in abeyance.

The book herewith now given to the public is fittingly entitled *Light on Early Methodism*, for it

opens a window that looks out upon scenes of which
the Church has had but very imperfect knowledge,
and which, as partially disclosed, have not always appeared in altogether truthful aspects. We have had
our heroic histories—stories of sacrifices and successes
—worthily achieved by heroic men ; but the time has
come for taking broader views, and for properly esti-
mating the purposes and the actions of those who,
under God, laid the foundation and began the con-
struction of the goodly edifice of organic Methodism ;
and as that structure is still in process of building,
the things here brought into view may be useful in
the prosecution of that work : and only good will
come from such efforts if they be made in the spirit
of devotion to the work of God and of loyalty to
Methodism which actuated him who stands forth as
the most prominent figure in these pages.

                                        D. C.

NEW YORK, *June,* 1887.

LIGHT

ON

EARLY METHODISM IN AMERICA.

CHAPTER I.

EARLY LIFE AND EXPERIENCE OF EZEKIEL COOPER.

THE history of the Methodist Episcopal Church has been carefully, eloquently, and, in the main, accurately given by her historians, especially by Nathan Bangs, D.D., and Abel Stevens, LL.D., and the library of no Methodist can be complete without them. But there are historic data, to which they had not access, that disclose facts of such importance as to render those valuable works deficient. The design of the writer is to supply the deficiency by giving to the reader facts gathered from the diary, documents, and letters, written and preserved by the venerable Rev. Ezekiel Cooper and his heirs at law.

The period embraced in the examination is, chiefly, from the year 1784 to 1809, and, as far as is practicable, the words of the authors quoted will be set forth as written by them. An outline of the early life and experience of Mr. Cooper is first in order.

In 1791, at the request of Bishop Asbury, he wrote,

A Short Account of the Life and Experience of Ezekiel Cooper. He says therein :

I was born in Caroline County, in the State of Maryland, on the 22d day of February, in the year of our Lord 1763. My parents, Richard Cooper and Ann, his wife, were plain people, in easy and plentiful circumstances in life. They were hospitable to strangers and benevolent to the indigent. They were of the Church of England by profession, into which they had all their children initiated in infancy by the ordinance of baptism. I was raised a member of that Church, as were all my brothers and sisters. But, sorrowful to relate, we were all too great strangers to any thing truly spiritual. We had a name to live while we were dead ; professing Christ, but in works denying him. Religion in those days, in our parts, appeared to be universally neglected. It was almost a miracle to find a man of real piety. The land truly mourned by reason of wickedness and the neglect of religion. Very few knew how to teach their neighbors, and those who knew very seldom attempted it ; but we were all members of the Church.

I was early put to school, where I made the usual progress in learning. Here I thought, to be like some other boys, I would learn to swear, and attempted it a few times ; but such remorse of conscience seized me that I renounced it forever, and ever after shuddered at the crime. I was, from my earliest recollection, remarkably attached to truth both in myself and others. I never could knowingly give way to lying, in jest or any other way, and felt a contempt of it in others. The principles of injustice, evil-speaking, slandering, etc., I ever abhorred ; also what were generally called the profane and scandalous evils of every kind, I flew from with indignation. I believe this was principally owing to my mother's fixing, by her instruction, in my tender mind, a prejudice against those things. She was very moral—what the world calls "a very good woman"—and had, I believe, a measure of the fear of God before her eyes. Her attention was particularly paid to the external conduct of her children ; she would always correct profaneness in any of them, and restrain us from what to her appeared wrong.

Though I was thus kept within tolerable bounds, yet I pursued many things that led me on in the way to death and hell. Many tempers in my heart and practices in my life showed clearly my depraved state, and that I was unfit to die and go to judgment. I believe a proud spirit was one of my most besetting sins through all my youth. My mother would frequently say, "Ah! Ezekiel, you are the proudest child I've got." I dearly loved my mother and truly feared her, by which principles I was led to carefully avoid giving her displeasure. This was a means of considerable restraint upon me. Nothing affected me more than to grieve her. I was also ambitious of securing her approbation as a dutiful child, which I obtained.

Very early in life I had divine impressions, and my mind was frequently drawn in a tender manner to fear, love, and serve my Maker; but I knew scarcely any thing about the matter, more than I would have awful thoughts of God, of another world, of death, etc. The first people that I remember taking notice of as a good people were the Nicholites, or Reformed Quakers. But I had no conception of a change of nature, or the new birth. I concluded that their religious life was by the force of natural resolution not to give way to sin, but to attend to their religious duties; I thought they all had the same desires or propensities to evil that other people had. This was my ignorance, not knowing the things of God, nor the power of grace in changing the heart.

It was early in my youth, about my thirteenth year, when I first had an opportunity of hearing the Methodist preachers. This was at their first coming into our neighborhood. One came to our house, Mr. Freeborn Garrettson, whose life and conversation made a remarkable impression on my mind. He obtained liberty to preach the next day, but I recollect that my mother was very uneasy that he came at that time, because it was muster-day in one of our old fields, when two captains met together with their companies on Saturdays. For that reason she wanted to put the preaching off; however, it was fixed and the neighborhood notified. When the hour of preaching came on the captains marched their company into the yard and grounded their arms under two large shade-trees, and the people in general heard very civilly and decently. My conviction was more and more increased. I felt the drawings of the Spirit powerfully in my soul. I wished to be a Christian, felt much concerned that I was not as good as I ought to be, and resolved to try and be good. But O! I knew not what to do, and had no instructor among men. My father at this time was dead, and my mother married to her second husband, who was a violent enemy to the Methodists as a people, who, as he supposed, were enemies to the country. Preaching was not continued in the neighborhood near our house, so that I rarely heard preaching; neither had I any opportunity of conversing with any religious people or receiving any human aid whatever; but, on the contrary, there were many things to draw me from my concern and to lead me into vanity, which in time succeeded.

During this concern, which lasted for some time, I used to converse freely with one of our Negro men, who was also concerned upon the subject. But he knew no more than myself; we could neither instruct the other in the nature of true religion. O, how I lamented my state! But I kept it all to myself, excepting the Negro man above mentioned. My secret mourning was, O that I was a Christian, and a righteous person, like the preacher—that servant of God. I believed the truth of that doctrine, the knowledge of sins forgiven, the witness of acceptance with God, etc., but how it was I could not tell nor conjecture.

In the neighborhood the people made a great noise about these new preachers, who were preaching up a strange doctrine, as they called it. Some would positively have it they were the false prophets. All manner of evil was busily circulated, to and fro, concerning them. It grieved me that those whom I believed innocent men should be thus slandered. But so it is; the most righteous are generally the hatred and scorn of wicked men. My love was very great toward the preachers. I thought them to be the holy ones of the earth.

Once I rode with J. H. and S. M. some distance as they were going to their preaching place. One of them fell into conversation with me about my soul. I was glad of it, but did not know what to say. I told him that I wished to be good. He gave me counsel which I hoped at that time to take. Before we parted he told me to read Eccl. xii, 1, which I did on my return home; where I found, "Remember now thy Creator in the days of thy youth, while the evil days come not, nor the years draw nigh when thou shalt say, I have no pleasure in them." The reading of those words and the conversation of the preacher rested upon my mind for a long time; indeed I never expect to forget it, in time or eternity. I believed the truth, but could not comprehend it. The mystery of godliness was great. I wanted a Philip, like the eunuch of old, to teach me, but I had no one. I wished further instruction, but could not get it. My cry was, "O that I knew the work of God! O that I was a child of God!" I was somewhat like Samuel; the Lord called, but I knew not the nature of his voice. I heard, but did not understand. By and by, having no opportunities, no preaching, no means of furtherance in the ways of truth, I began to grow cold and careless, and was by degrees led captive into wickedness.

When I reflect on my condition I sensibly feel pity for those who are in the predicament in which I was—wanting help and not being able to obtain it. I became quite careless, but often remembered those seasons of visitation with a troubled heart. Some time after this regular preaching was had in the neighborhood, but none of our family ever went, unless there was some particular meeting or burying. Indeed, we seldom knew the day of preaching, though within a few miles; such was our carelessness. I was now traveling on cheerfully in the way to eternal sorrow, pursuing my sin and vanity against the dictates of my conscience; though I must observe that the continual remonstrances of conscience, drawn from reason and Scripture, was a means of deterring me from many evils which otherwise I should, doubtless, have run into. My state was truly unhappy: I had fled from the Shepherd and Bishop of my soul, cast off his fear, was wandering in the wilderness, and knew not whither I was going, but felt conscious of the fact that I was not going to heaven. My propensity led me into young company, where my mind was, more and more, set on vanity and levity. I continued to go on in this way for four or five years.

In my greatest folly I felt a particular love for religious people, and watched their conduct very attentively. When in their presence I always felt strangely, and was almost afraid to speak or do any thing lest they should see cause to reprove me for wrong-doing. I looked for something very extraordinary in their life and conversation; if I saw any of them to be light or trifling in the least, I was ready to doubt their Christianity, believing that true religion made men holy, solemn, and devoted, that it delivered them from levity and from all unguardedness of word and action. I may here observe, that like many I feared the people of God more than God himself, inasmuch as I would do things in His presence that I would not do in theirs. However, I rarely went among them.

In the year 1780, being then in my eighteenth year, I ran into vanity more than ever. My greatest delight was to be where I was the most hurt; but now my race of sin was almost run. In the fall of the year I was so clearly convinced of my duty and danger, by a sermon which I heard, that I covenanted with God to set out once more to seek the way to life. There was something peculiar in my re-alarm, namely: A certain preacher, whom the people, generally, thought to be a great speaker, was to preach near us. Our family seldom went to preaching, but on this day several concluded to go. In the morning, about nine o'clock, I got vexed by some circumstance in the family, and resolved not to go to preaching that day; but when the time drew nigh, mother sent one of the servants for me to come and go with them. Here I was in a strait: was afraid to refuse, lest I should disoblige her, which I was unwilling to do. At length I submitted to go. While I sat and heard the word, the thought came very plainly to me that my repugnance to attend the preaching was the devil's work. That day the way of life was made so plain to my understanding that I formed a determination, by God's grace, to seek the salvation of my soul. It appeared to me that if I now refused I should never, hereafter, be able to return. I saw that hell was my doom forever unless I embraced the hope set before me. Now appeared "the acceptable time," and "day of salvation." I found a great struggle, but the sound through my mind continued, "Turn to God or bear his wrath." The world flesh, and devil were strongly against me, to draw me back from my purpose, to charm me into the neglect of duty, and to fill me with levity and the desire of company; but considering nothing more uncertain than life, and that the door of mercy might be shut, I resolved, "God help me, and I will serve Thee!" I took to reading the Scriptures, and to private prayer. I kept my resolution and concern to myself, being ashamed, as yet, to let any body know that I intended to be religious. But I found it could not be kept secret; that I should lose my concern unless I was bold and open. Various were my difficulties; I was like a ship upon the tempestuous ocean, at times almost overwhelmed with the billows of temptation.

I frequently got off my guard when among my young acquaintances; their influence led me to do that which grieved the Spirit, and filled me with condemnation. At length I saw I must give up my gay company or be prevented from going on in religion, and lose my soul at last. Thus I continued in an unsettled frame of mind until—at the time called Christmas—finding that the worldly companion-ship of my young acquaintances led me into unguarded and light conversation, I promised to leave such company. I then sat down in a serious pensive frame, and began to reflect upon my conviction, until I felt as guilty as a criminal at the bar. My trouble was like a flood, and my mind as the restless sea. That Scripture came to me, "If our heart condemn us, God is greater." I felt condemned, indeed, and wished myself away. I thought: Hereafter I never, no never, will give way. But a thought returned, How often have you concluded thus? and the next time may be as this, and the time after as that, and so you go on another and another day. It was then pressed on my mind to break off at that time, and leave them and their ways. Here I had a severe struggle, while I sat in silence speaking to no one. At length I concluded it would be no harder then than at any other time to break through, so I arose to take my leave of the company. They appeared to be surprised at my sudden movement, and wished to know what was the matter, and the cause of my departure. I had not resolution enough to tell them plainly that I was intent upon bidding such company farewell for the future; but, in fact, such was my purpose. I was importuned very much to stay, but I could not consent to their entreaties. "Escape for thy life," seemed to be sounding in my ears. They were very little acquainted with the rending distress I had in my soul. I had a cup to drink and bread to eat which they thought but little of. I bade them a solemn and final farewell; resolving, God strengthening me, never more to shun the cross, but to be in earnest, and unreservedly to give myself to him and his service.

In January, 1781, I went to live with my brother-in-law, in Queen Anne County. Here I was as destitute of religious acquaintance as anywhere else. I associated with but few, as religious people there were at that time very scarce. Now I was set down by all as a Methodist; and was thought by some to be needlessly strict. I thought myself to be unworthy of a name or place among the people of God. I stood alone, without joining any society, having God alone for my help. I was diligent in searching the Scriptures, and in private prayer; my understanding in divine things increased, and the more clearly I saw the state of my own heart. For months I went bowed down in mourning before the Lord, believing there was mercy for me, but not knowing how to secure it. By night I walked the fields in meditation, and brokenness of heart; or, when all were sleeping, would frequently pour out my soul in supplication. In the spring and summer seasons I made the woods my constant resort, walking and meditating, or reading and praying, sometimes prostrate on my face.

I resolved that, if I never found mercy, I would die crying and seeking for it. The world appeared as nothing to me, now; I was dead to almost every desire but that of the "one thing needful." I stood some time in this condition, but about the middle of the summer I grew more slack in my diligence and my concern decreased. Providentially, under my most careless and declining state, I had a sermon book put into my hand, in the reading of which my fears were alarmed, and, if possible, my distress was greater than ever. I now renewed my covenant, and set out with redoubled diligence, and nevermore rested until I found Christ formed in my soul "the hope of glory."

Between this last stir and my deliverance my sorrows were overwhelming. My heart was ready to burst asunder with inexpressible anguish. For several days I seemed careless about the things of time, scarcely ate or drank with any pleasure; I lay down and rose up, went out and came in, with my head bowed down under an intolerable burden. At length my bitterness of soul rose to its extremity. I was truly weary and heavy-laden. I used to prostrate myself on my face upon the floor and ground. My pain of mind was more than I knew how to express.

One day, as I was walking alone in the woods, I felt great encouragement. I knelt down and prayed fervently. Presently I had an opening to my mind of the infinite fullness of Christ, and of the willingness of the Father, through his Son, to receive me into his favor. I had such confidence in the merits of Christ and the mercy of God that I laid hold of the promise, felt my burden remove, and a flood of peace, love, and joy break forth in my soul. I was now enabled to call Christ Lord, by the Holy Ghost sent down from heaven. I am assured, to the present moment, that at that time the Lord forgave me all my sins, and owned me for his adopted child. My heart was enlarged toward all mankind. I was ready to conclude that I could convince any or every body of the great truths and necessity of religion. I wanted an opportunity to warn the world, especially a number of my irreligious friends. But I found them not to be so easily convinced. "I work a work," said God, "which ye will in nowise believe though a man declare it unto you."

It was not long before the devil came and powerfully tempted me to doubt my conversion and regeneration. Under these doubts I labored for some time; however, I felt the deliverance from guilt, from the fear of death and hell, a hatred to all sin, and an unspeakable joy in my soul. O how I needed the help arising from Christian communion! But I had it not. I resolved to form acquaintance with the Methodists, and to join society as soon as I conveniently could; to open my mind to them, hoping to be fully satisfied, yea or nay, when I heard their experience of the work of grace upon their souls. During the fall and winter I was considerably among the wicked, and, consequently, exposed to trials of divers kinds. I had resolution to reprove them for evil, and not to give way to their folly. My soul was grieved at evil, when or wherever I saw it.

In the spring I joined society. I found it to be a great blessing, and wondered that I had put it off so long. I believe it was a cunning device of the devil; the neglect had well-nigh proved very injurious to me, as I believe it had to many. Class meeting I found to be one of the most profitable meetings I attended. We had but a small class, in a new preaching place, but the Lord frequently refreshed us with his presence. I believe that I daily advanced in the divine life, was more and more established in the truth, and enjoyed a greater and more steadfast confidence in God.

My mind became much impressed that it was my duty to warn sinners to "flee from the wrath to come." I suppressed this thought at first, fearing it might not be a call from God. The more I resisted the more I was concerned to publicly declare the counsel of God among men. I used, frequently, to pray in the prayer and class-meetings, and had great happiness in so doing. The brethren, at length, made it a constant practice to put me to prayer among them. My soul was daily alive to God; the time between meetings appeared long—I was impatient for the time to come when we should go up to worship before the Lord. Frequently I felt a great willingness, and almost wished, to be with Christ in glory. I was bold in reproving, and zealous in inviting sinners in private to turn to the Lord and seek the salvation of their souls. My earnestness in this soon had such an effect that it was seldom that any of my acquaintances would sin within my sight or hearing. This was a particular satisfaction to me, for sin always grieved me to the heart.

My exercises about preaching increased very fast, until at length they brought about a real distress of soul. I consulted the most experienced friends, and opened my mind to the preachers, both local and traveling. They advised me to make a trial of my gifts. Brother Freeborn Garrettson, under whom I was first of all awakened, traveled our circuit about the time of my greatest exercises on this subject. He appointed me to be class-leader at friend P.'s, in Talbot County, about four miles from the class I had been in before, in Caroline. I found precious times in meeting the class, the Lord highly favoring us with his presence. I still neglected speaking in public as an exhorter or preacher, though a number of friends advised me to take up the cross; but it was so very great to me that I feared and trembled at the thought. At length I felt threatening impressions, as that God would enter into correction if I did not obey—that some judgment would befall me if I refused to do the work appointed by the Master. I feared that my gifts were not adequate to the task; that my abilities were so small and the work so great that I

3

doubted whether I could ever preach the Gospel of God. Then this was applied, "Am not I He that sendeth by whom I will send? Dost thou doubt my promise? Open thy mouth and I will fill it. Go forth and warn them from me, and declare salvation in my name." My uneasiness and anxiety of soul grew to a degree greater by far than I can describe. I put off the duty from time to time till I feared God would give me up to the devil to be bruised and devoted to misery. I fell into a languishing state of body, and a dull frame of soul. I wore away to a mere skeleton; many thought I would die. I continued in this low condition for several months, being incapable of any business.

It was forcibly impressed on my mind that this was a judgment of chastisement from God. I then entered into covenant that if the Lord would restore me to my former state of body and mind, I would preach, provided I felt the same impressions to it.

In January, 1784, I began to recover. As my bodily strength returned, my engagedness of soul returned; also, my impressions to call upon my fellow-creatures to turn to God.

I was now more than ever confirmed in the impression that it was the will of God that I should preach. My concern for souls was very great; my love encircled all mankind; I wanted to see men come home to God. I wept, as it were, between the porch and the altar; watered my pillow by night with tears, and went sorrowing all the day. I thought I could lay down my life, would it prove a means of turning others to the Lord. I was always sorrowing, yet rejoicing, and growing in grace. My peace of soul and love increased, and, as my love increased, I felt still more distressed for sinners who were "in the gall of bitterness, and the bond of iniquity." I reproved whoever sinned before me, and improved every opportunity of recommending religion to all with whom I had intercourse. Very frequently I was among the opposers of religion. We used to have many altercations upon the truth of the Methodist doctrine; but the Lord enabled me to support and prove the truth thereof from Scripture. It was my constant care to handle all such disputes in mildness and love, and I found it proved much more effectual in convincing and informing the opponents.

It was strange to think how I still put off speaking in public after that I had suffered so much in mind from that quarter, and was fully convinced of its being a duty. The cross! the cross! To stand forth, in the capacity of a gospel teacher, before a concourse of people, and warn them to flee from the wrath to come, seemed more than I could stand under. However, I prayed earnestly to God for strength, for power to take it up, lest, through neglect, I should bring upon myself swift destruction. At length, being encouraged by one of the preachers with whom I had been for some days, I ventured, after him, one Sabbath, to open my mouth in testimony of the gospel truths. Several hundred were in the assembly; it was at Brother Thomas's chapel. I spoke but briefly, and trembled under the cross. However, the Lord gave me matter and words to utter his counsel. I spoke again that afternoon at Brother M.'s, when I had more liberty, and spoke twice as long. The Lord attended the few hints to several hearts; a number wept considerably. I found great joy and satisfaction in thus submitting to speak for God, though it was not long before I was tempted that I had probably done hurt. However, I again, for a few times, spoke after others of our preachers in different places. I never attempted to have an appointment made for myself, feeling too much diffidence; nor at any appointment did I attempt to take a text until I went on the circuit. I believe I never spoke more than eight or ten times, at most, and then after some one else, until you (Bishop Asbury) prevailed with me to travel.

It is due to the memory of Ezekiel Cooper, that the above outline be given to the Church served by him for more than sixty years. He was one of the most eminent among the Methodist fathers, and, as will be seen in the further perusal of these pages, is entitled to the veneration of all who love the Methodist Episcopal Church. While no attempt is made herein to give a history of his life and work, yet he is so closely connected with the life and work of the Church that his name will appear, and his acts be recited, in almost every department of the Church's expansion and field of her operation. He has left to us not only documents that the Church will treasure up with gladness, but a personal history that will blend him with the Church as a husband with a spouse. To-day, where he is known, his name is as ointment poured forth.

CHAPTER II.

CAROLINE, KENT, AND LONG ISLAND CIRCUITS.   1784-1786.

IN the preceding chapter we have found Mr. Cooper, after a severe experience, yielding to the calls of the Holy Spirit to preach the Gospel; we shall now follow him in his highly interesting description of the work upon which he entered, at the very period when . it was determined to organize the Methodist Episcopal Church in the United States of America. It will be seen, from the record given below, that at the same Quarterly Conference, on the same day in which it was decided to call the preachers together at Baltimore the ensuing Christmas-day to organize the said Church, he was appointed by Rev. Francis Asbury to travel his first circuit. The reader will find items of historic interest in connection with the Church on the Peninsula, at John Street Church, New York, and on Long Island; items, which, sometimes, will serve to supply the hiatus so frequently occurring in the account of our early church life, and bring to light the names and actions of the Christian men and women who adorned the Methodist circles of a hundred years ago.

In the beginning of his itinerant career Mr. Cooper kept a diary, from which quotations, duly credited, will be made. Speaking of his call into the itinerant field, and of his travels thereunder, he says:

In November, 1784, I went and rode with one of the preachers about a week, before quarterly meeting. I spoke while with him. He asked me if I would travel if Mr. Asbury wanted me? I told him I thought not; for it appeared to me, that I was not capable of taking a circuit; and said but little more, having little thought of traveling at that time.   However, at quarterly meeting, at Barratt's Chapel, Del., Mr. Francis Asbury, our superintendent, was inquiring among the preachers "if they knew of any young speaker in the circuit that would travel."   One of them mentioned my name; and they sent for me to come unto them, which I did, and Mr. Asbury desired that I should go on Caroline Circuit and make a trial.   I consented: and thought if I could not stand it I could go home again.   So I got in readiness, and went on the circuit the 20th of November, 1784, and got to my appointment, at Johnstown, the next day, being Sunday, the 21st, and preached from 1 Peter iv, 17 : "What shall the end be of them that obey not the gospel of God?"   In the afternoon I buried a child.   In the evening I was much distressed in mind, but a word old Mr. Laws spoke unto me removed my trouble, and I found much peace.

The circuit on which Mr. Cooper had entered was very large, embracing St. Johnstown, Lewistown, White's Chapel, Abraham Collins's, Widow Hoskins's, Brown's Chapel, Ezekiel Smithers's, Thomas Layton's, Alexander Law's, Stradley's, and other places.   The service in Lewistown, Del., was in the Court-house, in which was assembled a large congregation to greet the young preacher.   Here, finding some that were disobedient to the rules of the Societies, he was subjected to the unpleasant task of "turning out" five or six disorderly members.   At Brown's Chapel a "black class" had been organized, separate from the "white class."   He remained on the circuit two months, during which time the Methodist Episcopal Church was organized.   He, in connection with the other preachers, was instructed to read to every congregation where he preached Mr. Wesley's *Circular Letter to Dr. Coke, Francis Asbury, and the Brethren in North America,* which he did. On Tuesday, January 25, 1785, the Rev. Hope Hull having arrived to be his successor, he prepared to go to his new field of labor, Kent Circuit, Md., having the

Rev. Richard Whatcoat as his colleague.   The following is from his diary:

Wednesday, January 26, 1785.   I set out for the circuit to which I **was** appointed — Kent Circuit.   I went as far as brother White's, and met the class.

Thursday, 27.   I rode to William Cannon's, on the circuit to which I was appointed, and preached, with great liberty, from 1 Tim. vi, 12.

Friday and Saturday.   Was very much cast down, and could hardly speak at all.

Sunday, 30.   Samuel Spry preached for me at Colonel William Hopper's.   I gave a short exhortation, but was still cast down.

Monday, 31.   I preached at William Ringold's, with tolerable comfort; I found much satisfaction, and got much encouragement to press on.   .

Tuesday, February 1, 1785.   I was at James Duhamel's and spake very short.   All this week through I felt but small freedom of speech.

Friday, 4.   I rode about eight miles after meeting, to meet brother Richard Whatcoat, who was appointed to travel the same circuit.   I was much affected while I was with him.

Saturday, 5.   I rode to Chestertown and met class.

Sunday, 6.   I preached in town at ten o'clock, with comfort; then rode about eight miles down Easter Neck and preached.   I lodged at John Hynson's, where my mind was comforted.

Monday, 7.   I rode to Easter Neck Island, where I went to the house of Mrs. Weeks—a happy old woman: it appears that she thinks but little of any thing except religion.   She has given up the world to her two daughters.

Tuesday, 8.   I preached on the Island, from John ix, 25.

Thursday, 10.   I preached in Quaker Neck; it was a happy day.

Friday, 11.   I met class at Worton Preaching-house, and rode down to the widow Frizbey's, where I found an agreeable family.

Sunday, 13.   I preached in Worton, from Gen. xxvi, 49.   My mind seemed quiet, but not so happy as I could have wished it.

Monday, 14.   I preached from Mal. iv, 1, at John Angier's. After preaching there were petition papers handed out for the people to subscribe; they were to send into the Assembly against poll-tax for the ministers of the Gospel.   I spoke against the tax, for I thought that they who preach the Gospel ought to be supported freely by their own society, and not to have a tax to force the people to pay, and, perhaps, some to have their goods confiscated on the account. For my part, I thought such things were not right.   I believe there was but one man who refused to sign the petition.

Tuesday. 15.   I found much peace with God, and liberty in speaking, at Francis Rutter's.

Thursday. 17.   I had a comfortable time in preaching at Frederictown on the Gospel Supper.

Friday. 18.   I preached at the Head of Sasafras, and then rode to Sudler's Cross -roads, lodged at Thomas Seager's, where I met class next morning.

Sunday, 20.   I preached at Mr. Pryor's with great liberty.

Monday and Tuesday.   Our Quarterly Meeting was held.   I found my mind backward and dull both days.   Brother Whatcoat preached two very great sermons.   In the evening, after our quarterly meeting was over, we had an opportunity of hearing Dr. Coke in Chestertown, and again next morning.

Having now given, in his own language, Mr. Cooper's account of his first tour through the circuit, a summary of his labors thereon is presented.   As on Caroline Circuit, so here, the colored people were formed into classes separate from the whites, though they were not until later reported in the Annual Conference Minutes in a separate column.   It is proper here, also, to state that the Minutes of the Annual Conferences for the year now under review give no account of the appointment either of Mr. Whatcoat or of Mr. Cooper to Kent Circuit.   The reason for this seeming omission probably is, that Mr. Whatcoat did not arrive in this country until some months after the close of the Annual Conferences of the year, and that Mr. Cooper, also, did not go out as a supply until after the date of those Conferences.   Hence neither could appear on the Minutes of those bodies.   The same is true, also, of Rev. Thomas Vasey, who also came to America with Coke and Whatcoat, by appointment of Mr. John Wesley.   Both Mr. Cooper and his elder, Rev. R. Whatcoat, were removed from Kent Circuit by the Conference of June

1785, the one being sent to Baltimore, Md., and the other to Long Island, N. Y.

Besides the preaching places mentioned above, as connected with Kent Circuit, meetings were held and classes established at Captain Kent's, Spaniard's Neck, Newtown, Smithers's, Richard Gold's, Kent Church (old), John Collins's, Georgetown Cross-roads, Gideon Clark's, Mr. Seaman's, Widow Featherstone's, Risden Plummer's; John Smith's, near Long Marsh; Mr. Bayley's, George Bolton's; Mr. Jerome's, near Rock Hall; Dudley Church (or chapel); Mrs. Woodland's; and other places whither the calls of duty pointed.

Toward the latter part of February the work of the Lord began to revive, and at various points on the circuit there were displays of power that rejoiced the hearts of the Methodists, but awakened the spirit of sarcasm and ridicule in those who opposed them. Under date of February 28, Mr. Cooper says:

> I preached in Spaniard's Neck. At night we had another meeting, and met the black class. We had a powerful time; under Brother Shears's prayer three or four fell to the floor under the power of God.

Speaking of the Society at John Angiers, he says:

> This class is more alive to God than any other in Kent County, according to my opinion.

Again:

> Sunday, April 24. At night, at Captain Kent's, we had a wonderful time. The power of God so fell upon the people that many cried out aloud; others fell dumbfounded to the floor. I had never before seen such a time among the people anywhere.

After giving several instances of conviction and conversion among the people, Mr. Cooper adds an account of the second quarterly meeting held during his stay on the circuit. It is as follows:

Sunday, May 15. Our quarterly meeting began. We had, I do expect, three thousand souls present. We held it at Dudley's Brick Preaching-house. The house was very large, but would not hold all the people. Some gathered under the trees, and so we had preaching in both places.

Monday, 16. Love-feast began at nine o'clock; the house was almost full of members of society. Then preaching, in and out of doors, began at twelve o'clock. Brother Whatcoat preached within, Brother Cloud outside. George Moore gave an exhortation in, and Harry, a black man, exhorted without. It was a good time.

With the close of the quarterly meeting Mr. Cooper prepared for his departure from the circuit, which, both to him and to the members of the Church, was serious and affecting. They were strongly attached to one another in the bonds of Christian love. During the period of his service among them one hundred and fifty persons had joined the Church, most of them having been converted within four months.

The Conference for 1785 was held in Baltimore, Md. It was opened on Wednesday, June 1, and was closed on the following Saturday. Mr. Cooper was admitted on trial, and was appointed to Long Island Circuit, whither he repaired as soon as was practicable, with a mind resigned to the work wherever he might be stationed.

In connection with his work on Long Island he was, also, during certain periods of the year, in the John Street Methodist Episcopal Church, of New York, as pastor. The meager history of that Church, as heretofore published for this period, decides us in giving an extended extract from Mr. Cooper's diary, both as inclusive of his labors on Long Island and in New York, in the year 1785; hence the following extract. He says:

Saturday. June 4. I left Baltimore; called at Mr. Gough's, and got dinner. From thence I rode to Abingdon. On the way I had to ride through a stream called Gunpowder, which was deep and very rapid. I found it hard work to sit on my horse and keep my feet dry. I think it was the worst place I ever rode through, and desire never to ride through such a place again, for it is really dangerous.

Sunday, 5. I was under the disagreeable necessity of traveling. Dr. Budd and I were to be in company as far as Philadelphia. We that night got to Mr. Hersey's, near the head of Elk. The doctor was very sick that night, but was better next morning.

Monday, 6. We arrived at James Barton's, near Chester, in Pennsylvania.

Tuesday, 7. We set out, and I forgot the second volume of Mr. Wesley's *Notes on the New Testament*, for which I was very sorry. I stopped in Philadelphia, and dined at Mr. Barker's, Market Street. I got to Burlington that night, and was kindly entertained at Mr. Sterling's.

Wednesday 8. Was such a day that I did not travel. At night I preached in the Court-house.

Thursday, 9. I set off again, having to ride a strange road all alone. I rode in peace of mind during the chief part of the day. When night began to come on I began to inquire for friends, but could not find any, of our Church, near the road. I was informed, however, that a Presbyterian minister lived at Cranberry, and was advised by one of his hearers to call upon him, which I did. I was used kindly, for which I esteem the Rev. Mr. Smith.

Friday, 10. I again journeyed on my way, and that night I got into New York about ten o'clock; but I knew nothing of the city, and the name of but one of our people therein, which was Mr. Stephen Sands. Providentially I fell in with a gentleman who conducted me to his house. He was in bed and asleep. I then began to think that I should have to go to a tavern for lodging, but, by knocking at the door, he was aroused, and received me kindly. I found much peace of mind to think that, so far from home, I had found such friends; but the spirit of truth reigning in the heart will cause union between strangers.

Saturday, 11. I was requested to stay in the city and preach until Brother Hagerty, who was appointed to New York, arrived; to which I consented, and found my mind much in peace with God.

Sunday, 12. I preached three times in our church, with a degree of satisfaction.

Monday, 13. I spent in reading, meditation, and prayer. In the evening I preached again, after which I was taken with much distress, which lasted until Wednesday night, when I found a comfortable time in preaching.

Thursday. 16. I preached in the Poor-house with liberty.

Friday, 17. I visited several friends in the city, andp reached at night.

Saturday, 18. Brother Hagerty got into York very early. I then went on Long Island with a tolerably composed mind. I lodged at James Harper's.

Having now arrived at his appointed field of labor he preached his first sermon at Jonathan Furman's, where one cried out aloud under a sense of his guilt and others were much affected. Thence he went to Searington, on Monday, and was assisted in proclaiming, "Who hath believed our report?" On Wednesday he rode through the Great Plains, saying of them, "I never saw such a place before. I am informed they are fifteen miles by five. The ground is level and clear, there being no trees standing on it, and but few houses."

Friday. 24. I preached at Nehemiah Brush's.

Saturday. 25. Led the class.

Wednesday, 29. I rode to Hempstead town. Mr. Eldred was very glad to see me come; had word given out for preaching to be at his house on the following day, at which time we had a small congregation.

Friday, July 1. I traveled about sixteen miles. By the way I called at Mr. Smith's, who had never heard a Methodist, and, I believe, was very much afraid of them. I opened to him many things about them which he had never heard before: but he had heard many things that were false. How often is this the case! The truth is left, while a false tale is told.

Sunday, July 3. I met the Newtown class very early in the morning. It was a dull time, but at ten o'clock the presence of the Lord was powerfully displayed; the word was like fire in stubble: the people cried and trembled, wept and mourned. I then rode about six miles, and preached to the gayest assembly, by far, that I have had on the island. Some of them were very attentive, though it is to be feared that the good seed will suffer where the thorns, stones, and birds of the air are so thick. After service was over a number of them joined in singing; but such singing is strange to me—four parts all going at one time, and each part on different words. This is what they call the new mode of singing, and my opinion is, it was instituted more to please the ear than any thing else.

Monday, July 4. I strove to keep my mind up to God, and to pursue my work. I preached from these words, "What shall it profit a man if he shall gain the whole world and lose his own soul?"

Tuesday, 5. I rode to Hempstead Harbor, and illustrated the word "Watch," that being my text.

Wednesday, 6. I rode to Robert Valentine's, and preached with satisfaction to an assembly who knew but little of religion. I hope some were stirred in mind. The next day I preached at Cow Harbor.

Saturday, 9. I met Brother Hubbs's class, and pressed it on them to seek a deeper work of grace.

Sunday, 10. I found my soul very happy while laying down to the congregation the value of our immortal part, and how we should take care of it, lest it be lost at last.

Tuesday, 12. I met the class in the evening at Comac. The Lord was present to bless and comfort us.

Wednesday, 13. I rode about twenty miles, and preached at Zebulon Smith's to a full congregation; several were convinced of the necessity of religion, some of whom are now pursuing the narrow way.

Thursday, 14. In the morning I went down to the sea—about five miles. I preached at Mr. Eldred's at four o'clock. I was much drawn out after the people.

Saturday, 16. I changed places with Mr. Hagerty. He came on the Island, and I went into York for two weeks. I preached in a private house, near Fresh Water Pump, at night, on the necessity of watchfulness; was much comforted then, and afterward, in private prayer.

As the Rev. Mr. John Hagerty fulfilled the duties of an elder both for the Church in New York and the Long Island Circuit, thereby bringing Mr. Cooper to New York once at least in every three months, it will probably render the history of his work in the city more coherent to present his account thereof in one continuous narrative. Having done this, we shall return to the narrative of his work on the circuit, and set it forth in one connected whole. Pursuing this course, the reader will gain a knowledge of the work the preacher stationed in the city was required to perform. Following Mr. Cooper's narrative, as given in his journal, we read:

Sunday, July 17. I preached three times in our church. I believe the Lord touched several hearts.

Tuesday, 19. I felt something poorly in body. I dined at Mr. Staples's; after which I was complaining, but Sister Staples encouraged me. I preached at night from "Behold the man." The Lord struck several hearts. Some dated their conviction from that service, particularly, as I am informed, Miss Cornelia Anderson, who is now a pious girl. I do not know that I ever felt more for souls than I did that night.

Thursday, 21. I still found my mind following after that which I thought would be for the good of myself and others. I preached at three o'clock in the Poor-house, and at night met the Band Society, in which we were powerfully blessed.

The following week he engaged in similar public services, thereby showing us that the preacher was expected to preach three times on the Lord's day in John Street Church, every Thursday afternoon in the Poor-house, and during other parts of the week in the church or in less conspicuous places. The congregation at John Street was supposed to number one thousand. He left the city on Saturday, July 30, and returned to Long Island, on which circuit he remained until the 24th of September, when, being again summoned by Mr. Hagerty, he repaired to New York. Of this visit and the work performed during his stay he speaks as follows:

Saturday, September 24. Was a stormy, rainy day, nevertheless I rode down to York. The wind blew so hard that we sailed across the ferry from Long Island to York in six minutes by the watch.

Sunday, 25. I preached three times with tolerable liberty; the people were serious and very attentive. My evening discourse was on the ninth chapter and sixth verse of Isaiah.

Monday, 26. I visited a prisoner who is under sentence of death. He appeared to be very penitent.

Tuesday, 27. I visited a few friends; had calm repose, longing for religion to prosper.

Wednesday, 28. My mind was lifted to God in prayer. I dined at Mr. Anderson's, where I fell in company with two girls who had la ely found peace with God. Both of them were alarmed when I was in this city, last July. I was much comforted in conversing with them, and exhorting them to stand fast in the liberty wherewith Christ had made them free. At three o'clock P. M. I met thirteen or fourteen children in order to catechise them. The Lord met us, and powerfully wrought on the dear children. I believe there was not more than one of them who was not in a flood of tears; the most of them felt a desire to have an interest in Christ. I do not recollect that I ever saw a number of children so wrought upon before. I found my soul unspeakably blessed, and was very happy all the evening.

On the following Wednesday he met the children again, showing us that the Church, in her earliest days, had given attention to the spiritual wants of the rising generation, and that, in our stations at least, weekly meetings were held in this interest.

As in his former visit to New York Mr. Cooper had the company and counsel of the Rev. Jeremiah Lambert, who had returned from his mission to the West Indies, so, on this occasion, he was cheered by the company of a local preacher by the name of Lynch, who was much beloved and sought after by the Methodists of New York. The presence and ministrations of Mr. Lynch rendered unnecessary the call of Mr. Cooper to New York as a supply during the after part of the ecclesiastical year; he was not, therefore, thereafter in charge of the Society until regularly assigned thereto by the Annual Conference of which he was a member.

However, he occasionally spent a day in the city, and has left some pleasant statements concerning the work. Of these visits he thus speaks:

Friday, November 18. I rode into New York—about twenty-five miles. The Lord is carrying on his work in the city. He is converting sinners and sanctifying believers. I found my mind much stirred to live more to God. I heard Mr. Lynch at night. I trust he will be made a great blessing to the people in York.

Again:

Saturday, December 31. Brother Hagerty sent for me to come into York in order to hold a watch-night, it being the last day of the year. I went; there were five preachers present. We held meeting until after twelve o'clock, thus ending the old year and beginning the new in the worship of God.

Toward the latter part of February, 1786, being in New York for a few days, during which time he preached and visited the classes, he, with the Rev. Mr. Hagerty, visited a woman who, being concerned for some time on account of her sins, became strangely affected. He says:

She was taken with frights, thought the devil was coming for her, and cried out from time to time, "How he thunders and lightens!" Then she looked up and said: "I see the angels. O, how beautiful! but the stairs are so narrow and straight I cannot get up to them." Friday, the 24th, she was taken speechless, and now lies like one asleep, noticing nothing. We went to prayer for her, then left and called at Mr. Harden's. His wife was much distressed for her soul, and had been for some time. Last night she thought she would give up all, and strive for the one thing needful. Her heart was so filled she could hardly converse on the subject. O that Jesus may bring her to the knowledge of salvation!

At the close of this conference year, 1785-86, Mr. Cooper spent nearly a month in New York, awaiting the arrival of the ministers who had been appointed to that charge for the new year. In this period he performed the work of a faithful servant of the Church, and endeared himself more and more to his brethren. On Friday, the 25th of April, a public fast having been proclaimed, he met his brethren in the church at twelve o'clock "for intercession," and had a refreshing season. He maintained the work of the pulpit as it had been previously ordered, preaching three times on the Sabbath; also on Tuesday and Friday evening of each week he visited, warned, preached to, and prayed with the prisoners with such effect, that on Sunday the 14th of May a note was sent from the prison to the church stating that "near one hundred desired the prayers of the congregation" in their behalf.

The Rev. John Dickins, the new appointee to John Street, having arrived on the 28th day of May, Mr. Cooper bade farewell to the city on the 31st, saying, as he looked back upon it:

O the consolation I have had among the children of God in that place! but now we are parted. I looked upon the steeples, and thought how many sermons have been preached by the different ministers of Christ, and yet how many poor sinners remain! O what an awful thought, to think of the great day when the grand decision shall take place; what shrieks and cries will be extorted from disobedient breasts when they are about taking up their abode with damned ghosts forever! O that sinners were wise, that they knew this, that they would consider their latter end!

Having thus laid before the reader the work of the Church in New York, in 1785–86, under the ministrations of Mr. Cooper, attention is now asked to his work, and the development of Methodism, on Long Island Circuit for and during the same period.

Leaving the city on the 30th day of July, he returned to Long Island, preached in a private house when about ten miles out, and also during the following day, it being the Sabbath. Here he was grievously tempted by Satan; of which he tells us in the following words:

Monday, August 1. In the morning I was much concerned in mind. A fear got hold on me that I should not make the promised land, but lose my all at last. I was tempted to leave off traveling and go home, but would not give up to it; so, soon found it to weaken. I rode about twelve miles and found great liberty in exhorting a small congregation to prepare to stand before God, and was set free from my temptation.

Wednesday, August 3. I preached at the East Woods, to a people who were strangers to religion. I explained unto them the nature of salvation. When I first began my faith was weak, but I was strengthened, and in the application had great liberty; many hearts were broken down, tears flowed abundantly, and I was much encouraged to hope that they would seek the salvation of their souls.

Beginning now a second round on his circuit, he preached at Nehemiah Brush's, when one of his hearers concluded that the sermon was specifically directed against her, and became offended with "the woman of the house," under the belief that she had told the preacher about her life and condition. On the following Sabbath, August 7, he preached in the morning at John Wicks's, his theme being sanctification. As soon as he was done speaking, a stranger arose and began to speak. Some thought his design was to oppose the teaching of Mr. Cooper; but, on the contrary, he confirmed it. At three o'clock P. M. he preached at Bread and Cheese Hollow with such power that many were affected. He says:

After I had concluded, a sister of the Baptist persuasion got up and confirmed, in the strongest manner, what I had delivered, and said, if they did not obey, it would appear in judgment against them.

On Monday, the 8th of August, he preached at Philip Ellis's, to a people some of whom had never heard a Methodist before. From thence he passed down to the

4

sea-side, when he was filled with admiration on beholding the wonderful works of God.   On Friday he rode
about sixteen miles to Esquire Edsell's, where he remained for two days, preaching on Saturday evening
and Sunday morning.   In the afternoon he preached at
Flushing, with much profit both to speaker and hearers.
Thence he moved toward Hempstead Harbor, where
was held the first quarterly meeting of the circuit for
the Conference year.   He thus describes it:

Wednesday, August 17.   Our quarterly meeting began at Hempstead Harbor.   I was much rejoiced to see so many friends from
a distance.   While Brother Hagerty was preaching my heart
burned within me, I longed so for souls to serve God.   After
preaching we appointed stewards for the circuit and settled our temporal business, and then repaired to our lodging.   I found my mind
to be in much peace.

Thursday, 18.   Love-feast began at nine o'clock; we had a profitable time; I found the Lord very precious to my soul.   About eleven
o'clock public preaching began.   I found myself much drawn out in
speaking to the people.   Many, I trust, will remember this meeting
all their days.

The quarterly meeting being closed, he pursued his
course, entering into every open door and gladly proclaiming the Gospel of our Lord.   In the course of his
progress he came, on Wednesday, the 24th, to Mr. Benjamin Raynor's.   He says:

I preached at Mr. Benjamin Raynor's, a new place, where. I trust,
God will begin a work.   I have not felt more love and desire for
souls to come to Christ since I have been on Long Island than I do
this evening.

Thursday, 25.   In the morning I felt my soul filled with love.   My
heart is much united to this family, that is, Mr. Raynor's.   I left
some sermon pamphlets for them to read, as they seem much inclined
to read.   I commended them to God, and rode to Hempstead town
and preached, at four o'clock.

Sunday, 28.   A rainy morning—but few people came out.   In
the afternoon, when I was done speaking, Esquire Johnson said,

"These are great truths you have delivered unto the people." We fell into conversation, in which I found much satisfaction. I rode unto Flushing school-house and preached on the Gospel Supper with much satisfaction.

Monday, 29. I rode about twelve miles, and exhorted a small congregation to be much engaged, for it appeared that but few would be saved. I held meeting at night over at a neighbor's house.

Tuesday, 30. I felt my covenant with God renewed. I preached in the evening in Hempstead Harbor school-house.

Friday, September 2, was rainy, but I rode to my appointment, where I met a few of our friends. We spent nearly an hour in singing and prayer.

Saturday, 3. I met the Wien Comac class in the evening. The Lord was present to comfort us.

During this tour he visited a Mr. Bryan, who, though both dumb and deaf, seemed to have great power to discriminate between the religious and irreligious when brought before him. His wife was at this time under conviction for sin. He was also called upon to attend the burial of Mrs. Bailey, one of his members, and greatly beloved by all who knew her. He says: "I don't know when I saw people take on more at the loss of a friend than at this burial."

About the middle of October, he, by appointment, visited a place down the island called The Old Man's, where, at a Mr. Davis's, he preached. From thence he went to Rocky Point. Of its inhabitants he said: "There are some Christians in that place, I believe, but they have many wild ways." The following day being Sabbath, he preached in Mr. Hallock's house in the morning, and in the afternoon in the Presbyterian Church. He also had an appointment near Manet Hill, at Searington, and Coram. Of the latter place he says:

There is a pitiful division among the people called Baptists in that place. The members have shut their preaching-house door against their minister. The door was opened for me; their minister wanted to prevail on me not to go in to the preaching-house, but to preach in a private house. I would not attend to what he said. Then he told me he could not hear me, because he was forbidden to go into the house. "But," said I, "you may go to hear, though not to preach." I took my lodging at Mr. Sexton's. Saturday I rode to the middle of the island, held meeting at night, and was invited home with a man who appeared to be under much concern of mind. Sunday I returned to Coram, and preached three times, with tolerable liberty, but the above-mentioned minister did not come.

Rejoicing in the spirit of revival which was manifested at Hempstead, Mr. Cooper went forward to attend his second quarterly meeting, which was held at David Furman's. Of it he says:

Monday, November 7. Quarterly meeting began in David Furman's house. Brother Lynch preached, and Brother Sands gave an experimental discourse. I have a hope it was profitable to many; it was to me.

Tuesday, 8. Love-feast began at nine o'clock. I found my mind much engaged with God for a down-pouring of his Spirit. At eleven o'clock public preaching began. Mr. Sands preached from John iii, 16. I sat under the word with great delight. After he concluded I gave an exhortation, found much happiness in speaking, and believe the word was accompanied to several hearts. I was but short. Mr. Lynch concluded. I believe it was a profitable meeting to many present.

Of this meeting it may be said that it was remarkable from the fact that there was no elder present, and that the sermons preached were by local preachers—both Mr. Sands and Mr. Lynch being of that order, and connected with the Church in John Street, New York. Mr. Cooper himself was not yet in holy orders, so the services were all held by unordained ministers. As there is no mention made by Mr. Cooper of a Quarterly Conference session, the presumption is that no such session was held at that time.

On the 13th of November he preached on the south side of the island, at Mr. Chichester's—a new appointment—to a large assembly. As he had no other appointment for that day, though it was the Sabbath, he, in the afternoon, walked into the woods to pray for a blessing on the labors he had performed.

On Wednesday, November 30, he preached again at Mr. Benjamin Raynor's, which had now become one of the regular appointments of the circuit. A class had been formed, and religious services had become delightful to some, though not to all, in that community. Speaking of it, Mr. Cooper says:

Wednesday, 30. I rode to Mr. Raynor's, a place where religion hath lately taken root. The opposers are very warm against those that have set out on a divine life: they have many lies told on them. One poor, careless man roars at such a rate as to tell one of our society that he would be glad to see me mobbed out of the place; for "it was his doings," said he, "that brought all the reproach on you." But I rejoice to see them bear it as well as they do; it appears that the more that is said the more they are engaged.

On Thursday, December 8, Methodism was introduced into Flemington, as may be seen from the following extract from the diary:

Thursday, 8. I rode to Flemington. Mr. Douglass invited me to his house, and insisted upon my staying all night. After some hesitation I consented, and he gave word to some of the inhabitants that I would preach. There came a few, some of whom had never heard a Methodist. They are so filled with bigotry and prejudice that the very name, Methodist, sounds like some monstrous thing. However, after preaching, I heard that one said he should be glad to hear such preaching often. But bigotry so prevails that the people are kept at a distance from us, and, it is to be feared, too far from God.

Being intent upon enlarging the sphere of his usefulness, Mr. Cooper entered every open door and preached Jesus. Five days after his work at Flemington he preached in Bethpage " with much satisfaction, to a house full of people," and then prepared to plant the gospel seed in Jamaica, as will be seen by the following :

Friday, December 16. As I rode through Jamaica I called at Mr. Nichols's, to deliver him a letter. We fell into conversation, and, before I left him, I made an appointment to preach in his house on the 30th day of the month. I then rode to Mr. Furman's. He and I, with some of his family, went about five miles to hear a black man preach. He had much zeal.

When the time arrived he fulfilled his engagement at Jamaica, but was fearful that bigotry and prejudice would prove to be the hurt of many in that place. In the meanwhile he preached at a Mr. Shadbolt's, at James Hubbs's, at Peter Van Nostrand's, and at John Combs's.

After his visit to New York, to engage in the watch-night services, December 31, he was accompanied to his circuit by the Rev. Jacob Brush, who, as will be seen by the extract presented below, preached several times, and was gladly heard by the people. Says Mr. Cooper:

Tuesday, January 3, 1786. As we went to our appointment we called at Mr. John Searing's. I trust it was a profitable visit. I trust his wife, son, and daughter are striving to give their service unto God. There was a full congregation at the Harbor, where we had a comfortable meeting. We then rode down Cow Neck, and held evening meeting; we had many hearers. I trust religion is going to take root here.

Wednesday, 4. We traveled to the East Woods. Mr. Brush preached. I spoke to them about joining class. I believe several are striving to serve God, and inclined to join. I preached at night from Ezekiel xviii, 27. Did not find much comfort, yet had words to expose sin and recommend religion. I lay down with a sorrowful spirit for the people.

Thursday, 5. I called upon Mr. Daniel Van Nostrand, on Mannet Hill. They were very kind. I found a great desire for them to obtain an interest in Jesus. His daughter is awakened to see the necessity of religion. "I hope," said she, "I may never live as I have done!" I believe she is intent upon leading a new life.

Friday, 6. I was to meet Brother Brush at Mr. Foster Van Nostrand's, at Sweet Hollow, by ten o' clock. I set off early in the morning. He was waiting for me. We set out on our journey, and called at Mr. Gilliot's, and took dinner. He is very friendly.

Saturday, 7. We met class in the evening at Brother Hubbs's. After we went to bed we were talking about a fit of laughter we had the night before, and, behold, in the meantime the spirit of levity broke in upon us to excess, which wounded me sorely. O that God may give me more power and make me more watchful!

Sunday, 8. There was a very large assembly at Brother Wicks's, gathered in order to hear Brother Brush; this being his native place, and he having been gone for some time, they were very fond of seeing and hearing him. We appointed for watch-night. The people did not know what it meant. A large congregation came together, and we held meeting, preaching and exhorting for nearly two hours. I fear some of them will yet live in sin.

Monday, 9. I parted with Brother Brush, and went to the south side of the island. I called at Mr. Smith's, where I fell in company with Mr. Carle. We had a smart debate about religious matters, but I fear he is not acquainted with the power of it. I preached at Mr. Chichester's from "Awake, thou that sleepest, and arise from the dead, and Christ shall give thee light." At night I was informed of one who, when I was this way before, wanted me to preach at this time at his house, and a few days agone had a frolic. Does this agree with preaching? I answer, By no means; but how hard it is with many to give up the sin of life!"

During this tour Mr. Cooper preached at night at Jerusalem, to a congregation which was much moved under the sermon, many resolving thereafter to lead a new life. Of these, one had resolved to visit the preacher the next day, to converse with him on the subject of religion, but, having indulged in his usual draught of rum, "got out of the notion." He also had a "comfortable meeting at John Searing's, where Methodist preaching never had been before." Near Crab Meadow lived a brother, Smith by name, whose wife, Hannah, was on the 22d of January called to her reward in heaven. Mr. Cooper preached a sermon over

her remains on the 24th, after which she was buried.
He thus speaks of her character :

I have no doubt but that our loss is her gain. She had, for some
considerable time, maintained an upright walk with God. I, from my
first acquaintance with her, took knowledge that she had been with
Jesus. She was of a patient, meek, and humble disposition ; her
conversation, practice, and countenance bespoke a sincere heart.
She always appeared grieved at the conduct of any who lived care-
lessly. Her heart was generally very tender, which appeared from
her frequent tears, and loving, tender conduct. I trust the loss of
brother Smith's wife will prove a blessing to his soul.

After the burial of Mrs. Smith, Mr. Cooper, having
to "bring up" the two days wherein he was detained,
hastened to his appointment at Jerusalem. A large
congregation awaited his arrival. Here Colonel Birdsell desired him to recommend the building of a
church. Said he:

I hardly knew what to do in the matter of the request, as I had
preached there but two or three times; I thought people might put
wrong constructions on my intention ; but I told the congregation
my reason for speaking, and left them to meditate upon it.

He was again at this place on Wednesday, the 8th of
March, and speaks of it thus :

I found great liberty in preaching at Jerusalem to a large congregation. The people in this place are much taken with our preaching.
I was solicited to go to Colonel Birdsell's. I accordingly went, and
found an agreeable time. His wife and daughter are under great
concern. I conversed freely with them on matters of religion. His
daughter thought she found comfort while I was at prayer.

Two weeks after this, on the 22d day of March, he
formed a society, the first that had been organized in
this town by the Methodists.

On Saturday, January 28, he preached at Rockaway,
" a new place," his text being, " Seek ye the Lord while
he may be found." The citizens were at this time

strangers to religion, and said he, "Satan reigns much in the hearts of the people." In two months he was there again, preaching to "a full, attentive congregation;" and thus the seeds of the Gospel were scattered which soon brought forth an abundant harvest. On the last day of January he preached at Searington, where a little flock had been recently gathered together by him, and a class organized, that they might watch over each others' souls.

The third quarterly meeting was held on Saturday and Sunday, Feb. 4 and 5, at Crab Meadow. He tells us:

It began in the evening; Mr. Hagerty preached, I exhorted. Several friends came from far. I was much perplexed in mind about lodging for them. but all were provided for, and I rested in quiet.

Sunday, 5. Love-feast began at nine o'clock. We had a precious time. The rain prevented many from coming, yet we had the house tolerably full, and, I trust, a profitable meeting.

The quarterly meeting having ended, he made a visit of two weeks to New Jersey. During this visit he preached at Chatham, where a Presbyterian minister demanded his authority for preaching; at Mr. Clark's, and Colonel Crain's, where some expected him to be arrested ; at Woodbridge Church; at Amboy, in the Court-house; at Bonham; and at Brunswick, in the Barracks, to a room full of people. While here he was the guest of Mr. Alvey. He says:

Fell in company with some who were strangers to all experimental religion: some of them spake up for such amusements as fiddling and dancing, etc. Mr. Freeman, a student of law, and Mrs. Lynn, the governor's daughter, who were present, spake for it, but soon gave up the point. The lady was very honest in acknowledgment of God's calls to her, and that she was ashamed of it to think he had called but she had refused.

Leaving Brunswick, he preached at Mr. Freeman's, at Samuel Jaques's, at Esquire Marsh's, and at Daniel

Terrell's. Mr. Marsh accompanied him to Mr. Terrell's, and during the journey sought an explanation of some of the doctrines held by the Methodists, and, though a member of another denomination, was so well pleased and satisfied that he said he did not know but that he should be a Methodist.

On Friday, February 17, he arrived at Elizabeth, where, at night, he preached and led the class. Speaking of the state of religious affairs in the town he says:

Satan makes a wonderful bustle in this place; the class has lately been formed; the opposers report such horrid things about it that some have withdrawn, and others are very near doing it, but I feel a hope that they will be more reconciled, for they begin to find out that the reports are false.

Having preached in Elizabeth, on Sabbath morning, February 19, he rode in the afternoon to Lyon's Farms, and preached; from thence to Newark, where he heard Mr. McWhorter preach at six o'clock, P. M., at the conclusion of which service the Court-house bell rang for him, and he preached, beginning after seven o'clock, to a full congregation. From thence he returned to his circuit on Long Island.

Pursuing his course through his circuit, he visited a family in Jerusalem by the name of Jones, where he preached, much to his own satisfaction and to that of the friends there assembled. Coming the next day to Hempstead, he found that the parish minister was busily engaged in stirring up opposition to the Methodists, and he took such steps as would be likely to counteract the evil sought to be engendered. At Flushing, having preached at night from the words, "I am jealous of this people, lest I have bestowed on them labor in vain," an old lady and her three daughters tarried until ten o'clock to converse with him. He says: "I dealt very plainly with them. I fear they are strangers to religion; but they are not to fashions, for they are a part of the gayest in the town." An appointment having been made at Matthew Wilkey's, he preached to a large congregation there gathered, and was encouraged by the prospect of both " the man and the woman of the house seeking to know Jesus."

As he was soon to be called to another field of labor, Mr. Cooper, in his last "round," preached his farewell sermons, and almost every-where left the people in tears. Coming to Mosquito Cove, he met and preached to a large assembly, saying of them: "I feel great love for the people of this place, and hope a work will take root in their hearts, though, likely, I shall not see them again."

The last quarterly meeting for the Conference year was held at Searington, on Monday and Tuesday, April 17 and 18. On the first day the Rev. Mr. Hagerty preached, and on the second, after love-feast, Mr. Cooper preached to them his last sermon as their pastor, and then, amid tears, took the parting hand of the many who had learned to love him. In reviewing the work of the year, he says:

I think I have preached three hundred and nineteen times; and on the circuit I rode. one hundred and ten members joined society. I find that my mind is much united to the Long Island friends—how hard it is for us to part! and more so when we do not expect, or, at least, part of us. to meet again in this world. O may we meet at God's right hand!

Great, indeed, had been the prosperity of the year, as may be seen in the fact that he entered upon the work of the circuit having less than fifty members, and left it with a membership of one hundred and fifty-four.

CHAPTER III.

EAST JERSEY CIRCUIT, 1786.

It is, probably, to most of the students of the course of early Methodism in America a matter of astonishment that, although the Church was represented in New Jersey in 1786 by more than twelve hundred members, our historians are silent in regard to it, insomuch that we are almost wholly confined to the early Minutes for any information we desire to gain. Under such circumstances it is both the part of wisdom and prudence to bring forth, from Mr. Cooper's documents, those data which may, in part, supply the deficiency. There were in 1786 four circuits in the State of New Jersey, namely: Trenton, West Jersey, East Jersey, and Newark. Mr. Cooper had been assigned to East Jersey Circuit, with John McClaskey as his colleague.

The number of members of the Methodist Episcopal Church within the bounds of this circuit were three hundred and sixty-five, who were in classes formed at the charges given below. There were but few churches or "meeting-houses" as yet built; so that public worship was, for the most part, conducted at the residences of the people. The following is a list of the preaching places in the circuit in June, 1786: Flanders, Esquire Dotey's; Captain Hall's; Mr. Moore's; Mr. Grandin's; Mr. Hasen's; Mr. Young's; Beman's Forge, Esquire Tuttle's; Long Pond, Captain McAmley's; Warwick, Mr. Roe's; near Florida, Thomas Smith's; The Clove, Jonathan Stephen's; Mr. Clark's; Samuel Knapp's; Robert McWorter's; John McWorter's; Mr. Benjamin's; Esquire Wilson's; Esquire Bechover's; Pepper Cotton's; Sussex; Mr. Hunt's; Mr. Wilgus's; Hackettstown, Samuel Pews's; Mr. Weller's; Esquire Opdyke's; Mr. Mellick's; Godfree Peters's.

Though thirty-three places of worship within the circuit indicated the fact that the power and influence of Methodism were being felt, yet there existed strong opposition, and it sometimes manifested itself in an ugly spirit, as the following will show.   Says Mr. Cooper:

Tuesday, June 13. I was informed of several things which appear to be worthy of notice. Mr. Egbert informed me that some time ago he heard a minister, after he had preached, speak to the congregation much against the Methodists: after which Brother Egbert said, "You have misrepresented the people to your congregation." A man standing by said, "You had as well say the minister told a lie," and began to swear badly. Brother Egbert said, "Is it not wrong to swear?" He said he did not know whether it was or not. Another spoke and said it was not so much harm to swear as it was to take the Methodists' part. Poor, stupid man! Are the Methodists such monsters as he makes them out? Again, some time after that, two Calvinist ministers appointed a day for fasting and prayer, that God might remove falsehood and error from among them, looking upon the Methodists as guilty of both. When their congregations met they preached and prayed against both. I do not suppose they either of them mentioned the Methodist name; but here is something to be noticed: God did not remove Methodism, but in a short time they both were removed from time to eternity. Who can account for this? But Methodist doctrines yet remain and prevail among men as much, or more, than ever. I found great satisfaction in preaching and meeting the class; my soul was happy all the evening.

Mr. Cooper found, also, in the Church, at some of the appointments, a state of irreligion that was a cause of grief to him. As an illustration, he tells us that the class which met at Esquire Bechover's was in such disorder that he " broke it up;" that upon hearing a cer-

tain Brother Smith—of the local order of preachers—
attempt to preach, and finding his utter unfitness for
the task, he told him of his condition, and advised him
to retire from that form of service. Soon, however, in
various parts of the circuit, the work began to revive,
and those who were enemies to Methodism began to see
their error, and to recall their former utterances of
opposition and censure.

Returning from the quarterly meeting on Newark
Circuit he received letters from New York and other
places, which, as they illustrate the state of religion in
their communities, are here presented to the friends of
those charges, among whom, mayhap, are yet surviving
relatives. The first is from Thomas Smith, a lay member of John Street Church, New York:

NEW YORK, *June* 18, 1786.

DEAR FRIEND: I take this opportunity of writing to you; and
think, by this time, you are no stranger to coarse fare, a hard bed,
and the contradiction of sinners, as I told you you were to expect.
But, dear friend, the love of God and Christ will make all this light
and easy. When you consider the cause you are engaged in; when
we think on these words of the apostle, "This is a faithful saying,
and worthy of all acceptation, that Christ Jesus came into the world
to save sinners," that this was the very end for which he came into
time, how can we doubt the willingness of God to save such, of whom
I am chief? My conscience often upbraids me for being so unbelieving; it makes me blush for shame. I am much prone to be very
diffident.

My dear brother, the Lord, who is ever doing good, hath sent his
servants among us, who have proved a great blessing to us, and I think
the work of God will prosper in their hands, as they are men full
of faith and the Holy Ghost. My dear friend, you cannot press
faith too much, as it is that which "overcometh the world," likewise
our sins. The Lord hath mightily blessed us since you left us, and
it is all pain and misery not to feel God in our hearts every moment.
Myself and my wife wish you well in the Lord.

That this work may prosper in your soul, as well as of those who hear you; that you may be made a blessing to all that hear you, is the prayer of your friend.

Sister Ryker remembers her respects to you.   THOMAS SMITH.

NEW YORK, *July,* 1786.

DEAR BROTHER: I have received your kind letter, dated July 6, and esteem it a great favor and a token of your love toward us, and hope we shall always rejoice to hear from you. We are all in tolerable health of body, and trust some have their faces toward the kingdom. O that we may be thankful, and diligent, and abounding in love toward God and one another more and more, till we all obtain that meek and lowly mind which was in Christ Jesus our Lord!

As to the state of my mind: sometimes I seem to have access to the throne of grace, and behold as in a glass (darkly) the Lamb of God which taketh away the sin of the world. At such seasons my soul is refreshed, Christ's name is as ointment poured forth; but it is like the visits of a wayfaring man, who turneth aside for a night to visit the tent of an unworthy creature. O that I may be more thankful! that the blessed Jesus would destroy every enemy, and come with his Father and take up his residence in my heart, and reign the Lord of every motion there. O, my dear brother, think of thy unworthy brother and his family; let us have a place in your prayers before God. My wife and family join with me in sending our kind respects to you. My wife was at quarterly meeting on Long Island, and Colonel Birdsell desired to be remembered to you, and said he would be glad to hear from you. We have forwarded your letter to him. Brother Cooke is gone out to preach on the island. Our Peter comes on very well in learning, and remains still serious and diligent in the means. He has written unto you.

The Lord keep you in soundness of body and mind, and preserve you to a good old age, and then, as a full ripe shock of corn, gather you into his garner to be with him forever.

From your affectionate brother,   ELBERT ANDERSON.

Mr. Anderson, in the above, refers to his son Peter, who, though a youth, had written a letter to Mr. Cooper. This letter, too, is at our command, and is of great practical value, in that it shows that our fathers in the ministry were, from the beginning of our existence as a separate Christian organization, instructors of

children in the ways of righteousness.   Here is the
letter :

NEW YORK, July 22, 1786.

MY DEAR SIR : Papa received your kind and affectionate letter. It
gave me great satisfaction to hear from you, and to think you had
not forgotten your unworthy friend, but affectionately mentioned me in
yours to papa. All our family are well at present, except mamma. I
cannot tell whether she is well or not, for Mrs. Housman and she are
gone to Long Island quarterly meeting. I am well myself at present,
and hope these will find you the same.

My dear sir, when I take a view of myself, and see how careless I
have been, it affords me reason to praise God that he hath not sen-
tenced me into everlasting punishment. I hope I may be more
engaged in time to come. I cannot, as yet, say I have received the
forgiveness of my sins, but hope I may soon be able to testify it.
I know it is not the Lord's fault, but my own, that I have not
experienced it before now.

I have reason to be thankful we have two very good preachers
here. Mr. Jefferson, who came with Mr. Dickins, is gone back to the
south. Mr. Dickins and Mr. Tunnell are with us this year. I hope
they will be the means of doing much good. I hope you will write
to me as soon as it will suit you.

I remain, your unworthy friend,   PETER ANDERSON.

While we have here given the above letters from
members of the society in New York, where Mr. Cooper
had acted the previous year as an occasional supply, the
following one was from a valued and honored member
of Long Island Circuit, where he had ministered during
the larger portion of the year. It is doubtful whether
we shall find a clearer statement of the condition of his
late charge than this letter furnishes :

NEWTOWN, June 30, 1786.

DEAR BROTHER : Pursuant to my promise, I take this opportunity
to inform you that, through the tender mercies of a gracious God, we
are in health of body, and, I trust, still desirous to press forward.
O that the desire of our souls may be to the remembrance of his
Name! I trust I see a daily necessity of cleaving unto the Lord with
full purpose of heart, and that vanity and vexation of spirit is written
upon every sublunary enjoyment. Remember me in your access at

the throne of divine grace. I have great need of an interest in the prayers of all the people of God.

Respecting our Society, nothing material has transpired since you left us. Williams and his wife, at Hempstead Harbor, have left the Society, owing, it seems, to some difference between his and Bumstead's family. That's their pretended reason; perhaps he may have saved the preacher the trouble of discarding him, which, it is more than probable, would have been the case, as he was (poor man!) a litigious person. Our quarterly meeting is appointed at Jerusalem on Sunday three weeks.

I hope you have strength of body and serenity of mind. May the Lord make you extensively useful in your day, that you may be able to teach transgressors his ways, that sinners may be converted unto him; that at some future day you may shine as one of the bright constellations in glory. That you may, with unwearied assiduity, finish your course with joy, is the sincere desire, and, I hope, will ever be the fervent prayer, of him who is, with inviolable affection, yours,

JAMES HARPER.

One more, a letter from a layman on Newark Circuit, is presented to the reader :

NEWARK, 1786.

DEAR BROTHER: I hope this will find you in the enjoyment of health, both of body and mind, and I trust you have the satisfaction of seeing the work of the Lord prosper in that part of his vineyard where you labor, and are thence encouraged by seeing the travail of the Redeemer's soul and the fruit of your own labor. I bless God I am still a monument of his mercy, and, by his grace, am determined to press after all the salvation of God, though at times I am ready to faint. O may the Lord chase this slumber from my soul, that it may never more return! A few more have joined the Society since you were here; I hope they all are sincere, and striving to enter the strait gate. There is a great deal of opposition, but this is what all must expect that will leave the world, flesh, and devil, and seek the salvation of their souls.

I trust you will not forget us at the throne of grace, that the Lord may keep and strengthen us, that we may do his will, and walk worthy of that vocation whereunto we are called. May the Father of mercy give you every needful blessing for time and eternity, is the ardent prayer of your unworthy brother, in our common Lord.

JOHN CHAVE.

Saturday and Sunday, the 12th and 13th days of
August, were spent in the exercises and associations
of the quarterly meeting on East Jersey Circuit. Besides Mr. McClaskey and Mr. Cooper, there were also
present Messrs. John Tunnell and John Cooper, who
took part in the religious services.

While in the performance of his circuit duties, Mr.
Cooper preached on Sunday, August 27, in "a new
church lately built for the Church of England, so-
called." The appointment was not entirely satisfactory, as may be seen from the following statement of
Mr. Cooper: "I was informed before I got there that
some were much opposed to my preaching in it [the
church], but all were peaceable." The congregation
was large, and attentive to the word. There was not,
however, at this time such a spirit of opposition against
the use of the churches of the Episcopalians by the
Methodists as was afterward developed. Mr. Cooper
preached, the following Sabbath, in Mansfield Church,
without meeting any opposition, and, in the afternoon,
for the first time, at Judge Hughes's Forge, where afterward a prosperous church was founded. Later in the
year he preached in the Church at Log-jail; in the Log-
church, near Esquire Opdyke's, etc.; but the most decidedly pronounced spirit of Christian affinity was manifested at Newburg, of which Mr. Cooper thus speaks:

Sunday, November 5. I preached in the church at Newburg.
Methodism meets with unexpected fellowship in this place. The
church warden said to me, "You have some enemies; but where one
is against you ten are for you." Blessed be God! the battle is not always to the strong. I rode about five miles, and preached at Mr.
Westlake's at three o'clock, then I rode back to Newburg, with
Mr. Graham, and went and heard a Quaker, who preached at night
in town. After all the exercises of the day, I found a comfortable
evening and took my lodging with ease. Glory to God for his kind
providence!

Monday, 6. After breakfast Mr. Graham and myself took a chair and rode about two miles to see Colonel Palmer; but he had ridden out, so that we did not see him; but in the evening he and his lady came to town where I was. I preached at six o'clock P.M., in the church, to a tolerably large congregation, then went home with Mr. Anderson and lodged.

We hail, with delight, the spirit of Christian brotherhood as manifested in the following section. Under date of November 11, he says:

Saturday, 11. The people were much affected while I preached from Luke xii, 32, "Fear not," etc. I did not meet the class, being in a hurry. I had to ride a considerable distance that night in order that I might meet the Rev. Mr. Ogden, next day, at Sussex Courthouse.

Sunday, 12. I set off from Mr. Hopkins's about nine o'clock, A.M. There was a large congregation to hear Mr. Ogden. He preached again at night. I lodged at Mr. Willis's, who informed me, by way of application, when the vestry and wardens met (being one himself) that they unanimously agreed to a proposal made by some of them to prevail on me to take orders and settle in their parish; but I gave them an answer, that, at present, I was not disposed to settle. I found my mind at peace.

Monday, 13. There was a large congregation at the church, likewise in the evening at Sampson Howell's. After Mr. Ogden preached I gave an exhortation.

Tuesday, 14. I continued with Mr. Ogden; he preached down by the Delaware River to a large assembly. At night he insisted that I should give an exhortation to a few people that were at the house. I did so, and he went to prayer.

Wednesday, 15. I had some satisfactory discourse with Mr. Ogden, before we parted, upon "election and reprobation."

Although, according to Simpson (see *Cyclopedia of Methodism*, p. 745), the beginning of regular Methodist worship in Reading, Pa., was not until the summer of 1823, Mr. Cooper preached in that town in 1786, as the following will show:

Tuesday, September 5, 1786. I had much satisfaction preaching in Reading town to a small congregation. The greater part were affected while I was showing the value of the soul and the danger of losing it, then applying a careful walk to them, lest the world, flesh, or devil should get an advantage of them.

While here he was also requested to preach at Germantown, of which he speaks thus:

Wednesday, 6. The congregation at two o'clock was small, yet I trust that God was present; the greater part were affected, the others very serious. I was applied unto to go and preach at Germantown that evening, which I gladly complied with. I had twice as many as I expected, for the people there are generally opposed to us. I had an invitation from Major Rhynehart to lodge at his house, which I accepted. I am informed that a certain gentleman in town, while his family were gone to hear me preach, fastened the door to keep them out; but his heart failed, and at their return he gave them admittance after some time. I was pleased with an expression that dropped from Esquire Rhynehart's lips, namely, "Germantown is like a fort, but the Methodists. I think, will at last take it." I must acknowledge I was much encouraged while preaching to see the attention of the people; and I felt, I trust, a measure of gospel authority. One said, after meeting was over, he was not afraid but that all who came prejudiced had their prejudice removed. O that God may display his power, and by his Spirit clinch the word in every heart! With God's blessing, I purpose trying them again in about six weeks.

Both Reading and Germantown were now added to the circuit whereon Mr. Cooper was laboring, and he visited them regularly once in six weeks, and had the satisfaction of seeing some fruits of his labors. That this may appear to the reader in an uninterrupted statement, the following is set forth from the diary:

Wednesday, October 18. We had a comfortable time at friend Melick's—the greater part of the congregation was affected. Then I rode to Germantown and preached to a large congregation; found much liberty in speech, and feel almost confident that good was done. There is a pleasing prospect of a good work taking place among them.

Tuesday, November 28. I preached at two o'clock in Reading town. We had a warm room, and the people, generally, were affected.

Wednesday, 29. I was very cold as I traveled, so I got off from my horse and led him a considerable way, then I rode again. The congregation was small at two o'clock. I preached again at night; then we had considerably more. I had a comfortable night's rest. O Germantown, when will you give up?

Tuesday, February 20, 1787. Was a very cold day. I tarried till about three o'clock at Mr. Grandine's (a family of kind people), then traveled to Reading town, where we had watch-night. I preached on the "Fruitless Fig-tree;" two exhortations were given, but I fear that some poor tree is barren yet.

While at Esquire Edsell's, on Friday, the 15th of September, he wrote a letter to a member of the New Jersey Assembly, against sin, in answer to his assertion that "no one could live without sin." The letter is so important that it is here given entire:

DEAR SIR: I am sorry to find one who professes to be a child of God, yet espouses the infidel's cause, and openly proves an advocate for sin, even while the word of God loudly demonstrates that "He that committeth sin is of the devil," 1 John iii, 8; and, verse nine, "Whosoever is born of God doth not commit sin."

But sin's advocate, in order to defend himself, infers from 1 John i, 7, that sin is unavoidable. But surely St. John does not contradict himself! It evidently appears to those who understand the apostle, that he means a natural man, for we hear him say, verse seven, "If we walk in the light, as He is in the light, we have fellowship one with another, and the blood of Jesus Christ his Son cleanseth us from all sin:" that is, they who come from darkness (in which is the natural man) into he true light of the Gospel, which proves the power of God unto salvation to their souls. Which could not be the case until they were delivered from sin, as salvation implies this deliverance. But then, lest any self-deceived one, who had not that experience, should build up a false hope, or affirm he had no sin to be cleansed of, he immediately speaks in the eighth verse, as unto such, "If we say that we have no sin, we deceive ourselves, and the truth is not in us." Then he beautifully addresses them, in verse nine, and shows how they may likewise get clear of sin, namely, "If we confess our sins, He is faithful and just to forgive us our sins, and to cleanse us from all unrighteousness." Then, in verse tenth, he explains the eighth, and endeavors to guard against our mistaking his meaning on this subject and so wresting the Scripture to our destruction; that is, "If we say we have not sinned we make him a liar" who hath declared that all have sinned. So none by nature are clear. But, now, he who hath experienced the work of grace above mentioned, is "dead to sin," and how shall he "live any longer therein" (Rom. vi, 2)? agreeing with verse fourteen, "For sin shall not have dominion over you: for ye are not under the law, but under grace." So, in verse eighteen, "Being then made free from sin, ye became the servants of righteousness." Again, verse twenty-two, "Being now made free from sin, and become servants to God, ye have your fruit unto holiness" (which doubtless is not sin), "and the end everlasting life." I would now observe, "No man can serve two masters (Matt. vi, 24), for either he will hate the one, and love the other; or else he will hold to the one, and despise the other." We may doubtless affirm from this, Ye cannot serve God and sin. If we would consider how different their commands are, I should expect every understanding and unprejudiced person to quickly see it is impossible to serve both.

But O! a melancholy truth; there are advocates for this cruel monster, sin, which is such an enemy to all God's creation! Surely, such cannot be friends to God's cause, for if they were servants of God they surely would be enemies to sin. It is again asserted by those who appear bold for sin's dominion, that "no man liveth and sinneth not." But I would ask from whence they get this assertion, or, have they read it in God's word? If so, let the chapter and verse be found, of which I know nothing at present. I see something somewhat like it; but I have not seen those particular words. But I make no doubt, if the antagonists of holiness and the advocates for sin would but read the context of all the passages that speak in the manner or likeness above mentioned, and compare them with other parts of Scripture, their beauty and meaning would appear quite different from that which those who plead for sin's remains hope or think they do; for, doubtless, the Scripture is consistent with itself; but you would make it otherwise, to explain it according to your mind, which, it appears, loves sin.

If we would understand the Scriptures, we should always notice, 1) the people to whom they are written; 2) the occasion on which they were written; 3) the subject; and, 4) the design of the writer. For want of this some condemn the true word, and say it is full of contradictions. O let not this be our case; let not Satan get an advantage from this quarter. I would now ask a solemn question, namely, What is the cause of your pleading for sin? Are you afraid or apprehensive that your neighbors will be too holy, and, thereby, sin be driven from them, that you plead, there is no entire victory over sin? Is it in order to discourage them from seeking it? Take heed that you do not lay a stumbling-block in your neighbor's way, or be instrumental, through your friendship to sin, in stopping any in the pursuit of holiness, by getting that dangerous notion in their heads "that there is no living without sin," and so they may say, "I'll not strive after that which is not attainable," and give way to sin, as (the more is the pity) too many do. O turn not the blind out of the way. (Read Deut. xxvii, 18.) O that I could find as many friends to holiness as to sin! What happy times should we then see, while, instead of pulling down, we would be building each other up! What love, peace, and harmony we should have, instead of envy and strife!

Now, if you will not yourself enter, hinder not others who are entering. Consider: we have shortly to give an account for all our conduct. O take heed; be not found fighting against God; read impartially, for instruction, the word of truth, with prayer, etc.

It may not be amiss to observe that there is great difference between sin and temptation. None can escape temptation, but sin is not committed until temptation is yielded to. The devil presents something of the world, or flesh, to the mind. Here temptation begins, but while the mind opposes the evil we do not sin: if we give way to desire of the evil, then sin is committed. But, now, cannot man (Christ helping him, by whose assistance Paul said he could do all things) do this: that is, overcome sin and the false spirit? Doubtless he can, for St. John saith, first epistle, iv, 4, "Ye are of God, little children" (speaking to Christians) "and have overcome them." In chap. v, 7, 8, we have an account of them that bear record and witness to truth, as witnesses to these things. O, then, do not rise up against them. Read verse eighteen, "We know that whosoever is born of God sinneth not; but he that is begotten of God keepeth himself, and the wicked one toucheth him not."

I have not time, at present, to enlarge upon this subject, and have been very brief. Volumes might be written thereon. I beg that you will serve God and prepare to meet him, for "without holiness no man shall see the Lord." Heb. xii, 14.

A man cannot be saved without holiness:
But he cannot be holy until he forsakes sin;
Then he cannot be saved without he forsakes sin.
No unclean thing shall enter into the kingdom of heaven:

But a man is unclean till cleansed from all sin ;
Then he cannot get to heaven till cleansed from all sin.
The wicked are to perish :
But he that committeth sin is wicked ;
Then he that committeth sin is to perish.
He who is from under the law may live without sin :
But the Christian is from under the law; Rom. vi, 14 ;
Then the Christian may live without sin.
" He that committeth sin is of the devil." 1 John iii, 9.
But the child of God is not of the devil ;
Then the child of God doth not commit sin. 1 John ii, 9.
He that denies the Scriptures denies the truth :
But the above assertion is Scripture ;
Then he that denies it denies the truth.

Take heed to what you do; humble yourself. May you know the truth of these things is my desire and prayer.

The sheet is full or else I would add a few words more; but be not offended at Scripture, I pray you.

Farewell.

The letter was not very favorably regarded by the Assemblyman, but caused him to attack Mr. Cooper on the following Tuesday in an enraged state of mind, wherein, also, he discovered to his opponent that he had very little love for the Methodists.

Mr. Cooper was at this time instrumental in planting the Methodist Episcopal Church in Newburg, where, as above stated, he preached in the Episcopal church of that town. Alluding to the opening for him there, he says:

Sunday, September 24. I preached at Newburg. I think I plainly see the providence of God working for us. Mr. Wagrant applied to me to preach a funeral sermon over his sister-in-law. Her death, very probably, drew out many that otherwise would not have come. I found much liberty in opening my text; the people expressed themselves as much satisfied, and pressed me to come again. Several gave me an invitation to their house; I met with unexpected kindness from the people. Mr. Ellis, one of the greatest men in that part, gave me a very affectionate invitation to his house, but I could not go by reason of my appointment in the afternoon in another direction. I gave them a promise, by the leave of Providence, to visit them again in six weeks. Some said the meeting-house (Presbyterian?) should be opened; others, the church; but I told them it was immaterial to me which.

This appointment, which was filled November 5 by his preaching in the church as above recited, served so to impress the preacher that it became thereafter a place of regular visitation on his six weeks' circuit. His next appointment there was on Sunday, December 17. He says:

Sunday, 17. We returned to Newburg. The day being cold, and the drifting snow having blown into the church, I preached in the house of Mr. Wagrant. We had a large congregation; I had great liberty; the people were much affected; the power of God rested upon us. I hope the day will be remembered. I preached again at night; found liberty of speech. I feel a great hope that the labor is not "as water spilt on the ground."

By reason of his attendance at the quarterly meeting services of a neighboring charge he did not preach in Newburg at the time of his next appointment there, but was promptly in place on Sunday, the 11th of March, and preached to a "serious, attentive congregation."

While the exact location of some of the new places wherein the seeds of Methodism were at this period planted cannot be determined, by reason of the fact that public worship was, for the most part, conducted in the dwellings of families friendly to our cause, yet there are some neighborhoods and villages, or towns, given, where afterward societies were formed and churches or chapels built. Thus we find Mr. Cooper in September preaching at Mr. Miller's, in Smith's Clove; then at the Lower Clove, where he was "much encouraged to think that some of the family would covenant to serve the Lord," and where he hoped good would be done in that place if they could continue preaching there; then at Bethlehem, Pa., of which he thus speaks:

Friday, September 22. I then rode to Bethlehem, and preached at three o'clock to a small, but fashionable, congregation. Some of the first rank were out; they appeared in a superfluous manner, yet waited with seriousness while I was showing the nature of salvation through Christ, and the danger of neglecting it. I trust that Mrs. Ellis (John) got her heart touched, for, soon as meeting was over, she inquired as to where I was to preach on Sunday. O what a blessed thing if the rich receive the word!

On the following day he preached at Captain Smith's, four miles above Newburg, with much satisfaction; and the following day, being Sunday, at Newburg, where Mr. Ellis, husband of the lady mentioned above, whom Mr. Cooper describes as "one of the greatest men in that part," was out to hear him, and gave him a "very affectionate invitation to his house," which Mr. Cooper accepted, promising to make the visit in six weeks, which he did, and received a cordial welcome. At four o'clock on Sunday he preached at Esquire Sands's, in or near Newburg, from whence, on Monday, he rode to Goshen, another new place to him. Here he met with an elderly woman, she being ninety-three years old, who told him she was longing to die. "She appeared," he tells us, "to have a witness of her acceptance with God." Having opened his mission here, he returned to them in six weeks, and thereafter continued to visit by regular appointment.

On Saturday and Sunday, 21st and 22d of October, the second quarterly meeting for the circuit was held near Warwick. This was in the upper part of Mr. Cooper's half of the East Jersey Circuit, for he and his colleague had divided the charge into the "upper" and "lower" half; and here he met with his elder, Rev.

John Tunnell, and his colleague, Rev. Mr. McClaskey. Describing the meeting, Mr. Cooper says:

> *Saturday*, October 21. We had about five miles to ride to the preaching house, where quarterly meeting began. We had a comfortable time. The congregation was much affected; a solemn awe rested upon them.
>
> *Sunday*, 22. Love-feast began at nine o'clock. Many hearts were much melted therein. At the conclusion of the love-feast the sacrament was given. I think the presence of God was very visibly among us. Preaching began about eleven o'clock. I was pitched upon to preach the sermon. The house was so full, and there were so many out of doors, that I did not go to the pulpit, but stood near the door. There were, I expect, near or quite a thousand souls present: some think more. The words of my text were, "Happy art thou, O Israel!" etc. Deut. xxxiii, 29. I trust our Quarterly Meeting will be remembered by many dear souls.

Having, as heretofore shown, opened public service at Hughes's Forge, Mr. Cooper became, on Sunday, November 26, the guest of Judge Hughes, and has left on record a narrative of the judge which is given to the reader. Says Mr. Cooper:

> He (the judge) told me that, sometimes, when thinking of the different religions in the world, and how small a part of the world is of the Christian religion, he is almost shaken in his mind whether Christ was the Son of God; nevertheless, he approved of public worship, if there was nothing more than civility to be had from it. I told him I thought the fulfillment of the prophecies in him (Christ) was one proof of his being the Son of God; and a second proof was, the fulfillment of his own prophecies. A third proof is this: His example, in word and deed, proved him to be a good man, which he could not be if he was not the Son of God; for, if he was not the Son of God, he was a very great impostor. Then, as his words, works, and prophecies proved him a good man, he was no impostor; and, if not an impostor, then he was the Son of God. However, I hope he is not quite shaken off from his belief in Christ. I have this to say: he is a sensible gentleman, and used me with great civility, for which I must acknowledge myself to be under obligations to him.

Mr. Cooper had planned to preach on Sunday, the 24th of December, at Pepper Cotton; but, being prevented by a severe snow-storm from reaching the town, he preached at night in the house of a private family where he lodged. It being on the eve of the Christmas anniversary, he took for his text, "A prophet shall the Lord your God raise up unto you of your brethren, like unto me; him shall ye hear in all things whatsoever he shall say unto you." In the application of his subject he exposed, with severe reproof, the habits of professing Christians who spend Christmas in wicked vanities. He said:

They profess to keep it in remembrance of Christ's coming into the world; but we see some go to frolicing, others to drunkenness, others to various evils. Strange, indeed! What! because a Saviour is born, will men be more wicked than on other days? If a Jew, Turk, or pagan were guilty of this, in derision of Jesus, we might not wonder; but for a Christian to be guilty of such things is very surprising. I must confess I am constrained to doubt the Christianity of such.

One of the hearers, after sermon was over, was heard to say:

If he had intended to speak next day (which was Christmas) at a frolic, he would not have heard the sermon for a great deal. O! when will all fear, and love to obey, God's word?

The third quarterly meeting for the Conference year was held on this circuit at Mr. McCullock's, near Reading, on Saturday and Sunday, January 20 and 21. The services on Saturday produced a very deep impression on many, and it was thought great good was done. Mr. Cooper was the guest of Esquire Bevers, who, having attended the meeting, was much impressed thereby, as was also his brother, who was brought under a state of conviction. The next day (Sunday) being rainy, there were but few in attendance, and the

love-feast exercises were rendered less inspiring by reason of the door being kept open for all who might
come, whether "members, outsiders, or others."

At the close of the quarterly meeting Mr. Cooper
accompanied the Rev. Robert Sparks, who had been a
partaker of the services, to his (Trenton) circuit, to aid
in the religious exercises of the quarterly meeting on
that circuit. In making the journey they spent a night
at Mr. Joshua Anderson's, near Princeton, where they
had a watch-night service, and where there seemed to
be a good prospect of a revival of religion. At Mr.
Outgelt's, near Monmouth, where one of them preached,
and at Monmouth, where, at Mr. Grandin's, they had a
large congregation, they held watch-night services.
On Saturday, January 27, 1787, they arrived at Mr.
Woodman's, and on the next day opened the quarterly meeting in Goodluck meeting-house, where Mr.
Cooper preached at 11 o'clock A. M. Rev. Robert
Cann followed in an exhortation. Some of his expressions were so queer that many of the congregation
laughed at him, and were subjected to a sharp reproof.
In the afternoon Mr. Sparks preached, and in the evening, several friends having gone to the place where the
preachers lodged, Mr. Cooper gave an exhortation.
He said :

We had a powerful time while at prayer. I thought the Lord was
about to sanctify some present. I do not know when I felt the
power of God more sensibly.

With a deeply-felt faith that God would be with
them, the next day love-feast was opened at nine
o'clock A. M., and they had "a very powerful time, some
crying out under the powerful influence of the Spirit,"
and all being happy or desiring so to be. At eleven
o'clock Mr. Cooper preached from the text, "Happy

art thou, O Israel : who is like unto thee, O people
saved by the Lord?" Deut. xxxiii, 29. Says he :

When I was treating on my third head, of doctrine, which was to
show in what respect this was a happy people, it appeared that
nearly all the congregation were in tears. In my application I was
much drawn out after their souls. Brother Budd gave an exhortation, and Brother Sparks closed the meeting with singing and prayer.

The meeting being closed, Mr. Cooper, with a number
of companions, departed for Freehold, and lodged at
Esquire Akins's with seven or eight of his company.
On the next day, with a company of twenty, breakfasted at a hotel at Meltetetonk, where they had family
worship, and awakened a desire of salvation in some
members of the family, who were left in tears, and
arrived at Mr. Grandin's, on his circuit, that night.
From thence, going to Mr. Leonard's and Mr. Throckmorton's, he came to Freehold for the Sabbath service,
but, as the day was extremely cold, had only a small
congregation present for the public worship. On Monday, having the Rev. Mr. Sparks as his companion, he
preached at Joseph Hutchinson's, who on the next day
took him and Mr. Sparks in a sleigh to his appointment
at Mr. Barclay's, and the day following to Mr. Outgelt's. Returning to Mr. Hutchinson's, they again departed, on Thursday, the 8th of February, to Crosswicks, where they met a small congregation in the
evening at Mr. Smith's. From thence they went to the
quarterly meeting on West Jersey Circuit. Of this
visit Mr. Cooper thus speaks :

Friday, February 9. The snow was about eight inches deep. We
concluded it would be good riding in a sleigh; so Mr. Smith and I
set off in one for Brother Brush's quarterly meeting, which was
nearly fifty miles distant. We rode to Burlington very comfortably,
where Brother Sparks appointed meeting, and insisted that I should

preach. I complied, and preached in the Court-house to a small collection of people.

Saturday, 10. We were fearful of riding any farther in the sleigh, for it was likely that the snow would soon leave us; so we borrowed saddles and bridles, and left the sleigh behind us. We reached Mr. Chew's about dark, where were several friends who had come for quarterly meeting.

Sunday, 11. Meeting began about eleven o'clock. The Rev. Mr. Wnatcoat preached, and administered the sacrament, after which Mr. Benjamin Abbott preached. Of all times, under preaching or prayer, I was now most plagued with laughter to hear the old man so queer in many expressions concerning the sinners. He may properly be called a son of thunder. We, the preachers, lodged at Mr. Dilks's.

Monday, 12. Love-feast began at nine o'clock. The Lord was with us indeed in a very powerful manner. I have not seen such a day for a long time. At eleven o'clock public service began, at which time a corpse was brought into the preaching-house, the sight of which called aloud, "Be ye also ready." After Mr. Sparks and Mr. Whatcoat were done speaking the corpse was interred. Then two young people were joined in wedlock. I think the most solemn wedding I ever saw. Some are dying, others marrying, but soon we all shall be laid in the silent grave. A little after, I preached; then brother Brush concluded the meeting. I have not a doubt but that many dear souls were much profited by the services.

Returning to his circuit, Mr. Cooper resumed his pastoral work, organizing, on Sunday, March 11, a class at Mr. Stanton's, near Newburg—a great reformation having taken place in that community; on the 21st, at Mrs. Smith's, at the Great Meadows; and on Wednesday, the 28th, after preaching at Captain McCullough's in that vicinity, met a class which had but recently been organized. Near Greenwich, at Mr. Henry's, who opened his doors for preaching, he established a new place for service on Friday, the 30th of March, feeling, from the concern manifested, that good consequences would result therefrom.

While Methodism was advancing at almost every

point on the circuit, the spirit of opposition was also manifesting itself to such a degree that the preacher felt himself called upon to defend the doctrines and principles of his Church. This he did, sometimes in the sermon, at other times by private controversy, and most commonly by reading to his congregations the Articles and Rules of the Church. One or two instances are here given by way of illustration. At one place between Redding and Newburg, then called the Paltz, he says under date of March 9:

Captain Woolsey took me in his sleigh up to the New Paltz, where I preached at two o'clock. The house was full of people. The minister of that place, who had striven to hurt us, was out to hear me. I found much liberty in preaching on the Gospel Supper; then read our Articles and Rules, which gave general satisfaction to the people. The Rev. Mr. ——, who was present, found that he had told the people wrong things about us. I am led to think that he has hurt himself by so doing.

Again:

Saturday, April 7. At three o'clock I had to preach in Mendon upon our principles, it being a meeting appointed for that purpose. There was a large congregation gathered to hear. I took my text from Rom. ix, 22, 23. After soliciting the impartial attention of my audience, informing them, as I had a complicated assembly in which likely there was a diversity of opinion, I should just advance my own sentiments on the subject, beseeching them not to condemn or applaud before the same should be judiciously examined.

It was expected that I should be attacked, but no one said a word in dispute upon it, while many expressed great satisfaction in hearing the subject treated. I heard of but one man who was offended, and he never came into my presence, though I am told the people wanted him to. They reckoned that the sermon ought to have convinced him, and would have done it if he had been reasonable. This is the center of Calvinism, but they are almost overset.

I lodged at Mr. Henry Clark's. In the evening three or four gentlemen came over to hear our Articles read. They appeared to satisfy them, finding that they were quite contrary to what they had been informed. They parted from me with a very friendly spirit, though some of them had been remarkable enemies to us a few days ago.

Again:

Wednesday, 18. I had to preach twice. It was expected that a certain minister would meet me at one of the places in order to attack me on some principles in which we did not agree, but he did not come. It was thought that many more were at preaching than would have been but for the expected dispute.

Thursday, 19. I traveled to Mr. Jacob Dayton's, up in the New Paltz, where, after I was done preaching, I was attacked by an old gentleman who had been, I am informed, a preacher for more than twenty years; but O, dear man! were I he, I would be ashamed of my conduct. I hope, indeed, he is. He both got angry and disputed very weakly. What weakness it discovers in people to conduct themselves as about six or eight of them did. I exhorted them to dispute and talk less, and to pray more. They acknowledge it to be right. Mr. Talleau, who was sitting back, said unto me: "But you are among a people that talk much and pray but little." He did not like their conduct at all.

As the Conference year was now soon to close, Mr. Cooper, as he passed through his circuit, addressed his congregations in sermons indicative of his expected departure to another field of labor. The scenes through which both the minister and his congregation passed were deeply affecting, and produced many tender expressions and tearful eyes. In the meanwhile he was called to New York to exchange with Mr. Tunnell for three weeks, at the expiration of which time he had planned to go to Maryland to attend the session of the Annual Conference of which he was a member on probation. He left the circuit on Monday, the 23d of April, and the next day entered the city. Here he found, by reason of the arrival of Bishop Coke from England, the Annual Conference had been called to meet on the 1st day of May, in Baltimore; that Mr. Tunnell, with

6

whom he was to exchange, must attend that session;
and that if he did not return to the circuit he had left
there would be disappointment generally. He, therefore, remained one day in New York, after which he
returned to his circuit, and gave up the thought of attending the session of the Conference in Baltimore.
Here he remained until summoned by Bishop Asbury
to New York to be ordained deacon; preaching at
John Allen's, Colonel Palmer's, Daniel Gedney's, Newburg, Mr. Van Duzer's, John Ellison's, Mr. Holmes's,
where, eight weeks before, a man who had been deaf for
a number of years, so that it was with difficulty he heard
any thing, had been asked to come to meeting and hear
preaching, being told that, though deaf, he might get near
the preacher, and hear some, if not all, the sermon. He
came and placed himself near the stand. When the hymn
was read he heard but little, but, to his great surprise,
in time of prayer his hearing came to him, so that he
heard all the sermon perfectly well, and has had his
hearing ever since, which has been about eight weeks.
He was sensibly struck under concern of soul at the
same time, and is now a member of society. Likewise he
preached at Florida, Warwick, John McWhorter's, Mr.
Benjamin's, Winan's, on Schooley Mountain, Esquire
Tuttle's, Benjamin Town's, Joseph Sweezey's, where
was held the fourth quarterly meeting for the year.
On the 19th of May he also preached at Mansfield, and
at other places, closing his work on the circuit at
Mansfield.

On Tuesday, the 22d of May, he set out for New
York to meet the Bishop, but found, on his arrival
there the next day, that he had left the city and
had gone to Long Island. Mr. Cooper followed him,
visiting Newtown, Searington, Mosquito Cove, and
Hempstead, where he overtook the Bishop, with whom

he returned to New York, where, on Sunday, June 3, 1787, he was ordained, in John Street Church, a deacon in the Methodist Episcopal Church. The next day he prepared to go to the new circuit to which he had just been appointed by the Conferncee held in Baltimore, and which was contiguous to the one he had just left. The reader is now invited to a sketch of Methodism in that field—Trenton Circuit.

CHAPTER IV.

TRENTON CIRCUIT, 1787.

TRENTON CIRCUIT, in New Jersey, had, as reported to the Annual Conference for that year (1787), three hundred and seventy-two members. These were divided into classes extending over a large tract of country, requiring six weeks to visit and minister to them all with regularity, and two preachers to serve them. Mr. Cooper's colleague was Nathaniel B. Mills, who was that year admitted on trial in the Conference. As was stated concerning the circuit last passed under review, we are constrained to say of this one: our Church historians have given so meager an account of this field at this time that we enter more into detail than we otherwise would. That the inquirer may have some data wherewith to be guided in his search into early history, the appointments of the circuit are here given, namely: Burlington, Crosswicks (at Mr. Smith's), Monmouth, Perrine's, Outgelt's, Kingston, Anderson's (near Princeton), Mr. Fiddler's, Pennytown, Hopewell, Penny Hill, Mr. Hancock's, Trenton, Mr. George's (near Burlington), Mount Holly, New Mills, Browntown, Edge Pillage, Speedwell Furnace, Francis Bodine's, Esquire Matthias's, Egg Harbor, Esquire Tucker's, Hawkins's, Wier Town, Good Luck, Mr. Brewer's, Mr. Woolley's, Colt's Neck, church near Mr. Morford's, Peter Barclay's, Mr. Higgins's (near Delaware River), Hanover (at Widow Job's), Hancock's, Bask River, Clamtown, Mr. Cook's, Cedar Creek, Dover, Mr.

Throckmorton's, Mr. Grandine's, Joseph Thompson's
(near Cranberry), Shrewsbury, Pleasant Valley (at Mr.
Stoutenborough's), Middletown Point (at Mr. Francis's,
a Churchman), Long Branch, Mr. Rowland's, Heightstown (at Mr. Shaw's), and Robert Pettes's. These,
comprising more than fifty in number, besides other
places where an occasional service was held, made both
the traveling and the preaching, with other ministerial duties, constant, laborious, and extensive. While
it would be highly interesting to many readers to give
Mr. Cooper's Journal entire, space will not permit it,
and such extracts only as are most serviceable to an
understanding of the work, times, and events will be
here given.

Mr. Cooper began the work on his new charge on the
6th day of June, A. D. 1787, of which he thus speaks:

Wednesday, 6. I reached Burlington, though the day was rainy
and the traveling very disagreeable. . . . I preached at night in the
Court-house, and was favored with a number of the Assembly to
hear me—nearly thirty of them, Mr. Sterling supposed.

Thursday, 7. I traveled in the afternoon about fifteen miles to
Crosswicks; at Mr. Smith's I found a sweetness in meditation, and
much love and peace in my soul.

Friday, 8. . . . About nine o'clock I visited a sick friend, who, I
believe, is near death, and he believes it, too; but 'tis a matter of
great comfort to see any one so near death and no more affrighted.
He appears to be quite willing to be loosed from earth, to leave this
tabernacle of clay and be with Christ, which is far better. We
joined in prayer, and I felt much satisfaction. I traveled to-day
nearly thirty miles (was much wearied in body), and had an opportunity of reading part of *The Lives of the First Emperors of Rome.*

Sunday, 10. I preached in Monmouth preaching-house to a large
congregation; I found a mighty inflowing of comfort, especially in
the class-meeting. In the afternoon I went to hear one of our exhorters, who undertook to preach. I sometimes fear that young
speakers are too fond of taking texts, even before they are capable of
doing justice to them.

Monday, 11. I visited friend Francis, who was very low in health, but appeared to have his mind given up to God. I then traveled into a desert kind of place among the pines and preached. I think here is a prospect of good. I then traveled ten or eleven miles farther, and preached; the Lord was present; the word was accompanied to many hearts in power.

Tuesday, 12. I was requested to preach at a new place, where Methodist preaching never had been. We had a large congregation. I preached from Luke xix, 10. The word was, I hope, sent with power to many hearts; the people generally were affected. After preaching I was informed that one man said to a young woman who was much affected, that I preached at the passions and touched them. She replied to him, and said I preached to the heart, and touched that; which stopped him, so that he said it was a good discourse. I then rode to Mr. Perrine's, and preached there.

Wednesday, 13. I preached at Mr. Outgelt's; some were much wrought upon by the word.

Thursday, 14. I breakfasted at Dr. Jaques's, then traveled to Kingston, where I preached to a large congregation of airy, careless people, the greater part of them being youths. Before preaching I was requested to give consent for them to sing without my reading line by line. I was not fond of it, but seeing their desire for it was so strong I consented for that time. I read off the Psalm, and they then took it and sung it through, but I do not know that ever I was so much beaten out by singing before; it almost put me out of order for preaching, and I am afraid it hurt many in hearing; it was so light and airy that I thought it looked more like a place of vanity than of worship. In the evening I rode to Mr. Anderson's, near Princeton, where I was to preach the next day.

Friday, 15. In the morning, after retirement as usual, I walked out to the carriage-house, where I sat down in a sleigh and read with a comfortable mind. In the time of preaching I was much drawn out after the people, and the word appeared not to be in vain.

Saturday, 16. Friend Outgelt and I set off early. We dined at Mr. Bunn's, near Pennytown. Preaching was at Mr. Fiddler's at four o'clock. We had a comfortable time, both in preaching and in class.

Sunday, 17. I preached at eleven o'clock in Hopewell preaching-house, and in the evening in Trenton. I sensibly feel for this people. O Lord, will it please thee to give the effective stroke, so that a work may break out among them!

Monday, 18. I was caught in a shower of rain as I traveled to Crosswicks, but did not get much wet. I preached by candle-light to a room full of people. In my application I was much drawn out, and the people appeared to be deeply affected.

Tuesday, 19. . . . I preached at four o'clock, at Penny Hill, to a small congregation. I hope good was done. After preaching I saw one who was under great distress of soul from hearing the sermon.

Wednesday, 20. I expected to preach at Mr. Hancock's, but had no appointment. I found the family serious, and, I trust, engaged with God. I rode that night to Burlington, and there met the class; we had a comfortable time.

Thursday, 21. . . . In the evening I preached, but found little encouragement. I fear that this place is in a woeful state, not far from being gospel-hardened—perhaps some nearly given up to a reprobate mind. I have a singular concern for them.

Friday. 22. Mr. Smith took me in his chair up to Mr. George's, where I preached at three o'clock. We had a comfortable time. We then returned, and I preached again in Burlington. I yet feel distressed for the people in this city. O Lord, our heavenly Father, let my prayer come up before thee on their behalf!

Saturday, 23. I traveled to Mount Holly; was much disappointed in the place, found it to be much larger than I expected; it is really a clever town, and I like its situation much. I met the class at six o'clock, and preached at about eight o'clock. We had a tolerable congregation; the Rev. Mr. Spragg attended with us, and led in prayer after preaching.

Sunday, 24. I preached at New Mills. I was disappointed in this place as well as in Mount Holly; for I found it to be a smart village. I preached the second time at five o'clock, from 1 John iv, 9; found much liberty in discoursing on the subject. I had the Rev. Mr. Wilson, A.M., and General Lacey, to hear me. I am informed by Esquire Tucker that the general said it was the greatest sermon he had ever heard in that preaching-house. O Lord, keep me humble at all times; let nothing lift up nor cast me down. I remember the words of a certain man: "If they say," said he, "I am an angel, I am none the better; and if they say I am a devil, I am none the worse." So say I, that through the grace of God I am what I am. O Lord, let nothing hurt me in my journey so as to prevent my making a safe arrival on Zion's heavenly shore at last! As I was returning to Brother Budd's a shower of rain came up; I set off to run, and got out of it soon, and in so doing am almost afraid I have hurt myself, for I ran too fast.

Monday, 25. I expected to preach at eleven o'clock A. M., in

Brown Town, but, when I got there, found the service was not till
three P.M. I rode to Silas Brown's and got dinner, then walked to
the preaching place. We had a small congregation, and, I thought,
attentive. We had a very comfortable time in class.

Tuesday, 26. Was a very warm day. About one o'clock I set out
for Edge Pillage. I had to ride a very lonesome road through an un-
inhabited country. I had to go alone, and was enabled to find the
way by limbs of bushes which were broken at every forked road.
We had a company of poor, simple hearers together, and I endeavored to speak accordingly; I trust it was not in vain. After preaching I walked about half a mile to Mr. Dickins's, where I had to
baptize a number of children.

Wednesday, 27. I had a long sandy road to travel, and was glad
when I got to my preaching place, which was at Speedwell Furnace.
I had to preach to a number of workmen, who generally, at such
places, are very wicked. I had liberty, and perceived that many
were affected. Colonel Randal, from Philadelphia, the owner of
the works, was there, and appeared to be very friendly. I then rode
about three miles to Francis Bodine's, and preached to a small
congregation.

Thursday, 28. I had to travel alone again, as I have had to do for
three days in succession. I preached at Esquire Matthias's to a tolerable congregation, but they appeared heavy. I fear that little or
no good was done among them to-day. I had to preach next day
at Egg Harbor, and, having an opportunity of company with Dr.
Baker and another gentleman, who lived there and were going home,
I rode down with them this evening. The doctor and I had a free
conversation as we traveled; he is truly a sensible man. O what a
blessing if he had but the knowledge of salvation by the remission of
his sins! But he is very friendly, and I live in hope that he will see
and feel the need of a closer walk before and with God.

Friday, 29. We had a large congregation out to hear. I preached
in the house of Esquire Tucker; found tolerable liberty, but not the
satisfaction I hoped for; yet I bless God, whose wisdom is infinite,
and who knows best in what manner to deal with his creatures.

Saturday, 30. I preached in Hawkins's preaching-house to a tolerably large congregation, and hope that labor was not in vain.

Sunday, July 1. I preached in the morning at Hawkins's; then
rode to Wier Town, and preached at eleven o'clock. The word of
truth, I thought, had free course to many hearts while I was showing
the unspeakable love of God to our world in sending his only Son to

bleed and die that we might have life through him. I lodged at
Mr. Chamberlain's. Here I saw a young woman who would not attend meeting. She reckoned that preaching would do her no good,
and she should only hear the faults of others and herself exposed, so
she would not go. I talked with her about it, informing her that she
would have to give an account to God at judgment for slighting and
neglecting his worship. Likewise, that it was the work of the devil
to keep her away, and, if she was not careful, she might grieve the
Spirit of God, causing him to depart from her, etc., to all of which
she listened attentively. Next morning, when I was going away, I
thought I would talk to her again. I then spoke of Christ's love to
us, and asked her if she could have so stubborn a heart as to slight
such love? and how she would appear to give an account before
Him at the great day? This seemed so heavy she broke into tears,
and I left her weeping. Blessed be God, that her heart is touched!
O that it may prove effectual! I preached at eleven o'clock at Good
Luck in the preaching-house; we had a large congregation. The word
ran like fire to many hearts. I hope the spark will not be put out.
When I was meeting the class many were around the house very attentive, and some of them much affected, as I could see through the
windows. O that a glorious work may break out here! Lord grant
it, for thy mercy's sake!

Tuesday, 3. I had the company of Esquire Pharo for about twenty
miles. He appeared like a civil man, but I fear he is in want of the
one thing needful. I told him I thought that rulers ought always
to be examples in religion to the people, which spoke louder than
precept. He replied: "That's good doctrine," and seemed to be
pleased that I spoke so plainly to him. I quoted that passage of
Scripture, "Have any of the rulers believed?" showing that the eyes
of the people were generally on the rulers. It appeared to produce
seriousness in his mind. I preached at Mr. Allen's from Rom. viii, 1.
Several were much wrought upon. O may God's work prosper
here!

In the evening I took a short walk, but the mosquitoes were so
swarming that I had no rest, and soon returned to the house. I
don't know that I ever knew flies and mosquitoes to be so thick anywhere; I was obliged to keep my horse in the stable for a week
except when I rode him. These insects are very troublesome all
along the sea-shore for a great distance; I don't know how the poor
beasts do exist among them.

I was much astonished to see the effect, and hear the narration, of a contest between Mr. Allen and a number of robbers, who in time of the last war beset his house. They broke open his doors and windows, yet he, alone, kept them off; declaring that the first that entered would become a dead man. They fired their guns about thirty times into the house, aiming at him, but he escaped the shot: it being dark in the house they had to aim at his voice. They then offered, if he would give up, and give them fifty pounds, they would go in peace; but he told them he would trust no such people. Then they declared that they would burn the house over his head, and began to set fire to it, by throwing the fire in at a back door, until the house in one room was all in a flame. When he saw that he must be burned, or give up, or turn out and run the risk of escape, he cocked his gun, and sprung out into the piazza, and cried out: "Life for life! I am determined to kill, and be killed." But their hearts failed, and they ran, and left him. With much difficulty he put the fire out; but the house is burnt very much, and much was burned up in it, yet he lived.

Wednesday, 4. I had much liberty at Mr. Brewer's in preaching, but had much trouble in class with the Society.

Thursday, 5. I preached at Mr. Woolley's to a tolerable congregation. I had great hoarseness, so that I spoke with difficulty.

Friday, 6. In the morning, early, I went into the sea, and bathed, then rode to Colt's Neck and preached to a congregation chiefly of women, for it being the height of haytime not many men can conveniently leave their work. The word appeared to have some effect. I rode to Mr. Leonard's and lodged, having a comfortable evening with a number of sincere friends, who spent the night there also.

Saturday, 7. I spent the greater part of the day at Mr. Leonard's; in the afternoon I rode over to Mr. Morford's, where I found them very kind.

Sunday, 8. I baptized Mr. Morford's wife, one who, I believe, is sincere in heart and soul. We then rode to the church, where we had a large congregation. Many, I presume, came in order to see some baptized by immersion. I baptized two thus.

Monday, 9. I preached twice. In the afternoon I had four to baptize by way of immersion; we had a number of Baptists out to see, who appeared to be very friendly to some of our members. I found my mind very happy in God.

Tuesday, 10. At ten o'clock I preached at Peter Barclay's; the house could not hold the people. I preached on the Gospel Supper, and believe there were but few dry eyes in the congregation. Here is a great prospect of good being done; many are under great exercise. At four o'clock I preached at Mr. Perrine's; the congregation was small. I found tolerable liberty. In class the power of God was with us, every heart appeared to be affected. O Lord, work for thy glory, and the salvation of souls! I was particularly rejoiced in speaking to three young women, who stayed in the society meeting, in finding their hearts so broken, and their minds so determined, by grace, to take Christ in his appointed way, and put it off no longer. They appeared to be penitent indeed, and wept greatly to think that they had slighted the call of mercy so long.

Wednesday, 11. As I passed through Spottswood town I met the Rev. Mr. Ayres, who is the stated minister there. We fell into a long conversation upon our separation from the Church. He contended that we had done wrong, and that our ordination was not valid. I contended that we had acted with an eye to God's glory and the prosperity of religion, and, from Scripture, reason, and our success under God, was confidently persuaded that we had done right; and, as to the validity of our ordination, I looked upon it that he could not disannul it. He contended: We had broken the chain of succession from the apostles, consequently we, and all who had done that, were in an error to think our proceedings to be right. I told him I thought it would be a difficult point for him, or any one else, to prove the uninterrupted succession of bishops from the apostles. However, we parted in friendship, and agreed in other points. I preached at four o'clock from Eccles. ix. 10.

Thursday, 12. I met with brother Cromwell, from Nova Scotia, at Dr. Jaques's; was very glad to see him, but could not stay long with him, and went on to Mr. Higgins's, and preached to a small congregation. Some were very attentive; I hope labor was not in vain.

Friday, 13. After preaching, when at tea, Mr. Anderson and I fell upon the subject of living without committing sin. I asked him if he thought it was our privilege to love God with all our hearts. He said, "Yes." I then asked if we could love God with all the heart while sin took up one part thereof or remained therein? He said, "No." "Very well, this is just what I contend for: That it is our privilege to love God with all the heart; consequently, to be delivered from all sin, as we cannot do the former without experiencing the latter." "Then," said he, "I believe there are very few of such to be found." "True," I replied, "for few find the narrow way."

Saturday, 14. I preached near Delaware River, from Psa. xxxiv, 19, to a serious people, who, I believe, fear God, and are willing to suffer for his sake.

Having in the above extracts from Mr. Cooper's journal given an outline of the circuit, with the exception of a few points therein which may hereafter be mentioned, we shall now confine our survey of the charge to those facts which will serve to illustrate the work there through the year now under review, premising that there were at least seven houses of worship under the control of the Methodists within the bounds of the circuit, some of which were constructed during the year.

On Saturday and Sunday, August 11 and 12, the first quarterly meeting for the year was held in Hopewell. On Saturday the Rev. James O. Cromwell preached, and the Revs. William Gill and Ezekiel Cooper exhorted. The preachers all were the guests of Mr. Bunn, who entertained, for the night, besides them about thirty other visitors. The love-feast, which was opened on Sunday morning, at nine o'clock, was a season of great power. Says Mr. Cooper:

The presence of the Lord was with us in an extraordinary manner. . . . I have not been in such a meeting for a long time. All the services were fruitful and inspiring.

The next quarterly meeting was held in Freehold, on Saturday and Sunday, October 27 and 28. It, too, was marked by the manifestation of the Holy Spirit. Of the third, held at Manahawkin Saturday and Sunday, February 9 and 10, the following interesting description is given of the Sabbath service:

"Love-feast began between nine and ten o'clock, and held till after eleven o'clock; then the sacrament of the Lord's Supper was administered; public preaching began after twelve o'clock. We had a glorious time, especially in the close of our meeting. The power of God came down in the most powerful manner that I have ever seen in the State of New Jersey. It is said to have been the greatest time that has ever been known in this circuit. All ranks appeared to be in tears; many were overcome in such a manner that they could scarcely stand;

some found Jesus, one man crying out to the congregation to help him to praise the Lord, for he had found him whom his soul loved. This increased the flame, and it ran through the house as fire among stubble. Soon as he ceased to speak a boy of about sixteen years of age broke out in prayer, after which we concluded our meeting.

The fourth quarterly meeting for the year was held at New Mills, on Saturday and Sunday, May 24 and 25. As it differed in some particulars from the others, a more extended quotation from Mr. Cooper's journal will be given to the reader. Joining with other friends on Friday, the 23d, a watch-night service was held at Crosswicks, where were assembled, besides several preachers, more than forty persons from a distance, on their way to the quarterly meeting, and a large number of the people resident in that vicinity. The next morning they continued the route to the seat of the quarterly meeting. Says Mr. Cooper:

There were more than fifty of us who set off from Crosswicks, and rode in company together. We were well off for preachers at quarterly meeting, among whom we had old friend James Barton, who formerly was a Quaker. He gave a sermon on the continuation of the ordinances in the Church, which, I think, was as much to the purpose as any thing I have heard. His text was in 1 Cor. xi, 24: "Do this in remembrance of me." He showed that St. Paul received this not from men, but from the Lord, as in verse 23, and that by divine revelation, and not personally from Christ; for he was not converted when Christ went home to heaven; and as this was revealed to Paul by Christ so long after the day of Pentecost, it doubtless was to be continued; for had it not been so Christ would not have revealed it to Paul so long after the discontinuance of all the Jewish ordinances which were to be abolished; or, at least, after the day of Pentecost, when they were no more approved of by the Lord; and though they might not be fully set aside, yet the Gospel dispensation had fully taken place, after which all that the Lord gave unto his followers by the hand of his apostles was to be continued in his Church to the end, even until he should come, which was the case here, for St. Paul received this from him.

Sunday, 25. At seven o'clock A. M. I met the local preachers, exhorters, and class-leaders for their examination, and to renew the notes of the preachers and exhorters, which kept me very busy until nine o'clock. I then opened the doors and admitted the members for love-feast; we had a great number. It was past twelve o'clock when love-feast and sacrament were over; we had about two hundred communicants; then public preaching began. We had the largest congregation that had ever been seen there. We set up all the windows, that the people might surround the house, which they did after the house was well filled. I don't know that I ever saw a house better stowed with people in my life. It was near, or quite, four o'clock when our services were over. I was kept there from seven o'clock to that time, and was not out of the door but once. I hope the meeting may be a blessing to the place.

For some cause not stated in our Church histories, the Annual Conference of which Mr. Cooper was a member, instead of meeting in the spring or summer of the year, as heretofore, was not convened until September. There was, therefore, a Quarterly Conference held, being the fifth for that ecclesiastical year. As, however, the preachers were now about to leave for the Annual Conference session, and Mr. Cooper had preached his farewell sermons through all parts of the circuit, this quarterly meeting drew together a very large concourse of people. It was held at Joseph Hutchinson's, a few miles distant from New Mills, on Saturday and Sunday, August 23 and 24. At eleven o'clock on Saturday the Rev. Mr. Budd preached "a beautiful sermon" to a large assembly. Of the Sabbath service we have the following from Mr. Cooper:

Sunday, 24. Love-feast began between eight and nine o'clock. We had the preaching-house well stowed with friends, and a glorious time we had. I don't know that ever I knew the people to get under a better way of speaking than they did to-day. The Lord's Supper was administered between ten and eleven o'clock; then we went into the open woods to preach, where we had near about two thousand people. We, the preachers, got into a wagon, and then the speaker stood in a chair, so that we could both speak to and see the people. I preached the sermon from Acts xx, 31, 32. I had a field opened to me, and both the people and myself were affected. The power of the Lord rested on us. I don't think I ever saw so large a congregation in the woods behave so well; every one appeared 'to be still and attentive, an awe rested upon them, and I am persuaded that much good was done. Brothers Mills and Cromwell exhorted, and not in vain. After preaching I was, I believe, nearly an hour in bidding the friends farewell. I don't know that ever I bid so many people farewell, by shaking the hand, in one day before.

While space will not permit a much more extended view of the circuit work, by Mr. Cooper and his colleague, a recital of a few peculiarities will be in place, and give pleasure to the interested reader. At Middletown Point a family resided by the name of Francis. They were strongly attached to the Protestant Episcopal Church. Mr. Cooper, however, preached at the house of Mr. Francis, on the 2d day of October, 1787, and thereafter. The services, as was frequently done, alternated between his and other families of the town as the years rolled by. Mr. Francis had a daughter who, for three or four years, had been demented, and who was subject, at times, to fits of violence. When Mr. Cooper first visited her father's family, she gave respectful attention to his sermon, and could repeat passages from it and from the sermon preached the next day in another house in the village. She behaved as quietly as any one, conversed seriously and intelligently with Mr. Cooper, and impressed all who knew her with the fact of the remarkable change that had taken place in her conduct. Again: At Mr. Richard Ellis's, where preaching was introduced by Mr. Cooper on the 13th of October, 1787, he found one of the old gentleman's daughters to be in a melancholic condition, fearing that there was no mercy for her. Her state being known to the community, the enemies of the Methodists cried out, "The Methodists have driven Mr. Ellis's daughter out of her senses." "Ah!" said one, "I am not going to hear them preach, to be driven out of my senses." The spirit of opposition was manifested, also, in other places, as, for instance, in Allentown, Pa., where, on the 3d day of January, 1788, Mr. Cooper preached to a large congregation, and on the day following visited the Rev. Mr. Clark, rector, in Allentown, who had opposed the Methodists. Says Mr. Cooper:

> I wished to know what objections he had to our preaching in that place, as I heard he had spoken against it. He said he had no objection to my preaching, but he did not think I ought to preach in his congregation without his consent. But I told him that I must preach the Gospel; and if he would not consent for me to preach, yet, if the people chose to hear me, I must not be silent. He signified that I might go to other places, where there was no settled preacher. I told him I thought some in his neighborhood needed preaching to as much as any people.

Such opposition was not, however, without its counterpart, as will appear in the narration following. A Mrs. Furman had died during the previous harvest season, and was buried at Upper Freehold. Having requested her daughter to have her buried in Shrewsbury, she was disinterred, in February, and brought thither, where Mr. Cooper preached a funeral sermon over her remains in the Episcopal Church of that place. In speaking of it, he says:

> Unexpectedly to many, they gave a grant that I should preach in the church, which I did—and a famous building it is.

The number of churches, or, as they were called, meeting-houses, was limited to four throughout the bounds of the circuit in the beginning of the year, and public service was, therefore, for the most part, held in private dwellings, or school-houses, or barns, or Courthouses. Of holding services in the latter, Mr. Cooper thus speaks:

Thursday. April 10. To-day we made an effort to get a house in Burlington to preach in; for I am quite tired of preaching in the Court-house. We have preached there so long, and no good scarcely has been done, I think it much better to preach in a private house until we can get a house built for that purpose. It is true that there is a considerable work here in Burlington, but the greater part, or all, has been in private houses. What can be the cause I cannot tell. . . . I refused to preach in the Court-house, and preached in the house of Mr. George Smith.

Of the Methodist churches then on the circuit some were too open and cold for the severity of winter, and were, for the most part, closed during that season. One, however, the church at New Mills, was better adapted to the wants of the congregation; and on the 14th of April, 1788, steps were taken to secure its incorporation according to law; trustees were chosen, and the papers made out in due form for the record in the county clerk's office. Near Middletown preaching was held regularly at the houses of Daniel Woolley, Mr. Drummond, and Mr. Brinley. On the 8th of June it was held in Mr. Brinley's barn, "where," says Mr. Cooper, "the people were much better accommodated than they could have been in the dwelling-house. I hope they will soon have a preaching-house built here; they have got about it." Measures were also taken to secure a church in Burlington, as the following quotation will show:

Thursday. July 3. I spent the day in the city (Burlington). I drew up a subscription paper to-day for the building of a preaching-house in this place, with an intent to hand it out among the people, which next day I did, and got more than £80 subscribed the first day. I hope it will go on. I walked with friend Smith to view several lots, of which he judged we might have our choice, in order to pitch upon one; two or three I liked, but one in particular I liked very much.

The membership had during the year increased from 372 to 526.

7

CHAPTER V.

METHODISM IN BALTIMORE, 1788, 1789.

THE session of the Philadelphia Annual Conference opened in that city on the 23d day of September, 1788. It was attended by Mr. Cooper, though he was too unwell to take an active part in its deliberations. On Thursday, the third day of the session, the ordination sermon was preached; four persons were ordained, and the Lord's Supper was administered. After this Bishop Asbury, the Rev. Dr. McGaw, "a Church clergyman," and Mr. Cooper, dined with Mr. Fitzgerald. The Conference was convened again at three o'clock P. M., when Drs. Rush and Clarkson met with the preachers, by invitation, to express their sentiments respecting the effects of spirituous liquors upon them that drank them. In describing this meeting, Mr. Cooper says :

At three o'clock the Conference met, and Dr. Rush and Dr. Clarkson met with us in order to give their sentiments respecting the effects of spirituous liquors. They bore a great testimony against it, judging that spirituous liquors never did any good, except in a very few cases, but that they were the greatest poison to both body and soul of any thing we had in our land. Dr. Rush said he found, by observation, that a great many disorders were principally created by the use of spirits. He further said, that he, for some time, had had the care of the mad people, and had discovered that two fifths of them were brought into their madness by the use of spirits. He judged it much the best not to use them at all.

By this Conference Mr. Cooper was appointed to the charge of Baltimore, with Francis Spry as his colleague, and the Rev. Nelson Reed as elder over the district.

The charge had reported to the late Conference a membership of, whites, 950 ; colored, 269 ; total, 1,219, and, being then a circuit, embraced the following preaching places: Baltimore, Fell's Point, Gatches, Austin's, Owin's, Perrigo's, Wheeler's, Carnan's, Gorsuch's, Orrick's, Marshall's, Tipton's, Vaughan's, Reistertown, Bozman's, Dorsey's, Jones's, Stone Chapel, Hunt's Chapel, Hookstown, and Evans's. For various reasons, one of them being that his colleague feared the smallpox, then prevalent in and about the city, Mr. Cooper took charge of the work in Baltimore and on Fell's Point, and Mr. Spry that of the circuit outside of the city, being aided therein by an occasional service by Mr. Cooper. As this pastoral term was a season of remarkable power, such as has rarely been witnessed in the history of our Church, the following account, hitherto unpublished, is given, which, though somewhat elaborate, will be perused with delight by the descendants of the Baltimore Methodists of 1788–89, and others who are inspired by the spirit of the past. Mr. Cooper prepared it at the request of Bishop Asbury, and for the Church in general. It begins, *A Brief Account of the Work in Baltimore;* written by E. C. in an epistle to Bishop Asbury:

My much esteemed Brother: Pursuant to my promise, I undertake the pleasing task of presenting you with an account of the great and glorious work of God which went on in Baltimore during my appointment and labors there. I am at a loss to determine upon the most eligible method of giving this narrative, so that adequate ideas may be formed of the admirable display of God's power and grace upon and among the people. Had I not been present myself to see, hear, and feel the work, I doubt whether any description could have given me just conceptions of it. It far exceeded any thing I ever expected to see in this vale of tears ; but blessed be God that I ever saw such a work of religion, and, to the great joy of my soul, was in the midst of it! I expect my narration of the matter will be but faint to those who were present. It may appear very wonderful to many who never saw such a work, but they may rest assured I shall not exceed certain facts; nay, I verily doubt whether my review will raise their ideas to the just magnitude of the incontestable truth of the various facts given.

The 1st of October, 1788, that worthy man, Brother Francis Spry (now at rest), and myself, who were appointed colleagues, entered upon our ministerial work in Baltimore—town and circuit. Brother Spry, from fear of the small-pox, together with some other circumstances, stayed chiefly on the circuit; consequently I stayed in town.

You must know that Satan and many wicked men had been made very angry by reason of a noisy, powerful meeting which was held in the close of Conference; and, indeed, several of our worthy friends were exceedingly tried, being prejudiced against what then appeared to them as confusion insufferable in places of divine worship. Also several were much tempted against you on account of some plain, severe reproofs which you gave, in such close, and, as they thought, general terms, that they concluded you called in question their sincerity in religion, and condemned them as hypocrites altogether. I have not the least doubt but that your rebuke was, in the end, productive of much good. Those who were tried generally soon got over it, and loved you as well, probably better, if possible, than ever. There were various concurring circumstances which caused me to labor under a series of severe exercises. I felt great need of the wisdom of the serpent and the innocence of the dove. The God of the Christian and the god of this world were at open war; the Spirit of truth was powerfully striving with saint and sinner; but the spirit of error and lies was diligently opposing them in all that was good. It appeared that Michael and his angels fought, and the dragon and his angels.

In all my measures I moved cautiously but steadfastly in all settled points of discipline. It never was my choice or wish to govern or rule—rather to be ruled—but whenever it has been your pleasure to set me as an assistant, I always found it my duty to hold the reins of, and use, discipline with exactness; also with mildness, or moderation.

Amid all my private and public trials and labors I felt a measure of faith that God would revive his work. This encouraged me, and increased my love, joy, and patience. I labored on, night and day, both in town and on the Point, under great weakness of body. Often the word, by divine energy, made a great move among the people, to the melting of hearts and flowing of tears. I can truly say my mind was exceedingly drawn out after precious souls. Frequently, while preaching and praying, my soul would feel as if it were melted, and flowing from the pulpit in streams of love through the house after and among the people. I thus continued without seeing much fruit come to maturity till the latter part of the winter.

In February, 1789, the glorious work broke out like a fire which had a long time struggled for vent, and blazed forth in a flaming conflagration. It first broke out on the Point: the friends there were unanimous in forwarding and encouraging it. Soon the same flame spread through town also. A general query passed to and fro among the citizens: "What do these things mean?" Our meetings, it is true, were very noisy, with penitential cries and shouts of praise. Many could not bear this, but reprobated it as insufferable madness in places of worship; some were afraid to say any thing for or against it; a few were indifferent; while others, with animated zeal and humility, supported it by argument and example.

On February 16 there was a most remarkable time on the Point at a watch-night service. held by Brother Nelson Reed and three or four others of our brethren the preachers. It is thought, at a moderate calculation, thirty or forty were converted. This was the time when Brother Reed fully entered into the spirit of this great and marvelous work. From the effects then and the fruits since seen. a most glorious and awful night it was. My heart, head, and hands now were full, and engaged on every side in this mighty cause and work of the Redeemer. I wanted help very much, finding more work than one could do; accordingly I wrote to Annapolis for Brother John Hagerty to come up with Brothers C. and L. to assist me, for one week. to besiege town and Point every night alternately. They came on Monday, the 2d of March, and stayed till the Friday following, in which time the Lord favored us remarkably every night; it almost appeared that every body was turning to the Lord, or thinking awfully upon eternal things. However. we were sorry to find that numbers braved it out, resisted the Holy Ghost, and opposed the progress and power of truth.

Every evening in our congregations, which were uncommonly large, the power of God was like a rushing mighty wind. The citizens who never came to our church at other times now flocked thither in abundance to see and hear what some called "the Methodistical rant and enthusiastical madness;" but, poor creatures! they knew not what they said, neither the power of God, nor what manner of spirit we were of. Very hard things were spoken of the work and all who promoted it. It always was the case; where God carries on a remarkable work, Satan, like a roaring lion, stirs up all his wrath and power against it. We pitied and prayed for our enemies and persecutors. There were very few who listened with candor and looked on impartially who were not seriously impressed with the conviction that the work was more than of man, and really something divine.*

No wonder that the noise should be very dismal to some, when so many were crying as out of the terrible pit, as under the pains of hell which they felt in their souls, to a provoked Sovereign for his favor, or else shouting praises to God for mercy and pardon found while others were exhorting and praying with mourners, pressing them to believe on the Lord Jesus Christ to the saving of their souls. The cries of the penitents strikingly put me in mind of the hopeless shrieks or screams of the damned beneath, who have passed from the reach of mercy, and cannot obtain a drop of water to cool their tongue, being tormented in that flame. But, O! these were in a state of probation, looking for and obtaining salvation. Also, when several would join in the praise together who had just entered into life, it raised my ideas of heaven, and the sweet chorus to be joined in there. But this was like fresh arrows in the breast of those still under distress; and as if their hearts were rending, and their hopes sinking, they would cry out: "Has the Lord no mercy for me?" "What shall I do?" "Am I a wretch undone and banished from God forever?" "Lord, thou art just, but Christ has died! Bless me, even me, O my Father and my God!" "Save! save! save! Lord save from the wrath to come! Save, or I sink into hell!" Who could hear this (infidels excepted) and not both pray for and exhort them to trust and believe in Jesus?

It is thought that one night there were four thousand people in and around the church in town; the street was crowded, and the church surrounded. The work, each night, continued till one, two, or three o'clock A. M., during the whole of which time less or more

---

* The heart-rendering cries and throbbing lamentations were truly awful to hear. In one circle on the floor thirty or forty at one time, besides many others in various parts of the house, lifting up their voices in penitential invocations: "Save, Lord, save or we perish!" their gushing tears, like fountains flowing, and writhing agitations, like convulsive throes on the human frame, were enough to make the stoutest heart feel and tremble. "What shall I do to be saved?" cried one; "Pray for me!" implores another; "Is there mercy for a sinner like me?" inquires another; others cry out, "Lord save, or I perish." Thus all kinds of pathetic addresses to Heaven for mercy, pardon, and peace were heard through the church.

were struggling into or after peace and pardon. Some were convicted one night and converted the next; others, the night after; and some, the same night; though the greater part had had awakenings before for some time, but had never fully given up their hearts to take the cross and follow Jesus. But, glory to the Lord! they now came like doves to the ark of safety. It verily appears that these times bear a great likeness to those of old, when it was said, " These people are full of new wine." Some, maliciously, either for diversion to them-selves or reproach to us, said we " worshiped God as if the devil was in us." 'Tis not doubted but that Satan was in many who cried so lamentably for him to be cast out. And out of many he was cast, by the power of the Holy Ghost, through faith in Jesus Christ. They were first torn by Satan, then healed by Christ; their cries were, first of sorrow, then of praise; and had these held their peace, the very stones would have cried out.

In the time of this work I thought, surely nearly all the Lord's people are prophets. From the foot to the head in the Church all seemed ready to cast in their mite and do their part in promoting the blessed cause. Now appeared to have come the days spoken of by the prophet, that sons and daughters were to prophesy, and the Spirit of the Lord to be poured out upon all flesh. The work thus went on, none being able to make us afraid, or daring to do any thing against it, more than with their tongues or lips, under which was the poison of asps. Some enemies to the cross, I apprehend, had malice and will, like tyrants, to slay and devour, but their hands were bound by our civil and religious rights and privileges. Lord, grant that these rights may extend to and be maintained in every nation! Hierarchy, supported by a civil establishment, scarcely ever fails to create a species of tyranny over the simple Gospel truth, as it would otherwise operate in the consciences of men. We, feeling the bene-fits of a deliverance from this oppression, and seeking the blessed ef-fects of a free, unshackled toleration in giving truth every advantage to defend its cause and gain the hearts of men, we most certainly should feel grateful, and ever praise the hand of Providence for knocking off every human compulsion over the conscience of men in our government. Some vainly thought, and were pleased to insinu-ate, that we were aiming at government. I told them, frequently, there was no such intention, nay, not the most distant purpose of such a thing, and that we would as freely oppose a measure of that nature as they would. And still I pray that our rulers may ever be inspired with love to liberty and religion, and maintain the right and

privileges of the people. Whatever community flourishes, let it be
by the purity of its doctrines, strictness of its discipline, piety of its
members, and diligence of its ministers, not by political or civil
establishments.

Sunday, March 8. I received a considerable number into Society.
There had joined, in about four weeks, upward of a hundred members.
My work as a preacher still increased; I had little or no time for any
thing but to seek after souls. From day to day I passed from one
part of the town to another, also on the Point, visiting, comforting, encouraging, exhorting, and praying with all I found under awakenings, or who had set their faces Zionward. This visiting to and fro
was attended with singular success; it was made a lasting blessing
to my own soul and to those whom I visited. Whenever I heard of
any under distress, I made it my business, as soon as possible, to seek
after them, lest through delay the enemy of souls should get the advantage and draw them again into vanity. Many times at night I
have been so exhausted that it was painful to walk or stand; nevertheless, the next day I pursued the same method and track. At times
I thought I must give it up, being so weak in body; but the love of
Christ constrained me to go on, and venture my body and life for
souls; so I pressed forward in my fatiguing labor, preaching five and
six times a week, meeting classes every day, holding prayer-meetings
frequently, and visiting as above. The Lord supported me, and
through him I found it my chief delight, my element, my meat and
drink, to look after and feed the flock of Christ which he had purchased with his own blood.

Many of the most abandoned offenders against God were brought
to the experience of true religion. Those who had, a little before,
been notorious sinners, could testify of the pardoning love of God in
the remission of their sins. This was "the Lord's doing, and it was
marvelous in our eyes;" instances of which had great effect in si-
lencing gainsayers. Indeed, what can be more convincing than to
look around and see upright, pious men walking circumspectly in the
fear of God, who a few months before were enormous perpetrators
of the most atrocious crimes? I frequently put this case to the people, and asked: "Who that have a regard for social virtues, and wish
the destruction of their contrary vices, would contemn a measure productive of such desirable effects?" The effects were visible to all who
would look around, not only upon one or two, but upon many. This
was enough to silence any reasonable man, though a deist, and did
generally shut up the mouths of opposers. I have cited these facts

when in conversation with persons of deistical notions, and they have candidly yielded that, to their knowledge, great and good effects, which are truly desirable in society, were wrought in our meetings.

Some asked: "Could not those effects be produced without the shouting and noise?" My reply was, generally, I did not know how that might be, but this was certain, they were not produced before, and I doubted whether they would have been, had not God worked in this extraordinary manner; for I did not see or hear of any such effects then being so extensive and general except where there was this noise and power attending them. I also observed it was not the noise that produced the effects, but the effects of the power which produced the noise; though the noise, being principally the effect of God's power among the people, might be attended with a great blessing to the hearers and spectators, as it certainly was.

Others said: " All who make the noise are not sincere." This I believed (neither are all who are still and quiet sincere); but I believe the greater part of those who were so powerfully wrought upon were sincere. I thought it resembled the good seed sown in the field, but an enemy came and sowed tares. Some said, "Pluck up the tares." I answered, " No, for in so doing we shall destroy the wheat also; let them alone, by and by we shall gather the wheat, and the tares will be left behind," which soon was the case: the sincere came in and the others were left.

Numbers expressed great sorrow that we, who before this work had become a respectable community, had brought ourselves into reproach. I remembered our Lord's words: "Woe unto you, when all men shall speak well of you:" also, "All that will live godly in Christ Jesus shall suffer persecution." I felt rejoiced that our reproach was not for evil doing, but rather for righteousness' sake, which if we suffer we are to be glad with exceeding joy. I am awfully afraid that many will lose their souls through fear of reproach, and for a good name among men. The cross is a mortifying thing to nature. A fashionable, honorable religion, allowing the maxims, customs, and pleasures of this world, many would like; but where gospel holiness, the pure religion of Christ, is preached and enforced—that we must deny ourselves of all vanity, and walk the strait and narrow way of humility and meekness, love and obedience— they pray to be excused. Happy for those who have consented to have their names cast out as evil: to be accounted mad or fools for Jesus Christ. For my part,' I would much rather go the way to heaven with a beggar than the way to hell with a monarch. We are willing to bear reproach so long as it is for the sake of righteousness.

My repeated advice to the people was, if they could not be reconciled to these shoutings and powerful conversions, to let them alone, lest they should be found fighting against God. If it was of man, it would come to naught; but if of God, they could not overthrow it. The longer it stood, and as it went on, more and more were reconciled, and believed it to be of God. Indeed nothing but prejudice or obstinacy could prevent our acknowledging it to be a display of God's glory and power among men. It is a dangerous thing to impute the work of God to Beelzebub, or the power of the devil; it borders very nigh to blasphemy against the Holy Ghost.

I often derived much happiness from seeing those who for a long time violently opposed the work at last come in and get converted in the midst of shouting. Time passed delightfully; every friend's house was like a church; the principal and delightful topic among them was the work of God. Love filled their hearts; prayer and praise employed their tongues, both day and night. Surely this was "Life everlasting, and heaven below." A remarkable union and fellowship reigned among the brethren; they seemed to think, speak, and act in conjunction; they strove to keep the union of the Spirit in the bond of peace—all concerned for the promotion of the cause, and the furtherance of each other in the divine life; they were hearty in the matter, bearing up both preacher and people in the arms of faith and prayer. Whenever we came together the fire of love seemed to be already kindled in our hearts, which would glow from breast to breast through the congregation. I am constrained to confess that if ever I saw love, zeal, and humility among a people it was here, through the course of this work, in Baltimore. O may these graces ever subsist among them! may they ever be found among all our community throughout the Connection! nay, among all the true followers of Jesus! 'Tis this that makes our light shine before men, so that they may see our good works, and be brought to an imitation thereof, and glorify our Father who is in heaven. This constrains a sinful world to say : "See how these Christians love!" Though this was the case in general, yet, nevertheless, there were some crooked sticks, or professors which were hard to make straight. A self-willed member is always difficult to deal with; but the truly humble are teachable, and always submissive to the regulated order of the Church.

We had prayer-meetings established through various parts of town and Point. Never a night but that there were meetings of some kind—the echo of prayer and praise reverberated to and fro through both town and Point, and from one to the other. There were several prayer-meetings, sometimes the same night, in different private houses, no one house being large enough to hold all, nor yet convenient to those who wished to attend. Our class-leaders, and others who prayed and exhorted in public, would divide, some going to one, others to another meeting. Poor sinners could scarcely walk the streets without being accosted by the sound of praying, singing, or exhortation. We had our regular nights and times to assemble in the church, at which times they came from every part of the town, having no other meetings—except that when we met in the town church there would be other meetings on the Point; and, also, when we met in the Point church they would hold their meetings in town. I attended both churches regularly, in course, and as often as convenient visited the prayer-meetings in the private houses.

In May, the time of Conference, you and a number of our brethren the preachers were present, and saw a little of this work. Numbers were then converted to God. The work on two nights continued till one or two o'clock in the morning; but great as the times then appeared, they were not to be compared with many others which we had, for a genuine, powerful shaking among the dry bones. Our brethren at Conference then saw what was frequently seen among us, sometimes in a less, at other times in a greater degree. We used to have less or more conversions every week. These glorious seasons are to be remembered through eternity; for it is morally impossible that what we then saw, heard, and felt, should ever be erased from thought.

My appointment from Conference was to Annapolis; but you directed me to continue in Baltimore till November, and Brother John Hagerty to stay in Annapolis. Some weeks after Conference Brother Thomas Foster came, by your appointment, to take charge of the Point; this lightened my burden, having then the town only as my charge. Through the summer the work still went on as usual.

Sunday, July 5. Was a great time on the Point, being the quarterly meeting. At the afternoon, three o'clock, preaching and sacrament it broke out, and continued till t-n o'clock at night. The weather was very warm, and the house crowded. We took out all the window-sashes to admit the air. Several fainted, and were carefully conveyed into private houses. The work was very deep and general that night. The cries of mourners were very piercing; the most careless seemed to be stunned and struck with awe; a considerable number were converted. That night, Sister N. H., who had been under concern for some time, was thoroughly broken in heart under deep distress, and a short time after found peace with God up at the Forest quarterly meeting, where was a great and powerful work. She still walks with us in the light and the enjoyment of grace. O what cause of joy it was to see so many coming home to the Lord!

Toward the end of July Satan had almost gained his point in setting some of our friends at variance, which would unavoidably have done great injury to the work of religion; but the Lord brought peace. I plainly saw, "Except the Lord keep the city, the watchman waketh but in vain." Blessed be God, that "the devil was disappointed, and hell missed her expectation!" The matter at first gave me great uneasiness, lest the evil should grow. I exerted myself to suppress it, and found great satisfaction in its destruction. O that our brethren would guard against giving way to temptation, and also be careful to give to each other no cause of trials!

About this time many of the professors of religion felt the need of clean hearts, and were concerned for holiness. There was an encouraging prospect of sanctification taking place in the Church. Some experienced it, but it did not go on to an extensive degree.

At our August quarterly meeting, and a few succeeding days, was the most extraordinary work of any. It exceeded any thing I had seen before, or, indeed, expect to see again.

The quarterly meeting began on Saturday, August 8. In the afternoon, at sacrament, Sister H. M. J. (a cousin to our worthy Brother P. R.), who had been concerned for some weeks, wanted to find rest to her soul, but resolved not to cry out or make a noise. However, feeling strangely, she went behind the pulpit, and there breathed out her desires to God for mercy till she could refrain no longer, but cried out aloud under deep distress. On the next day the Lord blessed her with love, joy, and peace, to which she continues to hold fast, and proves a pattern of piety to the young sisters, adorning her profession to the present. O may she continue humble and watchful! In the course of this work there were several instances, similar to hers, of those who thought if they were converted they would not cry out; some, that they would keep it a secret, and tell it to no one at all. But they were mistaken; some of them cried aloud, indeed; and all who got converted were ready to tell it (like David), saying: "Come and hear, all ye that fear God, and I will declare what he hath done for my soul." I verily believe there are none who feel this divine work in reality but are ready and willing to speak of it to God's children. They have no desire to keep it a secret, but wish to declare it to their brethren in Jesus. Hence it is a true sign that those know but little about conversion, internally and really, who pretend that it is a secret, to be concealed from all but God and themselves.   *Correct*

Sunday, August 9. Love-feast began at eight o'clock, and a feast of love it was. The flame kindled through the church as though every heart had brought the fire of love burning with them. I don't remember ever being in a love-feast where there was so general and powerful a glowing and melting among the people. Surely the Lord sent the angel of his presence with a living coal from the altar, and applied it to every heart and tongue. There seemed to flow words of fire from every mouth, while one after another, full of rapture and love, arose and humbly declared the great goodness of God to his or her soul. It was a pentecost indeed! We stood as on the top of Pisgah, and viewed the land of which the Lord had said, "I will give it you." The love, joy, and power which we felt exceeds what human language can fully express. We wanted wings to fly to "Life's fair tree, fast by the throne of God."

At eleven o'clock public preaching began; the word, like a two-edged sword, pierced as it went. Stout and hard hearts were brought to tremble, while tears flowed in abundance from almost every eye. It was awful and solemn to behold the visible effects of divine power which accompanied the preaching of the Gospel. Many who were seldom affected on such occasions before, were shaken as if to the center of their souls, and penitently wept as though they had been sitting at the foot of the cross. At night we had a great time, and a number of conversions. We continued till very late, and the whole time some were crying for mercy, others shouting for joy. Now quarterly meeting ended, but the greatest work was still to come!

Monday, 10. Early in the morning I was sent for by Mr. W. Buchanan, to visit his daughter, who was under deep distress of soul. When I went I found her almost exhausted, pensively lying in the arms of Sister R. R. (a young woman who had lately found the Lord), and there mourning and sobbing. She had slept none all night; but spent the hours in weeping and praying. My heart was sensibly touched at her situation; her sorrow was truly penitential. I exhorted her to believe, and with confidence to venture her all upon Christ; strove to press on her mind the all-fullness which dwells in Jesus, and his willingness that she should receive out of that fullness peace and pardon. I sung and prayed twice, and pointed her again to a bleeding Saviour. But she could not believe; no peace could she find till toward noon, when several friends had collected together who sung and prayed till the Lord removed her burden, broke in upon her soul, and filled her with peace and joy. Immediately a general shout of praise ascended to God. The acclamation being heard at a distance, and some one saying, "The fire has broken out at Mr. Buchanan," the alarm was given, "Fire, fire!" by some who thought that the house was on fire. Immediately the fire-bell was rung; the people came running to extinguish the flame. But, behold! it was the fire of religion and divine love which had kindled, and raised a shout in Mr. B's. house at the conversion of his daughter E. This flew through town like lightning, quickly extending to every part thereof. Little P. B., about nine years of age, who had found peace the day before, was so transported when her sister E. found peace that she cried out: "O, how merry I am! Sister is happy, sister is happy! I got happy on Sunday and sister on Monday!" The house was full of prayer and praise; the people would have crowded in too much, but were prevented; the passage was full; some climbed up on a pile of wood, which lay at the end of the house, in order to look in through the windows, being anxious to see and hear what was being done, and how the happy souls rejoiced together. O Lord, the good that is done thou doest it thyself!

The same morning, at ten o'clock, a few mourners in deep distress went to Brother N. Jones's, to get Brother and Sister Jones to pray with them. They sang and prayed together, the power of God came down, and a great outcry and shout was raised. This spread through town; the people, in amaze, collected from all parts, and soon filled the house both above and below stairs; the street also was filled with astonished spectators. In the house the mourners and believers were all in full expectation, the professors being on a stretch for purity of heart, and the penitents for pardon. The people came and went constantly throughout the day, for it never broke up, nor was there any intermission all day. Numbers were converted, and several professed sanctification. Some came with all the indifference about religion that careless minds could possess, and got convinced and converted before their return; particularly, a young man and a young woman experienced this. The young man, when he came up, appeared to be quite in a pet, and dropped some sarcastic expressions; but when he looked on and listened awhile his heart grew tender, and tears began to flow; he pressed in among the mourners, and down he came and cried for mercy till his soul was delivered; then he arose and praised God.

Toward evening I had a table set out, over the street from Brother Jones's house, on which I mounted and spoke for some time to a surrounding audience, who heard with profound attention. A sea-captain who was there had his heart reached, who had before been quite thoughtless about his soul. All the time I spoke from the table the house continued full, the prayers and cries of mourners were plainly heard across the street where I stood. It was, of a truth, a most awful scene. Solemnity and dread rested upon the countenances of the people.

When night came on we repaired to the church, as there were many still under distress, unwilling to break up without the blessing of peace and pardon. As we passed to the church with the mourn-ers, who wept as they went, the people flocked through the streets, and in a little time the church was filled with men, women, and chil-dren. The work went on till two o'clock in the morning, continually less or more struggling in fervent prayer after salvation. No un-prejudiced person could have looked on without feeling his heart to be, in some measure, affected. Numbers, after they passed through the house and listened to the cries and heard the prayers of mourners and compared them together, finding the agreement and similarity between them, were constrained to acknowledge the power of God— it being too wonderful to be of man alone. Some were two or three hours in constant agony under the burden of guilt, some on their knees, others prostrate on the floor, others in the arms of their friends; all bitterly crying to God for mercy. When such distressed souls found rest, who could refrain from feeling joy? As those deliv-erances were frequent, peal after peal of shouting praise ascended to the great Redeemer.

I apprehend that thousands of citizens came together that night. Some came and went several times, not being easy there or at rest away. Indeed hearts must be callous not to feel on seeing and hearing these things. O Lord, wonderful and great are thy works; marvelous are thy doings! Unto thee, O Lord, give we the glory! These sixteen hours, from ten o'clock Monday till two o'clock Tues-day morning, we had no intermission, except while passing from the private house to the church, which could hardly be called an interim, as the beginning of service in the church was before all got from the private house. On Tuesday it was much like unto Monday; at eight o'clock several collected in a private house in another part of the town, for prayer. They began, the news of it spread, the seekers came together, and soon the house was filled. This was a great day, also, though not quite equal to the day before. However, we had some as remarkable conversions as I ever saw. Numbers could testify that that was the day of their espousal to Jesus. The meeting continued all day, and at night we repaired to the church, as above, where we were till ten o'clock, making fourteen hours in all.

These two days the devil's kingdom suffered great loss; his power was sadly shaken. Religion now became the common topic of conversation through town in almost every company. You could scarcely enter a shop, walk the street or market, but that you heard the people on the subject of our shouting meetings and the numerous conversions among us. A panic had seized upon numbers, who knew not what to be at or do; some railed, others were afraid, while others approved of what had passed among us. It was the cry of some, "The Methodists, at this rate, will get all the people." To see thirty or forty join us on a Sabbath day, besides others through the week, which was frequently the case, was matter of grief and aggravation to those who envied our success. The work went on daily. The felicity which I enjoyed was very great indeed—hard ways seemed easy.

Sunday, September 27, was another very extraordinary time. The whole day was a favorable season, but at night the Lord poured out his Spirit in a powerful manner. We had several conversions. This night young Jon. Dagan and Jacob Welch had a long struggle for peace, but found rest soon, one after the other, when a general acclamation of praise passed through the church. A most affecting sight it was to see these young men embrace each other, also their friends, and mingle together their tears of joy and voices of praise. It was enough to melt a heart of stone. Another young man, in the transport of his soul, cried out, "Glory! Glory to God! He has pardoned my sins! I have been a captain among devils, but now I am happy in God! What I feel is worth more than ten thousand worlds. O, what will heaven be, since such a paradise is here? I would sooner go in extreme poverty and be thus happy, than have the church full of gold and be a sinner as I was!" That night I received upward of forty members into society, who came up in the usual way, one after another, and gave in their names. The work was very genuine and powerful. As general a solemnity rested on the people as at any time through the work; though the work of conversion was not so extensive as it had been before.

Monday, September 28. I preached the funeral of Sister Killen, in the Dutch Church, to not less than a thousand hearers. To take her all through her illness, she was one of the happiest souls I ever saw on a sick bed. She had a long spell of sickness, but, blessed be God! she had set out in religion and found peace a few months before her death. She, likewise, was a witness of perfect love. After the burial I rode up to Captain C. Ridgley's, in company with not less than one hundred people, where we had a watch-night service. Seven or eight preachers were there, and a large concourse of people. Brother Wilson preached a most moving sermon, and soon after we had a general shout. The services continued till about two o'clock in the morning. A number of souls were converted to God, and more than a hundred persons stayed all night at the captain's.

Some time in the month of September was the singular conversion of Sister A. R., in time of family prayer, at Brother J. H.'s, while Brother Nelson Reed was at prayer. When the Lord broke in upon her soul she seemed quite carried from earth to heaven. "O Brother Reed, Brother Reed!" she cried, "you have prayed me to heaven." She asked, "Am I in heaven?" She still says that for some time she knew not where she was, but thought she could see into heaven. When she got recollected a little she flew to all the family, in ecstasy, to declare the glory which she felt, and to press them to fly to Jesus for the same. I was not present at the time, but Brother Reed, and she herself, gave me the information. The first time (after she had found peace) that she saw me was as we were meeting; at some distance she reached out her hand toward me, and hallooed aloud, "O, Brother Cooper, I have found peace! I have found peace!" This seemed strange to those who knew not what divine happiness was; but who can hold their peace when full of joy? This was frequently the case—those who found the Lord, when they saw me, published first of all what God had done for their souls.

Nothing could have been so delightful as the seeing of old and young, male and female, giving up to serve God; quitting their former delights, pleasures, and vanities, and boldly taking up their cross and patiently bearing it after a once crucified, but now exalted, Saviour. It exceedingly mortified the wicked who stood it out that their companions and associates should quit their company and refuse any longer to go with them in vanity. How worthy of a probation for eternity, to have fortitude enough to leave the company and practice of wicked men! And how amiable in youth to devote the bloom of their days to the service of God, willingly foregoing all the pleasures and vanity of this world, in order to follow their Saviour through

8

the regeneration to true and permanent happiness! In the time of this work, while I was there, about two hundred young people set out for heaven, and joined in society. In all, upward of four, if not five, hundred, old and young, were added to our Church, the principal part of whom were living witnesses of Jesus's love. Many others who had not joined when I left there were engaged in the pursuit of joys eternal, and have come in since under my succeeding brethren. Under Brother H., upon the Point, and Brother W., in town, the work prospered and went on, there being many convictions and conversions, of which I can say but little more than the Lord made these brethren a blessing to the people.

Through the course of this work it was very admirable to see children engaged, as many were. Little girls and boys were enabled to praise the Lord and intelligently to speak their experience, to the wonder of those who heard them. Out of the mouths of babes and sucklings the Lord ordaineth praise.

I have given you an account of this work in concise terms, which I have taken from minutes made in the time of it. Many occurrences which might be worthy of notice I have forgotten, they not being minuted; others I have passed over for brevity. Were I to be minute or particular it would fill a considerable volume. I wish it may ever again be my happiness to see such another work. Surely it is very desirable to behold hundreds turning to God! daring sinners becoming humble saints! lions becoming lambs! enemies turning into friends! The work spread through the country around town, some distance in the circuit. Some few are, since, fallen away; but the greater part stand fast, and I hope will till the day of eternity.

To close this epistle, I beg leave to add a few sentences relative to myself and the friends of whom I have been giving you this account. It was a season of great labor, trials, and happiness to me. My heart was particularly united to the friends whom I loved, and still love, in the truth. But when, by appointment, I was called to leave them, with resignation I bade them "Adieu," commending them to God and the word of his grace.

It is still my prevailing desire to live to God, and spend my days to some purpose under the sun. I feel myself to be a feeble child of mortality, subject to the numerous and various infirmities of mortal life. I am also a necessitous creature; 'tis by grace through faith alone I stand. My heart is much united to our Discipline and Church. O may it ever be the Church of Christ! While preachers and people remain humble, loving, teachable, and little in their own estimation, and strong in union, the Lord will bless and prosper our connection.   But, should we ever turn aside, or relapse into the spirit of the world, or formality, the Lord will remove our candle-stick out of its place.   He will take the blessings from us as a people, and give them to another.   O may preachers and people be one in heart and life!   May the Lord preserve us by his power!

My esteemed friends in Baltimore, Brother Philip Rogers in particular, and all others whose fellowship, friendship, and kindness I experienced, after gratefully thanking them for their instances of brotherly love, I must admonish to keep in mind the grand end of their calling.   This may be read by some of them when I am laid in the tomb to mingle with my native dust.   If so, being dead, I shall then speak; and now I speak, yet living, pressing them so to run that they may obtain.   O, brethren, if these lines come under your notice, remember my labor of love among you!   Watch carefully! Pray fervently!   Live humbly!   Suffer patiently!   Continue lovingly!   Walk circumspectly!   Fight the fight of faith manfully, that you may come off victoriously, and reign triumphantly in heaven, where I hope to meet you when all our toils and sufferings are over. Amen!   Lord grant it!

Now, my much esteemed brother, I subscribe myself, affectionately, yours in Jesus Christ.   E. C.

MARYLAND, *December* 1, 1790.

The history above recited gives such a glowing account of the development and growth of the Methodist Episcopal Church in Baltimore during the pastorate of Mr. Cooper, that but little more need be said in connection with the period under review.   As has been stated, though Mr. Cooper's pastorate, as by the Minutes of the Annual Conference, is represented as closed in May, 1789, he was continued in the charge until October of that year, Fell's Point having been formed into a separate charge, and put under the pastoral care of Rev. Thomas Foster.   Also the Rev. Francis Spry, who by the Minutes aforesaid is represented as if having died previous to the session of the Annual Conference in Baltimore, was still living when that body closed its session, as will be seen by the following statement made by Mr. Cooper. The Annual Conference opened on Tuesday, May 5, and was closed on Thursday, the 7th. Says Mr. Cooper, under date of Saturday, May 23:

About half after eleven o'clock I set off to see Brother Spry once more, who lay on the Point with the small-pox; but I had not gone far before news came to me that he was dead. I can truly say that I was much affected, more so than I had been at any death for some considerable time.

Sunday, 24. We met at eight o'clock in the morning for the funeral of Brother Spry. We were attended by an uncommonly numerous train of sorrowful friends and respectable citizens—thought to be a thousand who followed to the grave—and then we returned to the church, or preaching-house, when I preached on the melancholy occasion from 1 Tim. iv, 7–8, to, I judge, fifteen hundred souls. We had an affecting time, especially in my improvement. All this day was a solemn season to me. I don't know that I ever more sensibly felt the death of any one than of this promising young man. His death, according to human appearances, is a great loss to the Church of which he was a member; but our loss is, no doubt, his gain.

In the Baltimore Society was yet continued that early association of Methodists known as the bands. These were met regularly, from month to month, and were seasons of the display of the Holy Spirit's power. Fridays were observed as days of fasting, or abstinence, and public intercession. At the latter children as well as adults were cared for, as may be seen by the following quotation. Says Mr. Cooper, under date of November 7, 1788:

Friday, 7. At intercession I think there were more than fifty children, the oldest of whom did not appear to be more than ten years of age. Dear little children, how my heart was set upon them! I addressed them for, I suppose, fifteen minutes, in a plain, persuasive way, teaching them that they should be good and serve the Lord while young. While I was speaking in a tender way they gave

great attention, and some I saw weeping; their dear hearts appeared
to be tendered.

It was Mr. Cooper's privilege, with all the fathers of
our Church from her earliest days, to guide the children associated with us into the paths of righteousness,
and to witness in numberless instances their conversion
to God in the days of their youth.

CHAPTER VI.

METHODISM IN ANNAPOLIS, MD., 1789, 1790.

WE have seen that though Mr. Cooper had been appointed to the charge of the Methodist Episcopal Church in Annapolis in May, he was, by Bishop Asbury's instructions, continued in charge at Baltimore until October, 1789. He assumed the pastorate in Annapolis on Friday, October 9, and held it until the 20th day of January, 1791, when, by the instructions of the bishop, he repaired to Alexandria, Va., for pastoral work in that field.

He had visited the town previously, as the following extract from his diary will show. Says he:

> *Tuesday*, March 31. Mr. Lynch and I rode down to Annapolis. I was weary of my ride before I reached the city. We continued there till Friday. I preached the first evening, Brother Lynch the second, and I, again, the third. We had a considerable number of hearers, and pretty good times.
>
> *Wednesday*, April 1. I dined at friend Ridgley's.
>
> *Thursday*, 2. At friend Wilkerson's, and was sent for to drink tea with Dr. Murray. Annapolis is a small place, but 'tis an agreeable situation—a beautiful prospect. But it is lamentable that the *great* generally reject religion.

Annapolis was at this time a station having a membership of two hundred and sixty-nine, one hundred and forty of whom were colored. Of the latter the vast majority were slaves, and, as such, enlisted the sympathy of the Church, which from her organization had denounced the system of Negro slavery as vile and

wicked. The Rev. Abel Stevens, LL.D., is in error in
the statement made by him, to the effect that Methodism as early as 1787 failed to fight courageously in the
contest against slavery; for it will be seen that,
notwithstanding the threats of pro-slavery men, the
preachers of that day dared the violence of their enemies in proclaiming, "All men are free by nature."
An illustration of this will appear in the details of the
period now under examination.

The religious services of the Methodist Episcopal
Church in Annapolis, at this time, were: preaching
on Sunday morning, afternoon, and evening; prayer-
meeting on Tuesday evening; preaching on Thursday
evening, and class-meetings on Friday evening. The
"society at large" was met on Sunday morning before
preaching; and other meetings were held—bands and
classes—on Monday and Wednesday evenings.

One of the first public evils that Mr. Cooper had to
encounter was the annual public races, of which some
one falsely reported that Mr. Cooper and several of the
Methodists attended them; the former seeking a private place wherein he might escape public observation.
The following is his account of the whole affair:

Monday. October 12. I was not a little sorry at beholding the preparations for the races which begin to-morrow in the fields. What
pains the children of this world take to do wickedness! O Lord, have
mercy on them! Since last year's races a number in this town have
deserted Satan, are converted, and will not go this year. Glory to
God for it!

Tuesday, 13. There was a great hurry through the town, it being
the time of Satan's work. The wicked had collected from various
parts. The races held three days, in which time I found it almost a
cross to walk the streets. I could look no way but that I saw cause
of lamentation. O Lord, when will the wickedness of the wicked
end, and thy cause universally flourish? In the evening we had a
prayer-meeting, a number collected, and, I hope, all was not in vain.

Wednesday, 14. I heard that the wicked were propagating lies about the poor Methodists and the races. Somebody reported that I inquired of a gentleman whether I could not get a private place to look, and that some of the Methodists were there, etc. Blessed be God that these reports are not true!

Having spent about three weeks on the Peninsula, among his friends and relatives, he returned to Annapolis on the 16th day of November. He was visited in the evening by two gentlemen of the Maryland Assembly, then in session, and the next day attended the session of that body to listen to a debate by them on the subject of freedom. He thus set it forth in his diary:

Tuesday, 17. I attended the House of Assembly to hear the subject of freedom debated. Petitions had been sent in for the abolition of slavery, which caused considerable debate in the House. A certain Mr. Pinkney, from Harford, espoused the cause of the poor slaves, and defended it powerfully. He is truly an orator, and spoke to the feelings of men in behalf of the poor bond-race that struggles under the yoke of oppression and discouragement by reason of unjust and inhuman laws, depriving them of that which the laws of nature allow to every man. The majority of the House appeared in favor of abolition in some way or other, believing it to be cruel to have a hereditary slavery entailed upon any part of the human race. I had great satisfaction in finding the poor oppressed had so many on their side, and the ablest speaker in the House among them. There is a fair prospect of gaining the point for them.

Mr. Cooper further showed his aversion to slavery by publishing a series of articles in the *Maryland Gazette*, a weekly newspaper then published in Annapolis, in advocacy of the freedom of the colored slave, under the signature of "A Freeman," in which he boldly denounced American slavery as a vile sin from which the sons of liberty should free themselves, and, on the fourth day of July, 1790, with Rev. J. Chalmers, boldly proclaimed from his pulpit his opposition to the system. Thus he writes:

Sunday, July 4. When I arose and looked out at my window I saw the colors raised on the State-house dome. I called to mind Independence—this being the day on which it was declared, and the occasion of raising the colors. I was here led into a serious chain of meditation upon freedom. Is it not astonishing that a country so much devoted to freedom should act so inconsistently as to continue civil slavery in it? This subject was a little dwelt upon from the pulpit to-day : the inconsistency and injustice of slavery among us as a free people—the sin of it as a people professing the Christian religion. "If the Son therefore shall make you free, ye shall be free indeed." There was no better day to fall upon this subject than the day of Independence. May the Lord fasten conviction upon many hearts! Brother Chalmers did enforce the matter very homely and plainly, and charged the people if any impressions were made not to stifle them ; for he was certain that God would send some judgment upon those who were obstinate. He then mentioned a very awful circumstance which happened a little while ago, namely : A gentleman at a vendue where Negroes were being sold resolved to buy and send them to Georgia to make his market of them. One had a friend of his own color, who was free, that bid for him to free him. This man who wanted him bid on, till the poor black friend, having no more money, thought it vain to bid any more. The poor slave was about to be struck off to him who intended to send him to Georgia, but, being encouraged by a person of feeling who was present, the black man's friend bid once more. This gentleman, being resolved to have him for his Georgia market, was going to run the bid on, when on a sudden he was struck with a judicial stroke from God, and fell dead on the spot. What shall we say to this well-attested fact? Let none make light of it.

After we had borne our joint testimony upon the subject of freedom, I felt as if good was done. When going out of the preaching-house I met a young doctor who has Negroes. "Well." said I, "This is Independence," and took him by the hand. He replied, "The matter's settled ; mine go free." Walking in the street, I fell in with a lady of the city with whom I was acquainted. "Well," I spoke, "what thinkest thou of freedom?" She replied : "When the subject was taken up I felt uneasy, and was sorry to hear it ; but I soon got reconciled that it should, must, and would be so. But O that I was free myself!" Here, she alluded to the state of spiritual liberty. "Well," said I to her, "give up your heart to Christ and he will make you free." This has been a favorable day among us from morning till night.

The effect of these bold utterances upon the citizens who heard them may be inferred from the following. Says Mr. Cooper:

Wednesday, 7. I was told in the afternoon that the people in town were alarmed by our speaking up for freedom last Sunday night—the day of Independence. They fear it will hurt the Negroes; some are simple enough to fear an insurrection. If they fear, the ground of their fear must be their own injustice in keeping those poor creatures in slavery whom God made free. But, let them fear and be alarmed as they may, I must plead the cause of the innocent, and in so doing I have the word of God, and our own civil principles to uphold me. "Liberty is the theme." Our country and the Gospel, the principles of humanity and religion, cry out, "Take off the yoke of oppression, and let the captives go free." I am ready to defend what I advanced last Sunday night from the pulpit, and I believe Brother Chalmers can readily answer to what he advanced. The justness of the subject is what gives the panic to those who wish to keep themselves quiet in the act of injustice. (See Addenda.)

Not only did Mr. Cooper witness the manifestation of the spirit of the Maryland Assembly against slavery, but he was called also to see that before that body a bill had been presented providing for the incorporation of the Church in the State with the State, thereby rendering the State an ecclesiastical political institution. Against this measure there was raised a voice of opposition which in the end, after a sharp contest, secured its defeat. The Methodists of the present day will read with deep interest the following letter from the pen of Bishop Asbury, addressed to Mr. Cooper, and now published for the first time.

FISHING CREEK, *November* 16, 1789.

MY DEAR BROTHER: I am of opinion that the Act of Incorporation will, probably, stand a prosperous poll. If any thing can be done to let * it, I wish you to move every spring against it. You have just ideas of this political scheme. It will not do for us. We

---

* The word "let," is here used in its former sense, namely, prevent, hinder.

have no church property but our churches; who will contend with us for these, or put us out of the possession of them? I am persuaded that many of the members of those churches who pray for incorporation, when they feel the effects, will cry out against it. You can do something with the Eastern Shore members, as a native, and you have some acquaintance with Western Shore members, and you may use all your influence if it is not too late. God has been wonderfully with us at all our quarterly meetings. I think we shall have wonderful times.

I am thine in haste and much love,   F. Asbury.

P. S. It may plainly be declared what this bill is: that it is a Jesuitical plan. Why did not the people form and present this bill, and not the ministers? I doubt not but that the people will feel properly when it comes into operation, and they will cry under their burdens.

If you could be spared to go to Philadelphia I should be glad, for Satan is strongly forted in that city. There is heavy work, you may be sure. I was thinking we should see more about these matters at the Council.   F. A.

This letter, which was received by Mr. Cooper three days after its date, and answered on the 30th of November, found him in such a situation that he could not personally urge the adoption of its suggestions, nor could he attend the session of the Council in Baltimore because of his embarrassments. He had a brother who, with his family, lived a few miles out from Annapolis, who was suddenly called to eternity. On Tuesday, November 24, he rode up to visit his sister-in-law, expecting to find her bearing her grief bravely; but lo! he found her dying. She died before night, and left two children, without father or mother, the care and charge of whom fell on him. On Thursday, the 26th, both husband and wife were buried at Captain Warfield's, and the afflicted brother was left to care for the family and possessions left behind. As the relatives of the deceased were residents of the Peninsula, Mr. Cooper deemed it the better course for him to convey the surviving members of the family, as soon as possible, across the Chesapeake Bay. He thus describes the course he pursued:

Friday, November 27. I got all aboard the boat and went down the river to Annapolis, ready to cross the bay as soon as possible. I found it a sorrowful time indeed. I scarcely ever met with such a trial before as the care of the children and effects are to me; having the bay to cross, knowing very little of the water, having watermen to get to sail us over, provisions to procure, and various matters hurrying in upon my mind.

It was a great satisfaction to me that the brethren in Annapolis were so kind. I got little Tommy and Nancy, my brother's children, at Brother Ridgley's. I shall not forget the kindness of my dear Sister Ridgley in receiving the dear children. She is, indeed, an amiable woman. Likewise Sister Packer, who lives with her, was very loving to the little ones. I feel myself under great obligations to them; likewise to that mother in Israel, Sister Small, who took the Negro woman and her two children into her kitchen till I could get a good day and fair wind to cross.

While waiting for a favorable opportunity to convey his charge to the Eastern Shore, on the Sabbath intervening he underwent a course of labor unknown to the present generation of preachers, of which he thus speaks:

Sunday, November 29. This was a hard day of labor to me. Love-feast at nine o'clock, preaching at eleven, preaching again at three followed by sacrament, after which I met the stewards and leaders, by which time I was truly weary.

On Tuesday, December 1, he embarked, with those under his charge, from Annapolis for the Eastern Shore. He had a successful passage, made arrangements with his relatives for the children and goods, and every-where met with utterances and acts of sympathy from those who before had known his departed brother and himself.

On Sunday, December 13, he preached the first sermon that was delivered in the new Methodist Episcopal

Church built at the Head of Wye, and two days thereafter returned to Annapolis, where he had the satisfaction of meeting with Bishop Asbury and Rev. Messrs. Whatcoat and Reed, from whom he learned of the proceedings of the Council held in Baltimore.

In October, 1789, Mr. Cooper received a letter from Rev. Jesse Lee, then a pastor in New England, of which a copy is here presented:

August 11, 1789. STANDFORD, N. ENGLAND.

DEAR BROTHER: I received yours of June 6, 1789, and was much pleased at the account you gave of the work of God in your parts and among my old friends. Would to God the same increasing flame was seen and felt in this place! I should be exceedingly glad to be with you, if I could think I ought to be there. But I feel as if I was just where God would have me to be. I feel happiness in God, my constant friend, though much deprived of Christian company. I find but few lively Christians in these parts, and I go on for many days together without seeing any one on his knees.

I have a pretty little two-weeks' circuit to myself, about one hundred and thirty miles in circumference, and in that distance I see upward of twenty preaching-houses. The Presbyterians have a large meeting-house, with a large steeple, and a great bell, for every four, five, or six miles. Withal there are a good many churches. But it is to be feared that many of the ministers are not engaged in the work. The Presbyterians are the established religion, and every person is obliged to pay to them, unless he has a certificate from some other society; but they are obliged to support some minister or other. I think the time is come to favor New England, and, if I had acceptable preachers with me, I believe we should soon cover these States. I have some thought of writing to Brother Asbury to send you to this place after the meeting of the Council. If you are desired to come, I hope you wont object. If you knew this place, and how many souls are ready to sink into hell, it would make your bowels yearn over them, and I think you would wish to come over and help us. I never knew the want of help, both from God and man, more than I have done of late. Give my love to my old friends in town. I am your sincere friend and loving brother,   JESSE LEE.

P. S. If you can send a letter to the preacher at New York it will soon come to me.   J. L.

This letter, not hitherto published, gave Mr. Cooper to see that his services were desired east and west, north and south, but he was still continued in the station at Annapolis, looking and praying for the revival of God's work in the Church, and the salvation of the many who were "without Christ and without God in the world." To aid him in this work were many others—"Mother" Small, Messrs. McCubbin, Chalmers, Steward, Ridgley, Wells, and Swift, while the good-will of some who had not been converted was unreservedly expressed, to the satisfaction of those who had found Christ to be their Saviour. In illustration of this the following is presented, as found in his diary:

Wednesday, January 20, 1790. Major Daniel, of St. Thomas Jenifer, sent his servant and carriage for me. I rode up in the afternoon and found particular satisfaction there. By candle-light I met a black class at the major's. He attended with very serious attention, and, I hope, thinks of his latter end. May the Lord change him! Nothing is too hard for the Almighty to do.

This old gentleman's home became a place for preaching by Mr. Cooper, who formed a class of appointments outside of the town where he was stationed, among which were Beard's (over South River), Watters's, Steward's, Weems's, and Mrs. Watkins's. At the latter Methodism had not hitherto been introduced.

As the work advanced the devoutly-prayed-for spirit of revival was manifested, and citizens who before had stood aloof from the assemblages of the Methodists became converts to Christ, and patrons of those who proclaimed the necessity of holiness of heart.

While Mr. Cooper spoke with great plainness and force against the vices of society, he was equally bold in denouncing all pageantry among the people. An instance of this is presented in the following extract. A Mrs. Allen, who had become a member of the church in

Annapolis, having died, her friends looked to Mr. Cooper for counsel as to the burial ceremonies. He says:

Friday, July 9.   I preached a funeral sermon at the burial of Mrs. Allen, from Eccl. xii, 7.   We had a large congregation in the preaching-house, and a great number accompanied us to the grave. Her friends consulted me as to the mode of her burial.   I requested no pall-bearers, which I think is nothing but a parade, the pall on the coffin is sufficient.   I desired no hat-bands (crape) or any thing which was of no service and bore the aspect of vanity or pride.   And as to the use of spirituous liquors at funerals, I despise the custom as unbecoming the solemnity of the occasion.   It is out of character and a great evil.   Many are glad of a funeral that they may get something to drink.   I bore my public testimony against it to-day before some hundreds of the people.

At this time a letter was received from Dr. Coke, though it had been written more than eight months before.   It is here given:

BRISTOL, *October* 30, 1789.

MY VERY DEAR BROTHER: When on board the ship which brought me from New York to England I prepared a letter for you, which I sent by the captain of the same ship, and hope you have received.

The work of God in these kingdoms still goes on, but not with that rapid progress as in the States of America, or with the singular outpouring of the Spirit with which we have been favored in Virginia and Maryland.   There were about three thousand added on the balance last year to the societies in England, and about two thousand in Ireland.   I have sent over to Bishop Asbury about three hundred copies of the *Minutes of the English Conference,* etc., and, therefore, you will probably receive one.

I long to hear of the continuation and further increase of the work of God in the United States.   Write to me a couple of letters at least before I have the pleasure of seeing you again, which will be, God willing, next spring twelve months.   Indeed, I shall set sail, if the Lord please, for the West Indies about next September or October. And I should be glad if you would write to our dear old friend and father, Mr. Wesley; for he complains of his hearing very seldom from any of his sons in the United States. He seemed much pleased at the account I gave him of the preachers preaching early in the morning in the different cities and towns which I visited the last time I had the pleasure of seeing my American brethren.

I bless the Lord I do feel an unremitted desire to glorify him in the salvation of souls. But, O how little do I do for him in comparison to what I would; and, for that little, to him be all the praise and all the glory!

Our work in the West India Islands prospers very much among the Negroes. We have now above six thousand in society, a few of whom only are whites.

And now, my dear brother and friend, let me entreat you to continue your zeal for God and his cause. Be much in prayer, much in the exercise of the presence of God. The enemies of the Church of Christ are, alas! too active. Let us be as active, and, if possible, more so, in the best of causes and for the best of masters; and our Lord will make us the honored instruments of wresting the prey out of the hands of the mighty! Never fear; God is, and will be, for us, and, I believe, will make the Methodist Connection the grand instrument of bringing on the much-to-be-wished-for, the most-ardently-to-be-prayed-for, millennium. O that we may be found faithful; that we may esteem it an honor to be instruments in any measure in the hands of God for the hastening of the accomplishment of his benign plan of general happiness!

Bear me frequently on your mind before the throne; lift up your feeble but faithful friend on the sacrifice of your faith. He longs to see the whole continent flame with the glory of God; and he never forgets the work in which you are engaged. Through the blessing of God he will see you face to face again, if the Lord permit; and through the grace of God we shall meet where parting shall be no more. Adieu.

Your faithful friend and brother,   THOMAS COKE.

In accordance with the suggestion of Dr. Coke, Mr. Cooper prepared a letter to send to the venerable Mr. Wesley, of which we present to the reader the following extract:

MY AGED AND HONORED FATHER IN CHRIST: I believe I should have written to you long ago, but for the following reason, to wit: I thought myself of too little account to intrude upon your golden and precious time. But, receiving a letter from Dr. Coke a few days ago in which your name is so engagingly mentioned, I venture to take my pen, with due reverence, and address the man whom God has made the leading instrument of spreading his name among so many thousands, both in Europe and America. Your sons and daughters are numerous on each side of the Atlantic, and I am certain that your distant children on this western continent most dearly love and esteem you. It is my happy lot to be numbered with your sons in the Gospel, who, in my feeble way, am striving to win my fellow-mortals to the embraces of a loving Saviour. . . .

The great work of God is still going on in America; as it slackens in one place it revives in another, then again re-revives in the same places. I apprehend that you frequently have accounts from the different parts of our Union as to how the work goes on. At present, in Baltimore and Annapolis, and the adjacent circuits, there is nothing very extraordinary, yet there is a gaining. In some parts of Maryland there is great power attending the word, and, generally, from north to south, from east to west, through the different States, the work bears a pleasing report. I give you here an extract of a letter lying before me, from a New Jersey presiding elder:

" We have a considerable work in most of our circuits in this State. I lately attended quarterly meeting in this circuit (Salem). Such a time I never saw before. [He was not among the work in Virginia and Maryland.—C.] Six or seven sermons were preached to the same congregation, and, I think, not less than a hundred converted. From thence, about twelve miles, I preached five sermons where a hundred more were converted. At nine places I preached upward of twenty sermons, and, 'tis thought, three hundred and fifty were converted. Our meetings frequently held from two o'clock afternoon till next morning, and twenty, thirty, etc., were converted." " This is the Lord's doing and it is marvelous in our eyes." We have good news from other parts, also. God is doing great things for America.

Our superintendent, Francis Asbury, is a most worthy man for his station; his concern is great, and he is very faithful in the discharge of his duty. If you were to write, and send over in print, an epistle or circular letter to your sons in Christ, it might be of use. I know their hearts are warm in love and esteem toward you as their father in the Gospel. It would yield me great satisfaction to receive a line from you.

I am, honored friend in Christ, yours, etc., EZEKIEL COOPER.

9

Here, also, is given a letter of value from one of the preachers on the Peninsula :

DORSET CIRCUIT, *March* 23, 1790.

MY DEAR BROTHER : May peace attend you forever! Through mercy I enjoy a degree of health, and my soul is happy in God. I received your letter the 21st ultimo. There is a gracious work in this circuit—sinners coming home to God. Since our quarterly meeting there appears to be a considerable stir among the people. I see as gracious times as I have ever seen since I have been in Dorset. The devil is roaring in a wonderful manner. My God, I trust, will bruise his head.

I suppose you heard of the work among the rich in this place. Henry Ennalls and wife and sister have been converted to God since our quarterly meeting; yea, his house-keeper and all his Negroes down to those but eight years old. Glory be to God for his goodness to the children of men! Cambridge appears to be up in arms about it. We have permission to preach in the Court-house at last. O that the Lord may make bare his arm! O, brother, let us live near to God, that we may finish the work he has assigned unto us. The Lord bless you! Farewell. Pray for me.   EMORY PRYOR.

N. B. Our quarterly meeting will be the 22d and 23d of May. I should be glad if you could come over, if it should be out of my power to attend yours.   E. P.

While these letters show the advancing course of religion in various parts, and are, for the most part, confirmed in their statements by subsequent historical records, they serve to supply, to those desiring it, an accurate account of the work of God's people. Mr. Henry Ennalls, on being converted, Bishop Asbury tells us, immediately manumitted his slaves. The opposition of the citizens of Cambridge, Md., to the Methodists, on account of his espousal to their cause, was like to that experienced in various places ; and Mr. Cooper has left an account of a scene within the bounds of his charge which will further illustrate it. Says he:

Tuesday, August 10. I breakfasted with Mrs. Johnson, who told me her experience; how that she had formerly laughed, much at the

Methodists and their conversion. One day being persuaded to come and hear, she unexpectedly was so cut to the heart that she could not refrain from crying through the street as she returned, though she kept it concealed as much as possible. From that time she could get no rest day or night. She visited Mrs. Rollings, a gay lady of her acquaintance, who, she thought, might cheer her up, and remove, by her flow of conversation, this distress. But, as God would have it, she could get no relief—had no heart to be trifling. At length they fell into conversation about religion. Mrs. Johnson said to Mrs. Rollings, " Why can't you and I be good? "

Mrs. Rollings replied, " O we are as good as we can be."

" That will not do," said Mrs. Johnson; "we must be better," and was struck with such a power that she fell on the floor in deep distress and prayers for mercy. Mr. Johnson was sent for, who was for having the doctor; but Mrs. Johnson said the doctor could do her no good; she wanted the Methodist preacher sent for. He wanted to send for the Church parson, but she refused to have him. So I was sent for, at which time the Lord blessed her soul with his love, to which she has held fast ever since. She went and joined Society this afternoon.

Again:

Wednesday, 18. I am told that at quarterly meeting, last Saturday and Sunday, a number of wicked fellows undertook to support one of their party in whipping a preacher who reproved him; but they came off very badly. The preacher got two or three strokes, and the man was caught by a friend. One of his party interfered, and a second friend to the preacher stepped forward, and with a blow sent him away staggering, and hurt him amazingly. Others engaged, but the preacher's friends were too hard for them. One of the young men who fought for the preacher after the others were beaten off told them to come again if they chose; that he was not angry, but he fought for God, and for God he would fight; he would not see his servants beaten by any man.

" What shall we think of this? " said Mr. Cooper. " Did he do right or wrong? ' He was not angry, but fought for God, and would not see his servants beaten.' The conduct of fighting most certainly is not right; but here was an uncommon principle to be found in a fighter: ' In good humor for God.' "

While there was opposition to the Methodists manifested in many places there was also internal strife within the body, over the Church Council and the Constitution adopted at its session in 1789. Mr. Cooper received letters on the subject from his brother ministers, some of whom sought to gain his influence against the organization. Being much concerned for the welfare of the Church, he addressed the following letter to Bishop Asbury:

DEAR BROTHER: Many and various have been my exercises since I had the happiness of seeing you. I have just kept my head above the waters. Nothing has given me more painful feelings than the predicament of the Church of God. Satan is a most subtile adversary—how apt he is to transform himself, and apparently to transmute right into wrong and wrong into right, good into evil and evil into good; and thus make us fearful of truth and zealously embrace error, even when we think we are sincere. I am certain, as to my own part, I know but little and see not far, which makes me doubtful of myself either in judging or speaking. How do you find the preachers to the southward upon the Council and its Constitution? Is all smooth? I wish the enemy may not make and take advantage of some upon this subject. I confess my mind is uneasy at seeing any thing so irritating among the brethren as this matter appears to be. If I know myself I wish whatever is best to be, and feel as if I want no voice or will in the case more than for unanimity to reign among us in the will of Heaven.

I find myself an infirm creature, subject to many trials, and see great danger of yet becoming a castaway. I scarcely have yet learned to know myself. "Know thyself" is a lesson I wish to learn, but I find it hard to get; nevertheless I thank God for what I am and what I know. May he teach me what I know not, and make me what I am not! I wish to live to some purpose while God gives me an existence in this scene of trial; but O, my leanness, my leanness! I find myself an unprofitable servant, and undeserving a name and place among his saints.

At times I feel willing to be any thing or nothing. I love God, I love his cause, I love his people; but am jealous of myself, lest I should err in answering the great end of my vocation and probation. I am as needy, perhaps, as any under your care and charge. What shall be done to subdue deistical temptations? then, Universalism? May God keep me from every principle which he doth hate! I feel a considerable desire to meet you at Leesburg, but fear I have no business; I want to do nothing but duty, and in faith.

We have a sifting time in this town. I have turned out about as many as I have received. The Society is in tolerable order at present. There is a delightful stir over South and Severn Rivers—south and north of the city. Some few are coming in in town.

I am, dear brother, most sincerely yours, etc.,　Ez. COOPER.
ANNAPOLIS, *August* 14, 1790.

The agitation in the Church concerning the Council, to which Mr. Cooper refers in the above letter, was growing, and there were fears of unpleasant issues arising from the discussions had in all parts of the territory. At the session of the Duck Creek (now Smyrna, Delaware) Conference, on Friday, the 17th day of September, it was thought, however, that a more peaceful conclusion was reached than had been anticipated. Says Mr. Cooper:

Friday. 17. At nine o'clock we had the Council business brought before the Conference, which was unfinished when we adjourned. At three o'clock P. M. it was resumed. A small debate was seriously entered into. After the matter was investigated properly but few opposed, and their objections were answered. When the question was put, to the joy of the Council friends, there were but two who voted against it. It was expected that there would be dreadful work among the preachers in opposition; but they came agreeably into the measure and closed the business very amicably.

Mr. Cooper attended the session of the Council held in Baltimore in December, 1790, where all things seemed to go forward in a pleasant manner, and the spirit of harmony prevailed in all the sessions.

Returning from the Duck Creek Conference to Annapolis, his charge, he soon began the series of articles against slavery of which mention has been before made. While preparing these he wrote a letter to Bishop Asbury, soliciting counsel as to his course, and received the following reply:

BOLINGBROKE, *November* 12, 1790.

MY VERY DEAR BROTHER: I am fully agreed that you should write as you dictate. We have been laboring by heavy strides through the Peninsula, with some living. others very dead. It seems as though the work will go on in Accomack in spite of Satan and the B——pts. We have a little stir in some parts of Somerset. I am fully convinced of the necessity of a constant spirit of prayer in private, in families, in societies, and in public. Strive, my dear, to push all you can to prayer.

I am in hopes that we shall have $200, or near, this trip, for the college; but I shall want nearly $400. Our house will fill swiftly. I hope we shall see matters in a more promising state. Many poor are pressing upon us, and this is my greatest consolation. I have pleasing prospects of employing a teacher or two, if I am not disappointed.

We have had perfect unanimity in all the Conferences, and great peace. The work revives in York, and goes on in Jersey. In the latter State it is thought that not less than six hundred souls have been converted in six months, and it still goes on.

My soul is in peace, my breast is pained. Long rides, large congregations, quarterly meetings every day.

Peace be with thy spirit! As ever thine,   F. ASBURY.

In December; while visiting that part of his work which was in the country surrounding Annapolis, Mr. Cooper received a letter from Bishop Asbury, directing him to go to Alexandria, Va., to assume the pastorate of that charge for some months. He did so, but was engaged for more than a month in attending to the duties of the pastorate in the charge he was about to leave. He left Annapolis on Tuesday, the 20th of January, 1791, and arrived in Alexandria on the 22d.

CHAPTER VII.

METHODISM IN ALEXANDRIA, VA., 1791, 1792.

INASMUCH as our Methodist historians have given no account of the introduction of Methodism into Alexandria, it devolves on the writer to furnish, as far as he can, such data as will correct the omission.

Alexandria was originally the capital of Fairfax County, Va., and was a part of Fairfax Circuit. In 1783 it was visited by Mr. Asbury, he preaching to a large congregation in the Court-house, and being entertained by a brother Bushby, who, with General Roberdeau and others, warmly supported the cause of the Methodists in that community. In 1785, after the organization of the Methodist Episcopal Church, Bishops Coke and Asbury met there in May, with a purpose to visit General Washington at his country-seat, Mount Vernon, seven miles distant. Says Bishop Coke : *

Wednesday, May 25　I set off again. We dined at a friend's house by the way, and reached brother Bushby's, at Alexandria, about seven in the evening. There I met, according to appointment, that dear, valuable man, Mr. Asbury. He had informed the people that when I arrived the Court-house bell should ring, and about eight o'clock I had a very large congregation in the Presbyterian Church, to whom I insisted on the necessity of the "witness of the Spirit."

Thursday, 26. Mr. Asbury and I set off for his Excellency, General Washington's. We were engaged to dine there the day before. General Roberdeau, an intimate acquaintance of General Washington's, who served under him in the war, paved our way by a letter of introduction. We slept at General Roberdeau's the night before, and he was to have gone with us, but Mrs. Roberdeau was so ill that he did

---

* *Arminian Magazine,* vol. i, pp. 395, 396.

not choose to leave her. His Excellency received us very politely, and was very accessible. He is quite the plain country gentleman, and is a friend of mankind. After dinner we desired a private interview and opened to him the business on which we came.

We returned that evening to Alexandria, where, at eight o'clock, after the bell was rung, I had a very considerable congregation.

Bishop Asbury, while silent in regard to the religious services and entertainment in Alexandria, tells us that General Washington gave him and Dr. Coke his opinion against slavery.

In November Bishop Asbury was again in Alexandria, and thus speaks of his visit:

Being disappointed in crossing the Potomac at Holland's Point, I shaped my course for Alexandria. I preached on my way on the Sabbath evening to an attentive congregation, and reached town on Monday, 14.

VIRGINIA, *Tuesday*, 15. I dined with Dr. Samuel Smith and Mr. McK——, at General Roberdeau's. Our conversation turned upon slavery, the difficulties attending emancipation, and the resentment some of the members of the Virginia Legislature expressed against those who favored a general abolition. I preached in the Courthouse. I took cold by coming out into the open air while in a profuse perspiration; this I seldom fail to do, if I preach to a large congregation in a close, warm place.

In April, 1786, Mr. Asbury again visited Alexandria and spent several days with the Society. They were days of industrious employment, wherein measures were taken for a more comfortable provision for the members of the church, and the permanent securement of a house of worship. After being thus occupied, he broke forth:

Sunday, April 23. Hail, glorious Lord! After deep exercises of body and mind, I feel a solemn sense of God on my heart. I preached during the day in the Court-house, on 1 Peter iii, 10, and in the evening at the Presbyterian Church, on Luke xix, 41, 42. Alexandria must grow, and if religion prospers it will be blessed. I drew a plan and set on foot a subscription for a meeting-house.

From this time forward Alexandria began to show marks of Methodistic care; was visited by the bishops of the Church, and in 1791 was the seat of one of the Virginia Conferences, made memorable by the certain announcement of the death of that venerable man of God, the Rev. John Wesley. Dr. Coke, receiving this intelligence, proceeded to Baltimore on Sunday, May 1, and the following day Mr. Asbury held the Conference in Alexandria. Here he found Mr. Cooper, who had been pastor of that charge for more than three months.

Alexandria was made a separate charge in 1791, Ezekiel Cooper being the first preacher stationed there. He was the pastor for a little more than fourteen months, when he was called by Mr. Asbury to the charge of Charleston, S. C., and Hardy Herbert appointed to succeed him at Alexandria. Mr. Cooper found between fifty and sixty members of "Society" in town, and a few more in the country societies connected with his field of labor.

On the day of his arrival at his new station his attention was arrested by two events which moved the town with excitement. The first was that of a trial going on in the Circuit Court, of which Mr. Cooper thus speaks:

When I reached Alexandria there was a trial in court of a man for murder, a black man who had killed his overseer in defending himself from his extravagant cruelty which the overseer had inflicted on many, and also on this poor creature. The trial lasted till in the night sometime, and the prisoner was cleared—judged not guilty of murder. The Court-house was crowded with citizens. When the judgment was given from the bench a general plaudit by a clapping of hands passed through the house. I apprehend this will be a check on the cruelty of tyrannical masters and overseers who can, by degrees, massacre and murder poor slaves as though they were beasts of burden. The case was difficult indeed; but surely a black man should have right to defend his life as well as a white man. If religion was general, and all influenced thereby, such things would be done away; nay, slavery itself would not exist long. Liberty justly belongs to all, and principles of equity or religion enjoin us to grant it to every man.

The second event, which occurred the same day, January 22, 1792, was the announcement of the president's proclamation in regard to the location of the Federal City. Says Mr. Cooper: "It filled the town with great bustle, as the lines of experiment were to include the town of Alexandria." Nearly three months afterward, namely, on Friday, April 15, he says:

To day the corner-stone for the Federal District was planted on Jones's Point. The bell rang, and the people marched down to the Point in procession, with the town sergeant before them. They planted meal under the stone, and broke a bottle of wine and a bottle of oil on it.

The religious exercises in the new station were as follows : Preaching on Sabbath, morning and night, also on Wednesday night; prayer-meeting on Friday night; class-meetings on Monday and Thursday nights, and a class-meeting of females, about thirty in number, on Tuesday afternoon at four o'clock. The church building, begun five years previously by Bishop Asbury, was so far completed as to permit its use for these services; however, some of the meetings were held in private houses, as for instance, one of the Thursday night classes was held at the residence of a Sister Shores.

Mr. Cooper's "place of board and lodging" was with William Hickman, whom he describes as "a good man," and his wife as "an amiable little woman." Besides these among other members of the church were the Ramsey, West, Minor, Simmons, Hickman, and Hunter families in town; and in the country, John Moss, Esquire Simpson, William and Samuel Adams, Gunnell, Mrs. Dulin, and Bates, all of whom were deeply in earnest in maintaining the cause of Methodism in their several communities. The country appointments of the circuit were at John Moss's, Simpson's, William Adams's, Fairfax Chapel, Gunnell's, Dulin's, Summers's, and Bates's.

A happy spirit of Christian union and brotherly regard was manifested by the ministers and members of other churches toward the Methodists and their pastor. Mention is here made of the Rev. Mr. Muir, of the Episcopal Church, who set a noble example before all. He invited the recently appointed Methodist pastor, within a week after his arrival at Alexandria, to supper with him ; and finding that he would probably be kept away by reason of the arrival of a brother minister who was his guest, invited him also. Mr. Cooper was urged to accept the invitation, which he did, taking with him his brother, the Rev. Mr. Breeze, and Mr. Hickman, his host. The evening was passed in comfort and ease at Mr. Muir's. The Rev. Mr. Muir continued to show this brotherly spirit, as will be seen as we proceed further in this history.

On Thursday, February 10, *en route* for Montgomery quarterly meeting, Mr. Cooper preached to a crowded audience at Mr. Adams's, and the next day, having dined at Mr. Waters's, a local preacher, he, with Mr. Waters, proceeded on his journey and arrived at Mr. Awfort's, where in the evening Mr. Waters preached and he exhorted. On Saturday, having a large congregation at Mr. Nichols's, the seat of the quarterly meeting, Mr. Cooper opened the quarterly meeting by preaching, after which the Rev. Mr. Reed, the presiding elder, exhorted, and then administered the sacrament of the Lord's supper.

Many descriptions of these grand quarterly meeting services have been given, but there are points in the history of the one now before us that make it advis-

able to give the account as it has come down to us.
Says Mr. Cooper:

Sunday, 13. The love-feast began at nine o'clock; we had a good
time. But several were tried by the application of different people,
not members, to come in. Some got in; others did not. Some
wicked young men attempted to break in violently; one got in, but
was put out through the same hole at the end of the barn where he
bored his passage through. He was very angry, but we cared very
little for that. I was very happy in love-feast. I thought seriously
on the increase of Methodism for several years past, and was thinking
of opening my thoughts when Brother Waters arose, and seemed to
have the very same ideas that I had on the subject.

The congregation was so large we divided it for preaching. The
barn and private house both would not hold near all, I don't know
whether much more than half, of the people. Brother Reed and myself preached in the barn; Brother Waters and Brother Chiles held
forth at the dwelling-house. It rained while we preached, and
hundreds of the people stood it out with great attention.

Having accomplished his mission in connection with
the Montgomery quarterly meeting, Mr. Cooper returned to Alexandria, visiting, on the route, Judge
Smith, who, with his wife and daughter, were members
of the Church; Mr. Warfield, where, on Monday, at noon,
he preached to a crowded congregation; Mr. Lacklin,
where a watch-night service was held; Colonel Ormes,
who, though a Presbyterian, received him and his
traveling companion, Mr. Waters, as cordially as if
they were ministers of his own denomination, and,
after family prayer was had, took each of his visitors
separately by the hand and said, "I gratefully thank
you" (they each had led in the prayer service); and
Mr. Waters, where he spent the night, and on the
next day arrived at Alexandria.

It was not long after his return to his station before
Mr. Cooper was called upon to preach a funeral sermon over the remains of Mrs. Harris, the mother of

Mrs. Hickman, with whom he boarded. She was not a member of his charge, but was associated with the church on Calvert Circuit, in Maryland. Such, however, were the circumstances connected with her burial that he assumed the duty, and afterward addressed the following letter to Bishop Asbury, describing her character and the scenes attendant upon the funeral:

CALVERT COUNTY, *March* 9, 1791.

MY ESTEEMED BROTHER: Being called down here, forty miles from Alexandria and about the same distance from Annapolis, to preach at the funeral of Sister Harris, one of our respectable friends, I feel impressed to give you some account of the circumstances of her death and burial.

She had been a member of our Church better than two years, and, as far as I can learn, invariably an ornament to her profession. Her clemency was experienced by the poor, and her fellowship esteemed by her Christian friends. She had but a short spell of illness in her death sickness, during which time she manifested the greatest resignation imaginable. And when taking her final adieu of her weeping, overwhelmed friends, she left them all triumphantly, and commended them to God in prayers and admonitions. The following account of her last hours I received from Brother B., the circuit preacher, who was then with her, and tells me it exceeded any thing he ever saw. Probably the relation is not and cannot be so striking as the sight:

"When I went to see Sister Harris, she was very ill, but could praise God with great happiness and resignation. We sang, and went to prayer. In singing, her voice was strong and clear, which was rather unexpected in her weak state. In the morning Brother Harris came out of the room with the aspect of gladness, and said she was better. We sat and talked about ten minutes, and he was called suddenly into the room again. When he entered, he found her dying. I also went in, and, at first, thought she never would speak more. Her friends surrounded the bed with bitter lamentations, and immoderate sorrow. I strove to pacify them, and told them to give her up to the Lord. Presently she opened her eyes and spoke as though one had spoken from the dead. 'Glory be to God,' she said, 'we can bear all things for Christ's sake;' then exhorted all present to love and obey God. She then lay as one dying, without speaking, for some time. She again revived and called her son G., and exhorted him to give up his heart to God; told him how that many tears she had shed in private prayer for him. It was a melting scene while she powerfully pressed him to turn to the Lord and save his soul, 'My soul is so happy that I can feel no pain,' said she. 'Glory be to God! I am resigned to his will. O the love that I feel! I am perfectly happy!' She lay still, again, for a time, then renewed her exhortation, till all in the room were melted to tears. When we went to prayer, she frequently cried ' Amen,' distinctly and loudly. Afterward she said, 'O sweet Jesus! Happy, happy! glory, glory be to God!' Then in about eight minutes her breath left her body, as one falling asleep without a struggle."

Her son G. has set off to serve the Lord, and appears to be much engaged. I feel strong impressions that her death will be a means of good to several. We had about a thousand people at the funeral; some suppose more, but I think not. We had a solemn time. I thought some of her connections were rather immoderate in their sorrow. I like for people to have sympathy, but it is not good to give too much way to our passions. May the Lord deepen the convictions and good purposes of those who resolve upon religion!

After the funeral we had a watch-night in Brother Chiles's preaching-house last night. The Lord was with us. We had a comfortable season.

I am, esteemed brother, yours, etc.,   E. C.

No mention having been made by our historians of the Rev. Mr. Chiles, the following account is given, as possessing historic value. Says Mr. Cooper :

At night we held a watch-night in Chiles's preaching-house. We had four or five hundred hearers, and a tender time. Brother Chiles was led out in exhortation very much. Brother Burgoon, also, and another preacher gave an exhortation. I lodged at Brother Chiles's. He is one of our preachers; formerly traveled, but now stays at home to manage his plantation. His two aunts, sister, and brother live with him; they appear to be a family of happiness. I was very comfortable there.

Returning to Alexandria, he resumed the work of his pastorate, strongly upheld and assisted by those who were in "Society," and by some who were not members, among whom was General Roberdeau, who was helpful in financial matters, and whose house was a home for the itinerant. While discharging the duties before him, both in town and in his country appointments, he received, in April, the following letter from Bishop Asbury :

PETERSBURG, VA., *April* 19, 1791.

MY VERY DEAR BROTHER: I am comforted to hear that the work goes on in Annapolis in your absence; that you revive a little in Alexandria, and your house is in better order. I heard by a young man that you were doing well. Brother Ward has lost his reason. Great exertions may wreck the system. If possible we shall be in town for evening meeting on the Sabbath. We must enter fully into business on Monday morning.

You, perhaps, have heard of the General Conference which is to meet instead of the next sitting of the Council. A letter from Mr. Wesley, the re appointment of Brother Whatcoat, the strange spirit of murmur here, and what can be done to amend or substitute a Council, and perhaps to implead me on the one part, and a presiding elder and conference on the other. No court is sufficient but a General Conference: and perhaps such a trial may make me and others take care how we take such rash, if not unwarrantable, steps.

You are a thinking, prudent man; a word to the wise—let it rest in thy heart.

I am, as ever, yours,   F. ASBURY.

Mr. Cooper had knowledge of the call of a General Conference in 1792, to be held instead of the Council and to supersede it, before he received the above letter; and he was so much affected by the disagreement existing within certain circles of the Church that he apprehended evil influences would arise from such a conference at that time. In speaking of it, he says, in his diary:

April 9. I fear some unfortunate end will come upon us before we get duly settled one way or the other. I am almost of a mind to say or do nothing, but submit the whole affair to Providence, and our brethren, who are so zealous about the matter, though I almost fear that some of them know not what they are about. Lord, direct us; superintend us in all things!

Being informed of the coming of the Bishop to hold
the Conference the following month, Mr. Cooper began to prepare the church for that session, and assisted
in planing the seats, which heretofore had been used in
their rough and undressed state. The state of the church
may be seen from the following entry in his diary:

Friday, April 29. This afternoon the preachers began to come in
town for Conference, which begins on Monday next, God willing.
We have got the seats, pulpit, and chandelier prepared. The windows will not be quite finished in their casings.

The Conference session was harmonious, and helpful
to the cause of the Redeemer. It began on Monday,
May 2. Besides the regular Conference business there
was preaching three times a day; namely, at sunrise, at
noon, and at night. At its close Bishop Asbury, with
Mr. Cooper, went forward to the Baltimore and Duck
Creek Conferences. "The former," says Mr. Cooper,
"was all love and union." On Sunday night Bishop
Asbury met the Society at large, "in order to speak his
mind upon some concerns relative to the Connection."
On Monday morning all the preachers were invited to
breakfast at Mr. Philip Rogers's. About thirty of them
were thus gathered together in one room, around one
table. Great love and brotherly kindness was manifested. From thence they retired into a room where
the Conference business was finished.

The Duck Creek Conference began on Friday, May
13, and was in session for three days. It was a season
of great power, and productive of much good, both
to ministers and laymen. The governor of the State
(Delaware), who had opened his house on the circuit as
a place for preaching, was present during the Conference
session, and partook of the spirit of love and faith that
animated his brethren; while the ministry of the word

of life, the love-feasts, and the various Conference sessions, all conspired to call forth the utterance of the
psalmist, "Behold, how good and how pleasant it is for
brethren to dwell together in unity!"

Mr. Cooper, having been continued in charge of the
work in Alexandria (Virginia), after visiting his friends
on the Eastern Shore of Maryland, returned to his station on Saturday, the 4th of January, 1791. On the
first Sabbath of the new Conference year the Rev. W.
Glendenning preached for him in the morning, and told
the audience the story of his exercises while he "lay
for five years under a state of melancholy and black
despair." The people were much affected, Mr. Cooper
himself saying, "I have not heard a narration more
affecting for a long time."

The disorderly walk of some of his members made it
necessary for him to divide the classes, both of men and
women, and to adopt such other measures as might
produce a higher development of a religious life, himself resolving to give more diligence to enter the kingdom and to enforce upon the people the realities of
religion. The first quarterly meeting was held on Sunday and Monday, June 12 and 13. The Rev. Mr. Bruce,
the presiding elder, preached both days with great satisfaction. The latter part of the week was given by
Mr. Cooper to his work in the country, he preaching at
Esquire Moss's, at Gunnell's, at the Falls preaching-
house, and at Adams's.

The country around him at this time was suffering
from continued drouth; the citizens apprehended a
famine. Says Mr. Cooper:

Sunday, July 17. I arose a little after four o'clock, and attended
meeting at five. This is a pretty morning; every thing looks delightful. The rain which fell yesterday evening makes every thing
bear a lively aspect. We have not had so refreshing a rain all sum-

10

mer. Such a drought has never been known in this country before by any I have conversed with. How thankful should they now be! But it is feared that the corn is so far gone that there will be scarcely any crops made.

While it pleased the Master to water the parched earth with refreshing showers, he was pleased, too, to pour out his Spirit upon the people in Alexandria, as the following, from Mr. Cooper's diary, will show:

Sunday, June 26. We had prayer-meeting at five o'clock A. M. At nine I met a class, at ten preached, and afterward met the Society at large. We had a precious time. At four o'clock I preached again, and found great liberty; the people were very attentive. Four joined Society to-day—Mrs. Brook and three others. I found this to be the best Sabbath that I have had for some time.

Monday, 27. My mind was happy in God. In the evening we held prayer-meeting at Brother Sanford's. A number were together; in the close we had a lively time.

Tuesday, 28. My mind was in a disposition for silence. I passed through town to see several friends, in whose families I sung and prayed. At five o'clock P. M. I met class at Brother Simmons's, and a most glorious time it was; the best class-meeting I have yet seen in Alexandria; every heart seemed to be overflowing with love.

At a prayer-meeting, held during the following week at the residence of Mr. Emmit, a man was so wrought upon by the Spirit that he declared his purpose of seeking the salvation of his soul, adding that he had been a dreadful sinner—a drunken, swearing, miserable offender, but from henceforward was resolved to reform.

Amid these manifestations of increasing spiritual fervor among the Methodists in Alexandria, their pastor was sought for by other charges and denominations. Among these was the congregation worshiping at Poheck church, until late under the ecclesiastical governance of the Church of England. Mr. Cooper arranged to minister to them on the 10th of July, having engaged the Rev. J. Ogburn to fill his appointment in Alexandria. On Saturday, the 9th, Mr. Dade, who resided a mile out from town, took him in his carriage and they went forward, dining at Mr. Bushby's, and spending the night at Esquire Moss's. The following is from his diary:

Sunday, 10. By eight o'clock we had a company of ten or twelve to start with us to Poheck Church, where I was to preach. We had about ten miles to ride; reached there a little after ten o'clock; began service about eleven. Brother Potts read prayers, and I preached. We had a very large congregation. Mr. Triplett said: "The church never had so many people in it before." I had great liberty in speaking: many were touched to the heart and wept. This is a well finished, pretty church. It is a pity that such a building should be idle for want of preaching. I hope that they will be supplied for the future by one of our preachers. I dined to-day with Mr. Triplett. He and his family were very kind indeed. Himself and one son appear to have their hearts touched. O Lord, hear my prayer; may they have their concern fastened on their minds, and may a work of religion take place at Poheck!

While the revival spirit was operating on the Church in Alexandria, two circumstances occurred that had the tendency to disturb her harmony and, for awhile, at least, to scatter her members. The first: the Baptists who were striving to establish themselves in that community sought to accomplish their purposes in part by traducing the Methodists. This course was so offensively pursued by them that at last Mr. Cooper was led to challenge them to a public discussion of the principles involved in the controversy. Speaking of it, he says:

Saturday, October 1. This evening, in company, we fell into a conversation about the challenge I gave the Baptists to have a public dispute. They have boasted and preached against us so long that I feel quite ready and willing to meet them before hundreds or thousands, and there defend our principles against the ablest preacher

they have in the State. I hope, now, they will either let us alone or
meet agreeable to the proposal. I am for, and would rather have,
peace; but they appear to be for war, so I wish them, if they will
have war, to come to an open-field battle like honest men. How lam-
entable it is that different denominations cannot go on in their own
liberty, and let others alone. They seem backward in taking us up.

Though the challenge was not accepted by the Baptists, it had the effect of causing them to cease their
abusive course toward the Methodists; and some who
had been disturbed by their tenets regained their soul-
rest and composure.

A second source of disquiet was occasioned by the
appearance and spread of the small-pox. It spread during the month of July with such rapidity that the citizens became alarmed; several families moved out of
town, and the congregations were much reduced. Mr.
Cooper himself, while the disease was most severe,
spent the most part of the week in the country, and
was only in town on Saturday and Sunday. During the
first week he visited and held service at Bushby's,
Esquire Moss's, Dulins's, Broadwater's, Hunter's, and
Gunnell's. Returning to town on Saturday, the 23d, he
preached the following day twice, and spent the week
in visiting the sick, meeting the classes, and attending
other religious meetings.

On Monday, August 1, the Rev. Mr. Bruce, the presiding elder, visited Alexandria, and stayed until Thursday, holding in the meantime, with Mr. Cooper, a watch-
night service, and visiting the prayer-meeting, at both
of which services was manifested the presence of the
Most High.

Accompanying the presiding elder Mr. Cooper made
quite an extensive tour through the district, attending
several quarterly meetings, and partaking, with his
brethren, of their varied services. The first attended

was the Prince William quarterly meeting, where, on Saturday, both preached, as also on the following day. At the service on Sunday morning Mr. Cooper, having an audience of near three thousand people, preached, declaring the "tenets, doctrines, and practices of the Methodists, and their agreement with Scripture." He was immediately followed by the presiding elder, Mr. Bruce, who gave a. "short and pointed discourse on the subject of predestination." Rev. Mr. Ellis closed the meeting with an exhortation. Returning to Alexandria, he had the Rev. Mr. Weems, of the Episcopal Church, to preach for him in the Methodist Episcopal Church on Tuesday night, to a large congregation ; preached himself the following evening, and on Thursday "set off for Maryland on a tour of several weeks."

On Friday service was held at Thomas Offertt's, during which, while Mr. Cooper was speaking, Mr. Offertt's daughter, who lay on a bed of affliction, was "so filled with joy in her soul," says Mr. Cooper, "that she broke out into praises, and, after I was done, she lay and exhorted the people very much to give up their hearts to God. The people were much wrought upon; almost every heart seemed tender; many tears were shed." From thence he went to Mr. Nichols's, where he lectured, and afterward spent the night. The next day, Saturday, August 13, being accompanied by more than twenty persons, he set off for the quarterly meeting at Joseph Pigman's. Of it he says:

At twelve o'clock we began public service. The congregation was very large—about two thousand—the greatest number, I think, that ever I saw at a quarterly meeting on Saturday. We went into the woods under an excellent shade. I preached from Matt. xxiv, 14; Brother Pigman and Brother Bruce exhorted. It was a time of great tenderness among the people. After preaching we gave the sacrament in the preaching-house. . . .

Sunday, 14. At eight o'clock A. M. love-feast began; the preaching-house, though pretty roomy, would not hold nearly all the friends. The Lord was very precious to us. At eleven o'clock it was laid upon me to preach again. I opened our Lord's words in John (ix. 4), to an uncommonly large concourse of people—some think six or seven thousand; I judge, at a moderate calculation, there were four or five thousand—I had to speak very loud. The Lord helped me; word fell with power on the congregation; truly it was an awful time! The word was like a sword in the hearts of some who cried out aloud to God; tears flowed on every hand; the countenances of the people bespoke the effect of the truth in their souls. Brothers Forest and Reed exhorted. There were three or four other traveling preachers who had not time to say any thing. This was a grand quarterly meeting. I hope great good was done. It was wonderful where the people could all come from; but such a concourse was hardly ever seen in those parts before.

Having closed the quarterly meeting services, Mr. Cooper, with other of his ministerial brethren, visited Captain Beall's family; old brother Holland, "an old, well-settled, good Methodist;" Thomas Howard; Mrs. Howard, widow of Dr. Howard, on Elk Ridge; and Mrs. Dorsey, widow of Colonel Dorsey; arriving in Baltimore, August 17, where he remained two days, and thence went forward to Annapolis, *en route* for the South River quarterly meeting. This meeting was held at Maccubbin's. The presiding elder, Mr. Reed, preaching on Saturday and Mr. Cooper on Sunday morning. After closing his discourse it was laid on him to beg money for the building of a " preaching-house," in that neighborhood. Mr. Maccubbin had been a very wicked man, but was now "a plain simple man, and very good."

A few days were now spent by Mr. Cooper among his friends in Annapolis, from whence, on Friday, the 26th, he "set off at nine o'clock for Calvert quarterly meeting," which was held at Chiles's church. Mr. Cooper " opened the quarterly meeting " on Saturday morning by preaching, then Mr. Reed exhorted, and the sacrament was administered. On Sunday, love-feast began at eight o'clock. The concourse was so large that the members were divided, the black people being sent to the barn, under the conduct of two of the preachers, and the whites convening in the church. At public preaching, however, they were all gathered together under the trees, there being about two thousand persons present. Mr. Cooper preached to them, having for his pulpit a hogshead with a board laid across the top. He says:

In the midst of my discourse, one of the devil's children disturbed the whole assembly, demanding of the Methodists a sum of money, which, some years ago, he had subscribed and paid to the preaching-house, but, taking offense, he demanded it to be repaid to him. I desired that he might be silent, but he declared that he would not, unless the money was paid to him. The disturbance continued some time, and then some person gave him $2 and he went off. I then proceeded in my discourse; we had a blessed time in the end.

After the close of this quarterly meeting Mr. Cooper returned to Annapolis, where he spent a few days, and then went to Alexandria, whither he arrived on the second day of September. The small-pox having abated, the congregations began to increase, and the religious services were much revived. Two weeks were now spent in the town, after which on Saturday, September 17, he attended the quarterly meeting held at the Fairfax Chapel. On Sunday morning, at nine o'clock, they had love-feast and the sacrament. While speaking to one another concerning their religious experience the following scene occurred: A Brother M., from Maryland, narrated his exercise of mind about slavery, which resulted in setting his slaves free. Mr. Cooper says:

As soon as he had spoken I rose and applied the subject; then Brother Watters, and then others, spoke on the same topic, which took up some time, and, I do believe, very profitably. Surely the captives will yet be set at liberty.

At twelve o'clock preaching began, the elder, Mr. Bruce, leading the way, and being followed by Mr. Cooper, both of whom preached. It was a profitable season. Returning after dinner to Alexandria, Mr. Cooper preached at night, spent several days in pastoral work, and then went up into the country, visited Captain Terrett, Captain Moss, at whose house he preached, and Major Powell; he preached on Sunday, the 25th, at Fairfax Chapel, visited old Brother Adams, leading the class there, and returned to town on Wednesday, the 28th, in time to preach in the evening. Among other pastoral cares which now devolved upon him was the work of repairing the church, by putting galleries therein. This work was begun on the 13th of October and completed within two weeks. Mr. Cooper now, for the most part, continued his ministerial work in town, with an occasional visit to the country appointments up to December 2, when he again was called forth on the district to attend the quarterly meetings.

In August the following letter was addressed to Rev. Dr. Coke:

ALEXANDRIA, *August* 11, 1791.

MY ESTEEMED BROTHER: From impressions of friendship, I take my pen to address to you a few lines. I have been, and remain, anxious to hear the result of the British Conference respecting their resolutions, government, etc. I have apprehended some circumstantial changes would take place, now our dear old father, John Wesley, is laid asleep.

I have forebodings in my mind relative to our General Conference, and could wish it was at hand, or over, for the minds of many are in agitation. What may be the end God only knows, but I fear that other principles are at work beside those singly to God's glory. Permit a friend to drop a caution to you, namely, when you visit this Continent again come with great care, with precaution, for you are suspected by some of your sincere friends to have conducted yourself, when last here, with a degree of unkindness to this Connection, and especially to our ever worthy Brother Asbury. It appears to them as though there were designs against Brother A., and, you must know, nothing will touch the majority of our preachers sooner and more powerfully than to seek the unjust injury of him who has served them so long and so faithfully. I am unwilling to say too much upon this critical subject, but, feeling sensibly for the cause, I drop a few hints. I fear our brother in the lower part of Virginia is too much prejudiced against Mr. A., and I candidly believe his ambition carries him to measures unbecoming a servant of Jesus, in filling other minds with his own prejudices to strengthen his party, and obtain a conquest for a conquest. Should you favor his scheme, it may be very unthankfully received by you that I thus speak; but let others mistrust as they may, I am unwilling to suppose you would unite with a party spirit which, if persisted in, will certainly make havoc, division, etc. The majority in any community should be submitted to by the minority as the voice of that community. But what shall we think when a few resolve and determine to stand it out against whatever number oppose their opinion, and never to submit? Is this not something like a conceit of infallibility, and does it not bespeak despotism in principle? and to what length would such a principle carry a man or men had they but the power? O Lord, give us humility!

Be assured there are strange spirits at work. I wish to be for no party but the blessed cause of Jesus, and to unite with that which appears just, wise, and scriptural.

We have nothing extraordinary here at present; in the work some few are coming in. I remain poorly in body and happy in soul.

Believe me, you share in my love. Pray for me.

I am, yours, etc., Ez. Cooper.

To this brotherly epistle Dr. Coke made the following reply, which, as a part of the history of the age in which he lived, will be now cherished for the points contained therein:

New Chapel, City Road, London, *November* 22, 1791.

My very Dear Brother: I would have written to you sooner, but a variety of circumstances have prevented. Soon after the English Conference I found it in my heart to visit France: and the Lord went with me. We have already formed a few societies in Normandy.

I left two elders behind me; and I believe we shall soon send a third preacher. I spent some time in Paris, and the Lord was with me there. I have received many encouraging letters from that city since I left it; but we have no established work there at present.

I had some design of going over to you for good and all, as the common proverb is; but I now feel such a desire of being the happy instrument of spreading the Gospel in France that I believe I shall never give up my labors there entirely to others.

I hope to see you at the General Conference. However, remember, I come as a man of peace. O, my dear brother, I only desire to live to be in some degree an instrument of uniting God to man, and man to man. The salvation of souls and the union of believers shall be, I am determined, my only points to aim at and pursue from this time forward. The time for every thing else is past. The Lord enable me to devote the remainder of my life's short day to his glory.

We are going to send missionaries to Sierra Leone, in Africa, where the English are establishing a very capital settlement. The company has chosen two chaplains; one of them is a zealous Methodist preacher of my recommendation. Four of our young exhorters are also going over.

Brother Black, of Nova Scotia, writes me word that he has been lately at Newfoundland, and gives me an account of a work there under his ministry something like the great outpourings of the Spirit in the States. O Jesus, ride on!

Remember me in your prayers, and write to me if you have an opportunity. Give my love to the preacher with whom you labor. May the God of love and peace be with you!

I am, your very affectionate brother,   THOMAS COKE.

I am confined, and have been for a month past, by a terribly scalded leg; but, I bless God, I am getting better. The Lord be with your spirit!

My love to my kind friends, Brother and Sister Rogers. Will you be so kind as to send me the Minutes of the last Conferences in the States, by a merchant ship.

On Thursday, November 10, Mr. Cooper visited Oxon Hill, of which he thus speaks:

I went over the Potomac and preached on Oxon Hill, in a small preaching-house, which has been built by a number of religious black people. I had considerable satisfaction among them. I preached at twelve o'clock, and again at night. The dear black people seem to be alive to God, having their hearts placed on things above. I lodged at Mr. Bean's. None of the family, except black people, are in the ways of religion, but they are a friendly, kind people. I had much satisfaction with them.

The line of quarterly meetings in Maryland having been arranged for the winter, Mr. Cooper, with other preachers, went forth to attend them. The first was in the lower part of Anne Arundel County, and was considered to be very profitable to those who attended it. It was conducted by Mr. Cooper, with the aid of ministers Ellis and Pigman. From thence, after spending two or three days with his friends in Annapolis, Mr. Cooper went forward to Baltimore, where, on Saturday, December 3, was begun the quarterly meeting for that city. Speaking of it he says:

At night. December 3. quarterly meeting began: Brother Morrell (who is in company with Mr. Asbury) preached to a considerable congregation.

Sunday. 4. Quarterly meeting continued. Mr. Asbury preached at eleven o'clock; I at three o'clock; and Brother A. again at night, when he preached the funeral of old Mrs. Triplett. She was the first who received our preachers in this town.

When these meetings had concluded he again returned to Alexandria, where he remained, in the discharge of his ministerial duties, until the 13th day of January, 1792, when, having secured the services of the Rev. Mr. Cook for his work in town, he made a tour in the country, being absent for six days. Thence returning, on Sunday, January 22, he performed a work that seems strange to the Methodists of the present day. Says he:

To-day I turned Sister S. B., that was, out of Society for marrying an unawakened man. It went right hard with some of her friends, but I must enforce the rules.

Continuing in town till February 5, he then responded to the call to make other quarterly meeting visitations, and, being uncertain as to the time of his return, excited no little anxiety among the members lest that he should not be with them more. He, on this tour, opened, on Wednesday, February 8, at Captain Burgess's, in Prince George's County, Md., a place for preaching, his being the first sermon preached in that neighborhood by the Methodists. Thence he went to Captain Beall's, where, on Saturday, the 11th, quarterly meeting began and was continued on Sunday; himself and the Rev. Nelson Reed led in the ministerial services. The next quarterly meeting was held at Magoty, where, on Sunday, great visitations of grace fell upon the audience. Describing it he says:

Saturday, February 18, 1792. We went on to quarterly meeting. The house was crowded. We had a tolerable time.

Sunday, 19. In love-feast the Lord was precious, but in the time of preaching he opened the windows of heaven and poured down blessings upon us. Sinners were struck as with hammer and fire, or like as if thunder flashes had smitten them. A general cry began, so that I was forced to stop preaching. I stood upon the stand and looked on, and saw them in every part of the congregation with streaming eyes, and groaning for mercy, while others were shouting praises to God for delivering grace. Numbers were converted—the season was truly glorious and very refreshing to God's dear people. The meeting never broke up till about sundown.

On Thursday, March 1, Mr. Cooper returned to Alexandria, where, as will be seen below, he was to spend nearly a month, and then to repair to another and distant field of labor. While engaged in his pastoral work, he received, on the ninth of the month, two letters from Charleston, S. C. He says:

One from the Bishop, the other from Brother Morrell, informing me of William Hammett's defection, of his separation from us, and that he has divided our Society there—a part having forsaken us and gone to him. The Bishop and Brother M., write in the strongest and most pointed terms for me to hasten immediately to that city, and take a station there the ensuing year. I feel it a cross to go so long a journey. well on to seven hundred miles; but as the occasion is so urgent, and Brother Asbury solicits me so powerfully, I consent to go off in a few weeks, God willing. But I have a horse, bridle, and saddle, together with other things, to buy for my journey.

Of these letters, that of Rev. Thomas Morrell, who was Bishop Asbury's traveling companion at that time, is herewith given:

MY VERY DEAR BROTHER: After a fatiguing, dangerous, and difficult journey we arrived here on the 12th instant, without the loss of life or limb, or senses, though each of them were exposed; but God preserved us. The Conferences in Virginia and North Carolina were all peace, love, and harmony; we found sweet, soul-refreshing seasons at each ; and the preachers went to their circuits in confidence that the Lord would bless their labors. From their tempers, piety, and prudence I believe their hopes will not be frustrated. When we were about seventy miles from this place, we first heard of the defection of William Hammett, with alarming reports of his having seduced the greatest part of the Society to join him, and separate from us. We found, on our arrival, that his not being appointed to be general assistant of the West Indies by the British Conference ; and that, perhaps being fearful of being brought to answer for some malicious and ill-natured reflections, not founded in truth, which he had spoken against Mr. Asbury and the preachers in general, inducing him to carve for himself, he accordingly, after some bitter and unjust reflections, separated from us, and persuaded about twenty-four whites and thirty-five blacks to join him. He has hired and fitted up a place for preaching, and holds worship at the same hours that we do. This hurt Mr. Asbury sensibly, that any thing like a division should take place, and he gave, last evening. a full account of his conduct toward Mr. Hammett in the presence of the Society, to their full satisfaction. When at the North Carolina Conference he appointed Jesse Richardson to this place, but when he came here, soon discovered that his want of knowledge of men and things (though an excellent man in many respects) rendered him unfit to fill this station, more especially at this juncture. At the request of the bishop, Conference, and Society, I consented to tarry here for two or three months, though I can only preach at most twice a week.

Mr. Asbury ruminated long in his mind to find a preacher suitable to the place and the present circumstances. At first thought yourself was impressed upon my mind as the very man; but, not being willing to appear to dictate, I forbore to mention you. After some time spent in meditation Mr. Asbury broke out, "I have found one that will answer in every respect," and immediately named you. I rejoiced to hear it, and am sure you are the man, through grace, exactly qualified for this place. He proposed your coming when I went away, as Richardson was on his way here, but—one preacher declining at Conference—Brother Richardson has orders sent him to repair to the vacant circuit, and this place is unsupplied only by poor unworthy me, who am so unwell that I cannot preach, as I said, more than twice a week at most. There is here a local preacher who tries to fill up; but you know what local preachers generally are, and how they are received. The time is critical; therefore Mr. Asbury repeatedly desired me not to fail in writing to you by the first post, in the strongest and most pointed manner, to come immediately, and consider Charleston as your station for the ensuing year. The last words were, "Hasten Brother Cooper; write post after post to him; beg him to come immediately."

My dear brother, a man of your understanding and zeal needs no motives to urge him to a compliance with a necessity so pressing. I am persuaded, therefore, that no delays will be on your part but such as are purely adventitious. Were the case not so urgent I would not be so pressing; but the cause of God, and the honor and prosperity of our cause so closely united with it, plead powerfully for your presence here. It has been mentioned to the Society, and they are extremely elated with it; do come shortly

Some of Hammett's party have showed a disposition to return. Those that are worth having we shall, probably, regain; some of them will not be received if they offer. Excepting three persons, he has only the chaff of the Society—for but those three among his adherents profess either to be awakened or converted—such is the curse attending the taking of unawakened persons into Society; they have always kept the Society here in disputes. Our party, far the most numerous, are, generally, really religious characters. To ingratiate himself he allows his members all the latitude of dress; and his communicants, some of them, are open swearers and common notorious drunkards. He is for money, show, and a worldly church. I believe he is fallen from God, if ever he had religion.

Our Society is more united than ever, and last night we received two members. I expect, through a blessing, we shall shake the devil's kingdom in this fashionable and luxurious city. I promised to tarry till the middle of May; but, if it appear necessary to us both, I will stay with you till the 1st or 10th of June, God willing. The people here are very kind; some of our Society are respectable merchants. Here is every thing that you want, and a field for exercising your talents to advantage. Once more, my dear, I urge you, entreat you, and beg you to come as soon as possible. What clothes you cannot bring with you you may send by water. to the care of Edgar Wells, merchant, No. 10 Broad Street, or John McDowell, merchant, No. 104 same street. Could we have preaching once or twice more a week I apprehend we should settle Hammett's business. My throat is very sore. I could not preach at all for five days past, and I am fearful not once this week to come. Do come! I am all anxiety till I hear from you. Write by the post when we may expect you. God give you a prosperous journey to us!

Adieu, my dear brother. Come in faith, in prayer.

THOMAS MORRELL.

CHARLESTON, *February* 20, 1792.

Remember me kindly to Brother and Sister Hickman, and all friends. If all our force is not directed against this first defection we may expect more European adventurers. Tarry not! The Lord calls!

In addition to this important historical letter, calling him to Charleston, S. C., another was received from Rev. Jesse Lee, a copy of which is now presented:

BOSTON, *March* 4, 1792.

MY DEAR BROTHER: Having an opportunity, I now write you a few lines. I am well. Brother D. Smith, who has been traveling with me, is still afflicted with the rheumatism. Brother Robert Bonsall, from New York, has lately come to travel with us. We are in want of a dozen more. Lynn is a great place for Methodists, and the work of the Lord revives among the people. We have a small class in Marblehead. and a few in other places. We don't preach in Salem at present. To-day I have preached three times in this town, in a school-house. for the first time. We have never preached here on the Sabbath. at the usual hours, before. We could do pretty well here if we had a preacher to stay constantly in town. I hope the Lord will send us more laborers. Calvinism is on the decline, though very strong yet. I hope to see good days in this part of the world yet. I believe it will be a great place for us after a little time. I still hope that you will come to see us before long. I wish it could be so that you could come and stay one year in Boston. I hear that the work of the Lord revives much in Connecticut, and greatly in Philadelphia. I shall be glad to hear from you at any time. Direct a letter to the care of Mr. John Taylor, merchant, No. 7 Long Wharf, Boston.

I am your real friend,   JESSE LEE.

Having determined to go to Charleston, in accordance with the urgent request of the Bishop, Mr. Cooper was aided by the members of his Church in Alexandria in making the needed preparations for his journey. They would gladly have retained him, but, being convinced of the necessity of his services and the value of his counsel to the Charlestonians, they yielded him up to them. A view of the parting scene may be had from the extract given below. On Sunday, April 8, he preached his farewell sermons, and bade the people adieu, shaking their hands while tears were streaming from their eyes, and the next day began his journey. He says:

Monday, 9. I arose very early and hurried breakfast, that I might start by eight o'clock. A considerable number of friends came up to take their last leave of me. When our horses were brought out and saddled it was visible that we should have an extraordinary parting. Every movement toward the setting off filled the hearts of the friends fuller and fuller. Several were in tears a good while before the most affecting moment of parting. When all things were ready I gave out:

> "Saviour, grant us now thy blessing;
> Send it now, Lord, from above;
> Grant that we may part a-praising,
> And rejoicing in, thy love.
> Farewell, brother, etc.,
> Till we all shall meet above."

But few could sing at all. My own heart got so full that I could not easily utter my words in prayer. Soon as we rose from our knees I went round to bid them, one by one, farewell; but I was so overcome that I could not speak a word to them, and they were too full to speak to me, so we squeezed each other by the hand, and with hearts full and eyes full turned our backs and parted. Several of the dear friends accompanied us for ten or twelve miles—Brothers Potts, Sanford, Rhoads, Summers, Donaldson, and one or two more. When we stopped to part, at Poheck, we were again beyond speaking. They returned and I went on, having Brother S. Williams for my companion, who sets off with the intention of going through to Charleston with me. He is a young man from Montgomery, and finds his circumstances and business will admit of his taking this journey. As it is suitable and convenient to him, as it is most acceptable and agreeable to me, I pray that we may have a good and comfortable travel together. We stopped at a Mr. Fowler's and fed our beasts, and got refreshment for ourselves. Mr. Fowler, it seems, is a Deist, but he was not at home; his lady was remarkably kind to us, and appears to be very sorry that he is unbelieving in revelation.

We started forward again, but Brother Potts would go a few miles farther with us; the others were gone back. When he stopped to return, it renewed the distress. We embraced each other as we sat on our horses, but no speech—so we parted—he returned and we went forward. He is one of our local preachers in Fairfax County, and a dear, good little man. I can but remark, to-day, when we were parting with our friends, Brother Watters was among them, a pious and useful preacher, one of the oldest American preachers in the Connection. He was the most affected that ever I saw him on any occasion whatever. Brother Williams remarked this also, and told me that, a few days ago, Brother Watters was observing to him that "parting scarcely ever affected him much;" but to-day he was as much wrought upon as others. O that the Lord may bless them all! We are now separated. I feel myself much attached to the dear friends in Alexandria and Fairfax; I have been with them for nearly fifteen months. The Lord has blessed my feeble labors in a degree. I leave upward of a hundred in Society in town, and found fifty or sixty when I came. All glory be to Christ my Lord! The good that is done the Lord himself doeth!

11

CHAPTER VIII.

THE METHODIST EPISCOPAL CHURCH IN CHARLESTON, S. C., AND IN NEW ENGLAND, 1792, 1793.

MR. COOPER began his tour to Charleston, S. C., on the 9th of April, having S. Williams for a traveling companion. The journey was completed by the 4th of May ; and he was received with many tokens of respect by the brethren of the new charge. Taking up his board with John McDowell, he entered at once upon the work before him, but soon had reason to feel that the water and climate of the city would not prove healthful to him, a truth that he was led more and more fully to realize, and that finally caused him to repair to another and more genial field of labor. He remained with them only till the 8th of September.

Of the condition of the work he says:

I find that William Hammett has written an appeal to what he calls *Truth and Circumstances*, in vindication of his conduct in separating from the Methodist Connection. Brother Morrell has written an answer to it, which is now in press, and is expected out next week.*

Mr. Morrell continued with him in the city as pastor, for a few weeks, and then returned to New York. The congregations, which at first were very small, began to increase, but there was little vital force among the professors of religion, so that Mr. Cooper was much oppressed, and mourned over the "deadness of the

* Cooper's Diary.

people." In referring to it, he says: "The people in this city are remarkably careless about religion." And again, when speaking of his resolve to return to Maryland, he says:

Charleston does not suit me. I fear I should never be fully reconciled to the climate, and hope I never shall to the customs of the place. Very little religion, either among clergy or laity, but luxury, fashion, and abomination in abundance.

During the few months of his pastorate at Charleston he twice visited John's Island, under the guidance of James Waddell, who resided there. The first visit was made on June 25, on which occasion, at night, he preached the first sermon that was preached there by a Methodist minister. The congregation was composed mainly of colored people, and Mr. Cooper was encouraged to believe that had they the opportunity of having gospel instruction they would soon become religious.

In July Hammett's *Defense* against Morrell's *Answer* appeared, and led Mr. Cooper to fear that it would "kick up the dust again." He visited Mr. Hammett, was received with much kindness, and, upon his requesting it, was shown a letter of Mr. Wesley with readiness and friendliness of spirit. The same evening (July 10) the Methodists were favored with the most powerful display of the divine power that had come upon them during the pastorate of Mr. Cooper. As presenting a faithful picture of the state of affairs in both religious and social life, the following extract is given: *

Tuesday, July 10. At night I preached from Eccl. i. 14: "Behold, all is vanity and vexation of spirit." After showing the vanity and vexation of setting our affections upon earthly objects, and of fol-

---

* Cooper's Diary.

lowing evil or vain pursuits, I made some pointed use of the subject. God gave me considerable liberty and faith. While I was address- ing the congregation pointedly upon turning from the vanities of the world unto the living God, several wept considerably. At length a woman of gay appearance fell upon her knees and cried out for mercy; another fell in the gallery, and appeared to be un- der deep distress. After closing the sermon I went to the distressed, who still was on her knees, near the pulpit, crying. She has been, it seems, a great sinner against God and her own soul; and now her cry was, "What shall I do?" I told her, "Jesus came to save sinners, even the chief of sinners." O that her conviction may be deepened and her soul saved! I repaired to my lodging very hap- py, excepting that I was grieved at the conduct of one of our sis- ters, who appeared to treat the poor distressed soul with contempt, and seemed tried because some of us attended to her. I don't know what to think of such people's religion. If sinners, under alarm and awakenings, are not attended to by religious people, what are they to do? But, says one, let them forsake their wicked company and ways. True; but there is a beginning, and whenever we see a sign of setting out, we should strengthen them by our admoni- tions and prayers, lest they should not be able to stand. The strong should help to bear up the weak.

This woman was opposed not only as above stated, but by others also. She had, until her conviction, been a member of the "Church of England, so called;" had a pew in the "New Church," where she attended in fashion, pride, and vanity; but, says Mr. Cooper, "never got any benefit from the sermons preached in that pulpit."

And how should she, when, to her knowledge, the minister was a vile sinner against God, who could drink, dance, play, and live after the flesh like other wicked men?

After her conviction she gave up her pew in the other church and sought association with the Methodists. Her former minister, on visiting her on her sick bed, derided her for "leaving her church, and going to the Methodist meeting, in such a mean way that she desired him to leave her room." Her mother, too, became her enemy;

and the colonel, in whose house she resided, also violently opposed her; but amid all she held fast to her
determination to renounce sin, and "spend her remaining days in penitence, prayer, and godliness." Telling
Mr. Cooper of her condition, from her sick couch, she
received such counsel and instruction that her faith in
the atoning blood of the Saviour was so intensified that
she cried out, as he was leaving her sick chamber, that
his work for her "was better than all the doctors and
medicine in town."

The presiding elder, Rev. Reuben Ellis, visited the
church in Charleston in July, and spent nearly a week
with Mr. Cooper and his flock, preaching several times,
and impressing the pastor (who had not met him before) with his great love for the Church and zeal in behalf of the cause of God.

In August a malignant fever broke out upon the city,
from the effects of which many died. Mr. Cooper himself was prostrated thereby, and both he and his friends
were impressed with the conviction that the state of his
health demanded his return to the north. To this the
presiding elder, who had again come to the city, assented.
Speaking of him, Mr. Cooper says:

Wednesday, August 30. To-day Brother Ellis came to town. He
is quite hearty, but 'tis likely he will get the fever, for almost every
body who comes to this place is taken with it. Such a sickly and
mortal time was hardly ever known here before.

His shipping stores having been procured, and all
things being in readiness, Mr. Cooper bade his little
flock adieu, and embarked, September 18th, in the sloop
Sally, under charge of Captain Doane, a Methodist, for
New York, where, after a stormy, dangerful, and in
part provisionless passage, he arrived on Sunday morning, the 30th day of September. Breakfast was served

to him, with the preachers, at the Chapel House. "Public thanks were returned," he tells us, "to Almighty God in both churches for our deliverance upon the seas." Eighteen days were spent with the Methodists of New York, during which time he visited the Houseman, Doane, Anderson, Browers, Smith, Bleecker, Russell, Staples, Fosbrooke, Clarke, Holliday, Jaques, Hazzard, Wainright, Mackeness, Mott, Newton, Valleau, Humbert, Mercein, Hervey, Matthias, Myers, Cooper, Snow, Shatford, Johnson, and Arcularius families, united with them in Christian worship, and listened to the delightful story of the growth of Methodism in the city as detailed by them.

After spending nearly three weeks with his old friends, and those who had come into the Church through their influence and example, he took stage toward Philadelphia.

Leaving the stage at Heightstown, he visited Joseph Hutchinson, where he met with Revs. Jesse Lee and Hope Hull, *en route* for the General Conference, to be held in Baltimore, Md. He also called upon Sister Holmes, living a few miles from Allentown. The next day Samuel Emley, who was the first person who received the Methodists in the neighborhood of Allentown, was visited by him. From thence he went forward, by Crosswicks and Burlington, to Philadelphia. Here two days were spent in religious and social entertainment, after which he went forward to Baltimore, where he arrived on Wednesday, October 31.

As the proceedings of this General Conference have not been before the Church in full, and additional particulars tending to show the work of the body will be favorably received, the following is set before the reader from Mr. Cooper's diary:

Thursday, November 1.   General Conference sat at nine o'clock A. M.   We had a large concourse of preachers from throughout the United States, and two from Nova Scotia.   In all we had in this Conference a hundred and fourteen regular members, besides a number who were not regular members.   Our business began in great love and unity.   We took up all this day in preparing our business, rules and regulations for proceeding through the Conference: the bishop to preside; a moderator to be appointed daily, to keep order; a committee of eight—two bishops and six elders—was appointed to prepare the business for the Conference.   We formed ourselves in a regular legislative order: motions made, seconded, debated, called for, put, voted, and carried.   We appointed for preaching to be every night and morning while Conference should hold, by the preachers in order—a new preacher every time.

During Conference we had much debating upon various subjects but still love continued.   We spoke plainly and freely what was in our minds; made several alterations and improvements in our form of Discipline.   I believe great good will result from this Conference, though there are four or five preachers much dissatisfied with some things that were done.   Several were ordained, a few missionaries were sent to different parts—one to Grenada, one to Newfoundland, two to Nova Scotia, etc.

Thursday, November 15.   We this day finished our business in Conference about five o'clock P. M.   We returned our unanimous thanks to Dr. Coke for his labor in serving the Conference.   This evening the Doctor preached his last sermon; an exhortation was given; then three or four went to prayer, and the Lord attended us in gracious power.   A work broke out and continued for a few hours; several were converted.*

From the General Conference Mr. Cooper went to Alexandria, Va., where was begun, on Saturday, November 18, the Conference for that district.   The session lasted through three days, after which the preachers repaired to their various circuits and stations.

Mr. Cooper had been appointed by the solicitation of Bishop Asbury, after the General Conference, to the charge of Boston.   He, however, did not immediately

* Cooper's Diary.

repair thither, but spent some time in visiting his relatives and friends in Maryland and Delaware.

On the 25th day of December he bade them adieu, and began his journey to New England, being accompanied by the Rev. Amos G. Thompson. Having to ride on horseback, and through wintry weather, the journey was not completed until the 2d day of February, 1793. In performing it he and his companion visited Wilmington, Del.; Philadelphia, where three days were spent; Milford, J. Barclay's; Mrs. Perrine's, Perth Amboy; reaching New York city on the 9th day of January. Here were spent five days among the old friends of Mr. Cooper, during which time he and Mr. Thompson ministered in the churches the word of life to vast congregations of delighted listeners. On Monday, the 14th, the trip to New England was resumed, and Nicholas Berrian (near Kingsbridge) entertained them the first night; after which they visited Stamford, Conn.; Norwich, where was living one family of Methodists, Mr. Dean and wife, with whom Mr. Cooper spent some happy hours, he having known them before while resident in New York; Stratford, where, at Capt. Peck's, they found it necessary to tarry for awhile that they might dry their garments, which had been thoroughly soaked by the rain through which they had ridden. While here they preached, Mr. Cooper on the first evening, at Samuel Ward's; and on the second evening Mr. Thompson, at Captain Peck's. The next day, Saturday, 19th, passing through New Haven and several other New England towns, they reached Middlefields, where they spent the Sabbath. Of Middlefields and its inhabitants, who were Methodists, Mr. Cooper thus speaks:

About seven o'clock P. M. we reached Mr. Seth Coe's, the first house in Middlefields. When we rode up to the door Mrs. Coe was the first one who appeared. We hardly had time to ask who lived there before she asked, with a warm accent, whether we were not Methodist preachers. I replied we were. She immediately pressed us to alight and stay all night. We did so, and found a very kind reception. Mr. Coe and his wife are both remarkably friendly to the Methodists. There is one young woman in his family a Methodist. At nine o'clock we had family prayer. After prayer Brother Thompson and I sang a hymn; then Mrs. Coe desired that we would pray again, and the Lord was graciously with us.

Sunday, 20. We had it published through town that we would preach at half-past ten o'clock and at half-past two. I preached in the morning, and Brother T. in the afternoon. Here is a Society of about twenty members. Friend Elisha Miller is leader, and appears like a steady man. In the evening we had a meeting at friend Ward's. I opened to them the subject of election and reprobation in the light in which the Scripture appears to hold it. Several came to me with expressions of great satisfaction upon the subject, and desired me to give them a discourse upon the subject of falling from grace, which I did. They all attended with great attention. I then had to answer several objections made against our doctrines. Brother Thompson added a few arguments. I trust this evening was profitably spent. All but one or two seemed to be entirely satisfied. Some expressed a desire that part of my lecture should be printed.*

The next day they rode to Middletown, Conn., called upon and dined with Benjamin Tarbox, a member and the leader of the Society in the city, and from thence went to Timothy Powers's and "put up for the day." Mr. Cooper preached at night, met the Society, and found that the church there was composed of about twenty members. "Poor things!" said he, "they meet with reproach for the cross of Christ, but they seem to bear it with patience and fortitude." Being detained another day by reason of a snow-storm, other families were visited, and at night a sermon was delivered, and signs of prosperity were manifested, much to the delight of the itinerant shepherds.

Leaving Middletown, they went through Glastonbury

* Cooper's Diary.

to East Hartford, dined at Esquire Pitkens's, and lodged at Thomas Spencer's. From thence they rode to Dr. Steel's, in Ellington, who, with his wife, had lately joined our Church. Here Mr. Cooper preached at night, and found a Society of about twenty members. The next day, accompanied by Dr. Steel to Mr. John Stanley's, and then by Mr. Stanley, they rode to Tolland, where at that time was a Society of sixty or more members. Being strongly urged by Mr. Thomas Howard, whose guests they were, and by Captain Robertson, to spend the Sabbath with them, they consented, and remained two days. The circuit preacher was the Rev. George Roberts, who also was the elder over the district. At his appointment—a school-house near Tolland—Mr. Cooper preached on Saturday, and, with Captain Robertson, spent the night with Mr. Grovers. From thence they returned on Sunday morning to Mr. Howard's, in Tolland. Here he preached, and also Mr. Thompson, as will be seen in the following extract from his diary :

Sunday, 27. At half-past ten o'clock I preached in the Tolland Court-house to an attentive set of hearers, with a good degree of liberty. At two o'clock I preached again with much freedom of speech and in faith. The people appeared to be all swallowed up with attention, drinking in the word with remarkable and uncommon eagerness. In the application the congregation was much melted, particularly the young people, of whom there were many. When I addressed myself to the youth, who I saw were much affected, many of them solemnly arose to their feet, in a respectful manner, to receive the address, and stood till I passed from them to the others. Poor things! some of their hearts appeared ready to burst, and their eyes were suffused with tears. This was a most solemn and blessed time of the Lord's goodness and favor. O may the impressions be lasting!

In the evening Brother Thompson preached at seven o'clock. It was with difficulty that we got liberty of the Court-house at night. A singing-school had met before us, and were backward in giving place

to preaching. Several spoke to them, and they stood out for some
time.   At length, after hearing them talk for some time, I was
distressed, and arose and addressed them upon the subject in the
following manner: " When we made the appointment for preaching
to be here to-night, we knew nothing of there being an appointment
for singing; so that we had no design against the singing whatever.
But, as both appointments are made, and the people are come together,
it is better so to accommodate ourselves as that both may be attended
to.   First, let the singers sing the hymns both before and after
preaching, and then, as the evenings are long, they may sing for a
season afterward."   To this they agreed, and we had a still and
quiet time."

On Monday, January 28, Mr. Cooper and his traveling
companion, Mr. Thompson, separated, the latter having
consented to stay on that circuit and help Mr. Roberts
to enlarge the borders thereof, and to increase among
the members the spirit of revival. The night was
spent with John Norris, who, the next day, set out with
Mr. Cooper to accompany him as far as to Providence.
At Ashford he found Mr. Jason Woodward, the leading merchant of the town, anxious to have regular
preaching by the Methodists established there, whom
he encouraged to believe that the Rev. Mr. Roberts
would "take that place into his circuit within a week
or two." Here, too, he met with John Allen, one of the
preachers among the Methodists at that day, and reported in the Minutes of the Conference of 1793 as
having withdrawn from our ministry and connection.
He was painfully impressed with the feeling that a
change had passed over the spirit of Mr. Allen within
the two or three years since they had met. During
the conversation had with him he found that he was
no longer engaged in ministering to the people on a
regular circuit; and afterward, while conversing with
Captain Cargill and his lady, at Pomfret, with whom
he and Mr. Norris spent a day and night, he learned

such facts concerning Mr. Allen as led to the following
record:

> This evening I heard of Brother Allen's having preached in this
> neighborhood several times; and some things were related of him
> that made me think that my suspicions of him were properly founded.
> He has agreed with the people to preach in this town as a hireling
> for some months, at $3 a Sabbath. So I am informed. No other
> preacher of our order has yet been here. What is his motive or in-
> tention the Lord only knows. I felt much distressed.

Mr. Cooper preached in Pomfret, at the residence of
Captain Cargill, and thenceforward sought to secure
a regular visitation there by the preachers in the adjoining circuit. From thence he went forward, passing
through Providence, Attleborough, Walpool, Dedham,
and Roxborough, and arrived at Boston on Saturday,
February 2. Here he sought the residence of Samuel
Burrill, where he engaged to board, and prepared at
once to set forward in the performance of his pastoral
work.

As the history of the period now passing under review has not been given by our historians, and as
especially some of the statements now issued may be
found to conflict with the records of the great and
valuable historian of the Methodist Episcopal Church,
the Rev. Abel Stevens, LL.D., it is deemed important
to set forth, as far as we can, the recital of these records
in the language of Mr. Cooper himself. It will be seen
that in connection with his services in Boston, other
towns contiguous thereto were visited by him, and that
from time to time he exchanged places with his presiding elder, Rev. Jesse Lee, who had charge of the
Society in Lynn, being assisted by Menzies Raynor, a
deacon. Mr. Cooper's movements at Lynn were of
such a nature as to convey the impression that he had
authority to exercise discipline while among them even

to the extent of changing the action of Mr. Lee in
some respects, on account of which he was severely
censured by the latter. The following is from Mr.
Cooper's diary:

Sunday, February 3. I preached twice in Boston and met the
class at night. Here is a very small Society, and, poor things! they
have labored under many and great discouragements. There are not
twenty in all who have joined us. I felt a little encouraged, though
the prospect at present is but small, and many obstacles appear in
the way. One joined to night, and another, who had become quite
careless, resolved to set out afresh.

Tuesday, 5. To-day I rode over to Lynn, about twelve miles, before
dinner, where I fell in with Brother Raynor, one of our preachers,
whom I had not seen for nearly six years. I put up at friend Benjamin Johnson's, who is the principal member of our Church there.
He and his wife are very kind; and some others of his family are
members with us. The Lord has done great things here among the
people. More than a hundred are in class, and they are still coming in. Here is the first Methodist preaching-house built in the State
of Massachusetts. I rode after dinner to Marblehead. and preached
at night to a crowded congregation of attentive hearers. I had considerable liberty and preached a long sermon; many hearts were
much tendered. I lodged at Mr. Martin's. Marblehead is a thickly
settled town of five or six thousand inhabitants.

Returning to Lynn, Mr. Cooper spent about two
weeks with the Methodists there, preaching, holding
class and prayer-meetings, and visiting the members,
among whom were Captain Johnson's and Mr. Mudge's
families. He did not find the Society to be acting in
conformity to the rules of the Discipline in some
respects, and he thus speaks of it:

Saturday. February 9. In the evening I met class. and enforced
an observance of our rules and order of worship; of standing to sing,
and kneeling to pray. They come into it pretty easily. I have
spoken to the classes in general, and believe all of the members
will come off from that old, careless way of sitting to sing and
standing to pray.

Another visit was made to Marblehead at the expiration of two weeks from the former, where a crowded house listened to the gospel message, and much encouraged the speaker to hope for a work of religious activity in that community. After visiting New Mills, and preaching in the school-house in that village, he returned to Lynn, where he had the satisfaction and pleasure of meeting with the Rev. Jesse Lee, who had returned and proposed to "tarry for some time" among the people. On Saturday Mr. Cooper returned to Boston, where he says he proposes to stay for some time.

Among the members of, and those friendly to, the Methodist Episcopal Church in Boston were Mrs. Wells, Mr. Clough, Mrs. White, Miss Costin, Mrs. Cambwell, Mr. Flavel, Mr. Switcher and wife, Mr. Tufts, who all were very earnest in their endeavors to advance the interest of the Redeemer's kingdom. By their cooperation the work began to revive and the list of members to be increased. A month was now spent in Boston, after which a second visit was made to Lynn and adjacent places. Of this visit, he says:*

Saturday, March 23. I visited several friends. I found that my dear Brother Lee has not enforced the Discipline in this place. It was a considerable exercise to my mind to think that an old preacher of his standing should introduce such a precedent in our Church as to dispense with a plain and positive rule as long as he had done in this town. Any who choose may come to the classes, and as long as they please, without joining. Six months, nine months, nay, a year, and not join. If our preachers thus make innovations upon our rules and Discipline, one, one part, another, another part, we may give them all up; for one has as much right as another to lay aside such rules or parts as he does not like. This will never do. We must keep our rules or lay them aside. If good, let's keep them; if bad, let's give them up; but let us all be one in practice. I have felt

---

* Cooper's Diary.

sensibly grieved at the omission of the rules here, and told the
friends that I thought not to meet the classes, unless the Discipline of
the Church was attended to.

Mr. Cooper spent a week during this visit with the
Church at Lynn, but was much cast down when called
upon to attend the classes, and finding great dullness
in those meetings, which he attributed to the mingling
with them of those who were not members, he was led
to declare :   " If Brother Lee does not attend to the
proper rule, I believe that when I visit Lynn I shall
omit meeting the classes."

After preaching at Gravesend, as well as several
times at Lynn, he returned to Boston, where he
preached three times on Easter Sunday.   On the 4th
of April, Mr. Lee having come to the city, he plainly
stated his objections to his course as above referred
to, thereby awakening a state of feeling which afterward caused unpleasant relations to subsist between
them.

The Boston Methodists had, at this time, hired a
lecture-room for their Sabbath services, and through
the kindness of the Rev. Mr. Murray and his flock,
the privilege was granted of Mr. Cooper's preaching
every Sabbath afternoon in their " meeting-house, after
their service was over."   This was a house of about
the size of the St. George's Methodist Episcopal
Church, in Philadelphia.   The Methodists were now
contemplating the erection of a church, and on the
9th day of April Mr. Cooper and Mr. Lee, who had
come to town, went through the city looking " for a
lot to build upon," but were not suited.

Another visit was made to Lynn April 15, and on
the next day to Marblehead; then to Danvers, where
he visited several families, among whom were the Rev.
Mr. Green, " the minister of the place," Mr. Hutchen-

son, Mr. Putnam, Mr. Carr, and Mr. Pindar. From
thence he rode back to Lynn, having in four days
preached eight sermons. At the end of the week he
returned to Boston.

On Tuesday, April 23, Mr. Cooper and his friends
prepared a petition to lay before the selectmen, asking
for the use of the school-house in which to hold their
Sabbath meetings. Forty subscribers' names were attached to it before its presentation, but such was the
spirit of opposition to the Methodists that it was not
granted for some time afterward. On Thursday, April
25, he went to Charlestown, spent some hours with Mr.
Wran's family, and at night, having obtained permission of the Charlestown selectmen, preached in their
school-house to " a large and crowded congregation of
very attentive hearers."* An appointment was now
made for preaching to the Charlestownians regularly
every week, on Thursday evening, and such was the
popularity of the movement that crowded assemblies
waited on his ministry. The pulpit of the Rev. Mr.
Morse, compiler of the *American Geography*, was
opened to him, and the Holden, Robbins, and Larkin
families, with others, kindly entertained him.

On Tuesday, May 21, a watch-night service was held
in Lynn, to which Mr. Lee called Mr. Cooper, inviting
him also to aid him in preparing a petition to the General Court in favor of the Methodist Society in Lynn.
These duties were performed, and he also preached in
Malden and Salem before returning to Boston. After
his return he attended the convention of the Protestant
Episcopal Church, which began in Boston, May 28,
1793. The services were opened by a sermon from
the Rev. Doctor Walter, on " the qualification and duty
of ministers in letting their light shine in knowledge,

* Cooper's Diary.

purity, and zeal particularly." The day following, being election day, " when the General Court meets, and qualifies for office, and the governor and lieutenant governor are declared," he attended at eleven o'clock A. M., at the old Brick Meeting, to hear the election sermon preached by Dr. Parker, an Episcopal minister, who, to a large concourse of people, "gave (says Mr. C.) a learned and very suitable discourse." The relations between the Episcopalians and Methodists of Boston at this time were very pleasant; an illustration of which may be seen in the following extract from the diary:

May 31.   Since I have been here in Boston, now four months, I have from time to time been reading various old books which belong to old Doctor Cutler's library.   The Doctor was the first Episcopal minister to the North Church in Boston, for whom the church was built and fitted out with a complete set of bells.   His daughter, Elizabeth, now upward of seventy years, is living, and lives in the house where I board, namely, at Mr. Samuel Burrill's, north end of Sheaf Street, near the North Church.   By this means I have recourse to sundry of her books, which were her father's.   An octavo Bible, which was his, with marginal notes and the Apocrypha, has been presented to me, which I accepted thankfully, and have had it newly bound, so that it is now an excellent Bible.

These books doubtless, some of them, were helpful to him in the controversies, arguments, sermons, and printed matter which he gave to the public against those who opposed Arminianism.

On Sunday evening, June 2, a new feature of Methodistic work was set before the Bostonians, in the use of a sea-captain as leader in the conduct of a prayer-meeting.   He says:

It was to be held by Captain Manning, master of a vessel in the harbor, and Enoch Mudge, from Lynn.   The people, hearing that a sea-captain was about to stand forth in the Lord's cause, flocked together to see and hear what they thought almost a wonder—a seaman pray in public.

12

The day previous he received a letter from his presiding elder, Mr. Lee, calling him to go to Lynn, Marblehead, Salem, Danvers, and Lynnfield to preach. He did so, arriving at Lynn on Thursday, the 6th of June. Here he found that the church was in great commotion by reason of an angry strife between their preacher, Mr. Lee, and the singers of the congregation. He says:

Almost every member of Society and of the congregation seems uneasy on one side or the other. It appears that both parties are to blame, and both seem set and stiff. I am resolved, by divine assistance, to commence mediator and moderator, and to do what I can to reconcile them. Our enemies, I understand, are ready to triumph over the disturbance that exists. O that peace may take place!

This disturbance, as we shall see further on, led to inharmonious relations between Mr. Cooper and Mr. Lee. A controversy was at this time raging between the Calvinists and Arminians of New England, and Mr. Cooper engaged in the discussion, using the Boston *Sentinel* as well as the pulpit in maintaining his Arminian views. Read the following extract:

Lynn, June 7. I was very unwell all day, nevertheless I wrote an answer to a piece in last Wednesday's *Sentinel* upon predestination. In it, among other things, I undertook to show that if all things were decreed then there can be no sin, for sin is opposed to the law of God, and consequently contrary to the will of God; but if all things are decreed, then nothing comes to pass contrary to the will of God, so that there can be no such thing as sin. I also showed that it was man's duty to do the will of God, and that no man would be punished for doing his duty, so that if nothing comes to pass contrary to the will of God there can be no punishment or blame, seeing that man has only done his duty in doing the will of God. I also undertook to show, that if all things were unavoidably fixed by an unalterable decree, then man had no freedom of choice, but was obliged to choose what was decreed, consequently was not a free agent, but only a machine, and in such case how could he be accountable? It would sound strangely to say, that man must be accountable for the decrees of Jehovah.

Saturday, 8. I preached in Lynnfield, at Mr. Munro's. We had so many people that I preached under the trees. After preaching I had much disputing to do with predestinarians and Calvinists. With one I combated the subject of the decrees. He very strenuously contended that every event, that all things whatsoever, were fore-ordained and inevitably fixed, so that they could and should come to pass, and nothing could be but that which was decreed. I, having been studying the subject the day before in answering a certain paper writer, was able to head him, and entangle him pretty well. At length I asked him whether he believed it was decreed that a man should cut his throat? for this sometimes took place among events. He stood a moment, and, to be consistent, he answered, "Yes." This had such an effect upon some that they spoke out against such a horrid idea, such an abominable opinion. This man is called the champion disputant in all the town of Lynnfield. But he was much embarrassed and confounded when I asked him the following questions:

1. "Is not sin opposed to the law of God and contrary to his will?" Answer, "Yes."

2. "Does any thing come to pass contrary to the decree and will of God?"

Answer, "No."

"Then," said I, "there can be no sin."

3. "Is it man's duty to do the will and pleasure of God?" Answer, "Yes."

4. "Will man be punished or blamed for doing his duty?" Answer, "No."

5. "And does nothing come to pass but the will and pleasure of the Deity? Then man will not be blamed or punished at all." *

Returning to Lynn Mr. Cooper continued his effort to repair the breach that had been made, by endeavoring to induce both parties to make some concessions to each other. He was unsuccessful, and thereafter abandoned the task of peacemaker. Marblehead was next visited; a sermon was delivered to a large concourse of people, pastoral visits were made, among which were calls upon Mr. Prentis and Mr. Bowlar, with the former of whom he ate breakfast and with the latter dinner. Thence

* Cooper's Diary.

he went to Salem, where, at half-past four o'clock on Wednesday, June 12, he preached "in the Rev. Mr. Hopkins's meeting-house. From thence he went to "New Mills, in Danvers," and preached. While riding out from Salem, *en route* to New Mills, a gentleman accosted him on the street, thus:

"How do you do, sir? I am a stranger to you, but have had the pleasure of hearing you preach to-day, and also heard you when you preached in the Court-house. I was ashamed," continued he, "to see no more of the ministers attend your meeting to-day [there was but one there], but I wish you to come again. I hope that I shall yet have such preaching in this town as I like. My name is Chamberline, and when you come again, call upon me."

Another term was now spent in Boston and Charlestown in pastoral work, after which, on the sixth day of July, he again went to Lynn, making thereafter a visit to one of the towns above mentioned. The Sabbath, July 7, was spent in Marblehead, where he preached three times in the Rock Meeting-house, the congregation increasing in numbers at each succeeding service. It had only been a short time since the chief proprietors of this church were so violently opposed to the Methodists that they said they would rather that the meeting-house should be burned down than that a Methodist preacher should go into it and preach. But they now gave up the key for Mr. Cooper. It is pleasant to note that prejudice was subsiding. Returning to Boston, the work was there resumed and carried forward with a view to the approaching session of the Annual Conference, which was to be convened at Lynn on the first of August. On Sunday, the 28th of July, he preached his last sermon in Boston for the conference year, and on the following Tuesday closed his labors by holding

a love-feast.   The Society during the six months of
his pastorate had increased from nineteen members to
forty-one.   Of the love-feast above referred to he thus
speaks:

> *Tuesday,* July 30.   This afternoon two preachers, Brothers Smith
> and Raynor, came to town.   At night we held a love-feast, and a
> blessed time we had.   The Lord was with us, of a truth.   This is
> the first love-feast that was ever held in Boston.   So noted as this
> great town has been for religion, nevertheless that apostolic and
> primitive custom of love-feasts was never introduced here till now,
> unless by the Sandemanians, a new and but little-known society.

On Wednesday, July 31, Mr. Cooper and his two co-
laborers, Smith and Raynor, went to Lynn to attend
the session of the Annual Conference.   This session,
the second Annual Conference held in New England,
was in some respects so unpleasant, and the historical
records thereof have been so meager, that it is needful,
we think, to give the record thereof from Mr. Cooper's
diary, in his own words.   He says:

> *Wednesday,* July 31.   We rode to Lynn, ready for Conference the
> next day.   We fell in with Brother Asbury, who had been at Lynn
> two or three days.   He soon informed me that it was his particular
> wish for me to continue in and to take charge of this district.   This
> was disagreeable to me, but, though with reluctance, I concluded, for
> the sake of good order and government, I would not refuse to stay.
> So I yield to take and bear the cross.   But it is as much as I can do
> to submit.   O Lord, I wish to do thy will, and nothing contrary to
> thy pleasure!

As Mr. Cooper was to be made the presiding elder
of the district over which the Rev. Jesse Lee had been
presiding the previous year, the continuation of his
narrative will be given in the following chapter.

CHAPTER IX.

MR. COOPER ON THE BOSTON DISTRICT, 1793, 1794.

BISHOP ASBURY fully sustained Mr. Cooper in his course of action in the controversy between him and Mr. Lee, and, becoming acquainted with the condition of the Methodist Society in Lynn, saw the necessity of making such an appointment for the ensuing year as would place that Society under the ministerial charge of some one other than Mr. Lee. The rule limiting the time of continued service by a preacher to two consecutive years in the same charge had not yet been adopted by the Church, and in a few instances the same pastor served the same people for a longer period. Mr. Lee, as we shall see below, desired to avail himself of this privilege, notwithstanding many of the church at Lynn were anxious for his removal.

The historical records concerning this Conference serve to awaken a spirit of inquiry on the part of the student of Methodist history. Mr. Asbury says: "Circumstances have occurred which have made this Conference more painful than any one Conference besides." What these circumstances were we learn from Mr. Cooper. He says:

Thursday, August 1. Conference began to-day and held all the week. Of all the Conferences I ever attended this was the most troublesome and trifling. So much accusation, cross-questions, dispute, and opposition, that I confess I was grieved and ashamed. The bishop found it a very difficult point to station the preachers. He wanted Brother Raynor to go to York and take a station from that Conference; but he (Brother R.), wished to stay in this district.

This was a matter of considerable trouble. Brother Lee the bishop wanted also to remove, which was a case of a disagreeable nature. There appears to have existed a jealousy between Brother Asbury and Brother Lee for some time: and, probably, what has passed at this Conference will not be soon forgotten; therefore I here think it my duty to minute down a chain of occurrences which relate to the conduct of them both in the present matter. 1. Brother Lee was made an instrument in gathering the Society at Lynn, somewhere about two years ago, as other preachers had done at other places and times. At the last Conference the bishop, to gratify the society and Brother Lee, appointed Brother Lee to stay at Lynn another year, and also to preside over the district. Brother Lee took a settlement among them, according to the laws and customs of the country, but to be removed according to the Discipline of our Church. At General Conference, last November, in Baltimore, Brother Lee strove very hard to have several parts of the Discipline altered, and the bishop's power reduced, but he could not succeed — the bishop's power was confirmed by that Conference. After General Conference, the bishop appointed me to come up to Boston, which I did. When I came to Lynn, I found that Brother Lee had neglected some parts of our Discipline, the rules about society meetings, privileges granted to strangers, etc., and that he had introduced some "new rules of his own," as he had before told Brother Hill. In those things I opposed his measures at my first coming, but could not prevail with him to alter. I told him we must defer them till conference. Such parts of the Discipline as he favored in the General Conference, such as not singing fugue tunes, etc., he was strenuous in and enforced, and required strict adherence; but such parts as he opposed in General Conference, though adopted by ever so great a majority, such as the reading of the Scriptures in the congregation, etc., he would not submit to. I told him it showed a stiff obstinacy. He wished every one to bend to him, and would not bend to any one, or even to the Conference.

Some weeks—about two months—before the present conference he was so stiff, and proceeded so improperly relative to the singing of fugue tunes, that he gave great dissatisfaction to the singers and members of the Society at large, so that there was a disturbance of a serious nature. Numbers of our congregation said, if he stayed another year they would return to the Congregational Society, from whence they came. It was generally believed that he ought to be removed. I spoke to him, and told him plainly, long enough before Conference, that I expected the bishop would remove him, and he might have held himself in readiness, if he would, so that he could have gone after a few days or a week's warning. But he laid out or left his matters in such a state that he could not, or pretended that he could not, move for some time. The bishop appointed me to take his place at Lynn and in the district, and desired him to go to York, for he was to be appointed to that city. But he said he could not go immediately, and would not agree to do so under three months. The bishop said that York must be immediately supplied, and provided for; nevertheless he would have agreed to his staying a considerable time at Lynn and among his other New England friends, if he would give assurance of his going thither at some given time. Brother Lee told me that he did not say he would not go in a shorter time than three months—but still he did not, and would not agree to go sooner—and gave no assurance or real satisfaction that he would go to York at all. He expressed a backwardness to succeed Brother Morrell, who is now at York, for sundry reasons. At length he proposed to go to the Province of Maine and take a station there. To satisfy him the bishop gave him his desire, and agreed to fix him there in the Minutes. Then he wanted his name printed to Lynn and Maine both. This was to keep his place and hold upon Lynn, which he seemed resolved to keep if he could. To this the bishop would not agree; and I am afraid this will be the foundation of evil. If he is printed to Lynn, I fear that he will be a trouble to us; and if he is not, I fear that he will resent it so highly that he may take some improper step. However, I resign it to the bishop; I scarcely know what is best or what to say. I truly wonder that a man of sense should be so troublesome and unreasonable and ungovernable, so stiff and set. He complains that the bishop never consulted him; but it seems that he never advised with the bishop, never gave him information of the state and condition of his district, and of the preachers therein. It appears as if he wished the bishop to come down to him and his desires, but he was not willing to submit to the bishop. He may think that the bishop was absolute, and dealt harshly with him; but I cannot see one absolute step. He yielded and yielded, but Brother Lee yielded in hardly any thing, so that the principle of absoluteness was more to be seen, I thought, in Brother Lee than in Brother Asbury. Conference closed on Saturday night.

Monday, 5. We all left Lynn, except Brother Lee, who is resolved to stay awhile. I propose to return there in about three or four weeks to see if he will go away or not. I expect he will then go. He is a man whom I esteem, and should more highly esteem if he would alter in some points. Still I love him, and wish him to regulate his conduct according to our Discipline.*

The unpleasant episode above set forth is explanatory of the hitherto unexplained embarrassments connected with the Conference at Lynn in 1793, as also of the fact that in the published Conference Minutes of that year the town of Lynn is set forth twice as a station for the preachers. On page 12 of the Minutes, in answer to the question: "Where are the preachers stationed this year?" Ezekiel Cooper is represented as presiding elder of the district composed of the following stations and circuits, to which are appointed the preachers whose names are also given:

Boston, Amos G. Thompson; Needham, John Hill; Lynn, Jordan Rexford; Greenwich, David P. Kendall and Enoch Mudge; Warren, Philip Wagar; Province of Maine and Lynn, Jesse Lee.

Thus it appears that Mr. Lee had obtained his request, though, as far as we know, no other appointment of a like character has been made in the history of our Church. As anticipated by Mr. Cooper, his appointment to Lynn was the occasion of renewed trouble. When Mr. Cooper visited that place, in the course of his travels over his district, he found Mr. Lee still there, and engaged in stirring up a feeling of opposition on the part of some against Mr. Cooper and Bishop Asbury. The charges against Mr. Cooper were, that of prejudicing the bishop against Mr. Lee, of being at the foundation of all the disturbance between him and the Society at Lynn, of raising or setting on foot certain reports prejudicial to him [Lee], of seeking to root him out from his station with the view of getting it for himself, and other taunting and harassing statements, all of which produced discussion and altercations. From

* Cooper's Diary.

time to time during the year unpleasant scenes occurred, thereby increasing the strife. Mr. Cooper having taken up his residence at Lynn, Mr. Lee, during his absence on the district, sought, says Mr. Cooper, "to fix matters so that I might not return or stay. And I now perceive, that if he can have influence enough, he will defy the bishop and the authority of Conference, and do as he pleases."

Under date of December 20, Mr. Cooper says:

Brother Lee and I had a plain conversation to day, in which I was pretty plain to him. I gave him to know that I would not consent that the authority of Conference should be trampled on by him. He appears to be resolved to oppose the regular government of our Church, and I am more and more satisfied that he only wants power and influence, and all would bend before him. He delights to exercise authority when and where he can, but cannot bear to be ruled or governed. I wish to love and be united with him, and am resolved to strive after peace and fellowship, but I cannot be reconciled to have the rules and government of the Church trampled on; no! not by a brother, or even the warmest or best friend I have in the world. Friends are near and dear, but the Connection is nearer.

As seen in the foregoing, the district over which Mr. Cooper was appointed to preside was composed of Boston, Needham, Lynn, Greenwich, and Warren Circuits. He visited them from point to point. Thus he went through Warren Circuit, preaching in Bridgewater at Mr. Churchill's, in Easton at Mr. Stoke's, in Warren, in a large barn which had been fitted up for a preaching-house with seats and a pulpit; in Bristol, where the Court-house was opened to him, and Captain Wardwell entertained him; in Providence; in Pawtuxet; and at Colonel Lippitt's. Returning to Lynn, on Sunday, August 25, he preached twice, met a class, attended a funeral, visited a sick person, and afterward drank coffee at Captain Johnson's, in company with Rev. Mr. Sherman and others. Mr. Sherman and he soon fell into a controversy about predestination, election, and reprobation, which lasted for two or three hours. The following account of the dispute is from Mr. Cooper's diary. He says:

Sunday, 25. He [Rev. Mr. Sherman] discovered as great prejudice against the Methodists as ever I saw in a man, and brought sundry great and false charges against us, which I was enabled to answer fully to his confusion and to the satisfaction of the company. He got violently angry, and spoke unbecoming a Christian minister or a gentleman. But, through mercy and grace, I was enabled to maintain a loving and calm spirit, which helped my cause as much, I suppose, as his temper and hard speeches hurt his. Several in company checked him from time to time for his bitter reflections instead of arguments, and wished him, if he could, to answer my arguments, which he called sophistry, assuring him that until he did, they must receive my opinion and arguments as scriptural and sound reasoning. I assured the company that it was my opinion that the Rev. Mr. S. would very freely answer my arguments if he could, but as it was out of his power to do it by Scripture or reason, the only come-off was to call it sophistry. I held that Christ died for all men, and that there was an offer of salvation to all; that unconditional election and reprobation by unalterable decrees was not a scriptural doctrine, neither was it true, together with several other points connected with them. He was violent against Arminianism, which led us to an investigation on that subject, and the arbitrary, unjust proceedings of the Synod of Dort against the Arminians, in refusing to give Episcopius and others the privilege of stating or defending their own principles and doctrines. So that the more we talked upon that the better did Arminianism appear, and the worse did Calvinism and the conduct of that professed assembly of Calvinistic divines look. Mr. S. was glad to make a retreat.

We then traced the antiquity of predestination. I followed it back to the beginning of the fifth and end of the fourth century, when St. Augustine wrote in favor of it; but I could not allow it to be of an older date in the Christian Church. I called upon Mr. S. to produce one of the Fathers, previous to St. Austin or Augustine that ever defended or believed in predestination. There were Irenæus, Ignatius, Polycarp, Basil, Simeon, St. Ambrose, Justin, Tertullian, Flavius, Clemens, Origen, Gregory, etc., none of them received it nor understood the apostles to mean it in the Calvinistic sense.

This he did not deny, but insisted that St. Paul wrote strongly upon it. I contended that St. Paul opposed the notion of unconditional election and reprobation, particularly in the ninth chapter to the Romans, when he was vindicating the goodness and universal love of God to mankind in calling the Gentiles as well as the Jews, and in offering mercy to both Jews and Gentiles, which was contrary to the Jewish notion of things, who thought themselves to be the elect and the Gentiles to be reprobates or accursed. St. Paul is oversetting this by a series of arguments, and showing, in a wise and deep manner, that the Gentiles were included according to God's purpose of predestination, which was not unconditional, as well as the Jews; so that both the one and the other might receive of that mercy which God showeth freely to all who accept it upon the Gospel terms. The old gentleman could not overset this observation, and therefore it stood that St. Paul was of my opinion, and that I held his doctrines and principles.*

On Sunday, September 1, Mr. Cooper preached in Salem, in the Rev. Mr. Hopkins's meeting-house, three times ; and though the citizens heretofore had so acted as to cause Bishop Asbury to decline to visit them, they seemed now to be in a better mood for hearing, and formed large congregations. Mr. Cooper was greeted here by Mr. Edward Johnson's, Mrs. Bickford's, Mr. Need's, Esquire Vann's, Captain Verry's, and other families.

From Salem he went to New Mills, and on Tuesday, September 3, formed a class in that town. From thence he went to Marblehead, preached, and found the people "open to and fond of the word and means of grace." From thence he returned to Lynn, where he spent the week, leading the class at Wood End, which met on Wednesday evening, preaching twice on Sunday and holding prayer-meeting, and meeting the class which was held every Monday afternoon. It was expected of the presiding elder that he should assume the

* Cooper's Diary.

pastorate of the Society at Lynn, and Mr. Cooper did so, having taken up· his abode at Captain Johnson's. When called off to other parts of the district his place at Lynn was filled by a preacher from an adjoining charge; as, for example, he says:

Monday, September 16.   I went up to Boston, and let Brother Thompson come down to Lynn for a week.

Again:

Monday, October 7.   This week Brother Rexford came to town, whom I propose leaving here eight or ten days, while I visit a few places fifteen or twenty miles round.

During this latter tour, he visited and preached at Marblehead, Salem, New Mills, Manchester, and Ipswich Hamlet. The preaching at Manchester was in the school-house, and at Ipswich Hamlet at Captain Patcher's. In the latter community a spirit of hostility was manifested toward the Methodists, of which Mr. Cooper thus speaks :

Friday, October 18.   I dined at Captain Foster's.   We have some warm .friends in Manchester, and I feel some encouragement.   This afternoon I rode to Ipswich Hamlet, and preached, by candle-light, at Captain Patcher's, to a full congregation of attentive hearers; but I felt uncomfortable in mind, and very weak in faith while preaching.   The family was kind unto me, and show a disposition of friendship toward the Methodists.   But in those parts we have our enemies,.and the standing ministers, I apprehend, are our greatest foes. They fear the craft is in danger, and if those itinerant men are encouraged, the salary of many will come down.   Nothing makes men so zealous as trade ; so those men, many of them, make a perfect trade of the ministry, and are more zealous to keep us away than to get the people converted.   I cannot refrain from thinking that they are like articles set up at vendue — the highest bidder takes them. Whatever parish gives the greatest offer gives the loudest call, and they strike themselves off to them; so that they are bought and sold.

After this excursion two weeks were spent in Lynn, where, also, on Saturday and Sunday, November 2 and 3, quarterly meeting was held. Five preachers were in attendance, namely: Messrs. Cooper, Jesse Lee, Thompson, Hill, and Rexford. It was a season of refreshment to all, and the spirit of revival gave encouragement to God's servants. The next week, quarterly meeting for Needham Circuit—Rev. John Hill, pastor—was begun in Needham; Saturday, November 9. On Sunday, the 10th, was held the first love-feast that had ever been in that community. Says Mr. Cooper:

Sunday, November 10. At nine o'clock love-feast began. This was the first love-feast ever held in Needham. We had friends from several towns who met together in great love and friendship; but few of them were ever in a love-feast at all before. The Lord was very good and present. Almost every heart was touched and melted into tenderness. And though the friends are all young in the way, yet they spoke very freely of their exercises and experience. I don't know that I have been in a better love-feast for a year past.

Needham Circuit was, at this time, made up of the following appointments, namely: Weston, at William Boyle's; Waltham Plains, at Mr. Travers's; West Waltham, at Mr. Bemis's; Firmingham, at Mr. Stone's; Milford, at Mr. Ball's; and Holleston, at Mr. Cutler's.

The next quarterly meeting was held at Easton, on Warren Circuit, the Rev. Philip Wager being the pastor. In going thither Mr. Cooper and Mr. Hill joined him at Mrs. Blanchard's, who lived in Mansfield. Of the reception by his hostess he thus speaks:

Poor Mrs. Blanchard was so rejoiced at having three preachers at her house that she shouted for joy, and praised and gave glory to God aloud. I hardly ever saw a person or persons so carried out with ecstasy at having preachers call upon them. "O," said she, "glory, glory be to God! O praise the Lord for sending his servants along! The earth is the Lord's and the fullness thereof. I have hay, oats, corn, and provender enough for your horses, and this house I want to be the house of the Lord."

The next day, Thursday, November 21, the company of preachers moved forward to Easton, where, at Mrs. Newland's, meeting was held in the afternoon. Here they spent the night, and the next day went to Mr. Goward's, where they were joined by their brethren Kendall and Mudge. On Saturday the quarterly meeting began ; the opening sermon was preached by Mr. Hill, and on Sunday Mr. Cooper preached in the morning; then Mr. Kendall; after which the sacrament of the Lord's Supper was administered. Then followed a short discourse by Mr. Cooper upon Methodism, love-feasts, etc., and the quarterly meeting was closed. Warren Circuit had within its lines, besides Easton and Warren, Rehoboth, which was connected therewith during Mr. Cooper's charge of the district ; Mansfield ; Bristol, where, on Sunday, December 1, 1793, the ordinances of baptism and the Lord's Supper were for the first time administered by the Methodists; Newport, Providence, Cranston, Pawtuxet, and Warwick. During this visit at Bristol, it pleased the Lord to call to his home on high one of their most valued members, a Brother Pearce, who, says Mr. Cooper, had long sustained a reputable character in civil and religious life, and was a useful member of either society.

After officiating at the funeral of this deceased brother Mr. Cooper went forward to Greenwich Circuit, then under the ministerial supervision of Rev. David P. Kendall, assisted by Rev. Enoch Mudge. While on this circuit he preached at Wickford, or, otherwise, Newtown, at Judge Philips's. The Judge he found to be a friendly man, and so much attached to the Methodists that he proposed to contribute as much as or more than any other man for the building of a Methodist Church in Wickford. Thence he went forward to Greenwich and to Cranston, where he preached on Sunday, December 8; and on the following Wednesday at Mr. Oliver Buckland's, in Pawtuxet; and the next day at Mr. Campbell's, in Raynham. Among those at and near Raynham who indorsed the Methodist movement were Colonel Leonard, the high sheriff of that county, with his wife and daughters; Mr. S. Williams and family, where was a stated service in connection with that circuit (Warren); Mr. Starr, living near Easton; and Mr. Stokes, Mr. Churchill in Bridgewater, and Mr. Monk.

While to Mr. Cooper the charge of the Society at Lynn had been committed, the circuit outside of the town was called Lynn Circuit, and was under the pastoral supervision of Rev. Jordan Rexford. One of its chief appointments was Marblehead, which is thus spoken of by Mr. Cooper:

Monday, December 23. I rode to Marblehead and met Brother Rexford. At night I preached to a large congregation of attentive hearers. Here is a good prospect. Blessed be God! I hope that this town will yet be flaming with religion.

Tuesday, 24. I dined to-day at Mr. Bootman's, in company with Brother Rexford and one or two others. One simple man was there who wanted to dispute about the ordinance of baptism, but he exposed his folly in introducing a controversy which he knew little or nothing about. It is strange that men cannot be more sensible of their ignorance, and not so fondly engage upon subjects which they know so little about. He went away, I believe, ashamed. A gentleman there told him he was surprised to hear a man like him attempt to dispute upon such points. I drank tea at Colonel Bootman's. To-day I visited several families with satisfaction. At night we had prayer-meeting at Mrs. Barker's. The house was crowded, and we truly had a blessed time. The Lord moved upon us; almost every heart was melted. I then took rest at Mr. Prentice's, the place where the preacher boards in town.

Wednesday, 25. When I arose in the morning I felt poorly; but was thankful to the Lord for the privilege of another anniversary of our Lord's birth. At eleven o'clock I preached from Luke ii, 10, 11. We had a large and attentive concourse of people. The Lord deigned to be present, and many hearts were melted before him. At three o'clock we assembled again; I then preached from Acts iii, 22, 23. Our congregation was larger than in the forenoon. The Lord was present again, and the people seemed unwilling to leave the house, and numbers stayed till the evening meeting began. At night our meeting-house was much crowded; we had. I suppose, six hundred or more hearers. Brother Rexford preached with much life and zeal. I then read the Rules of our Societies, and commented upon the same; which, I understand, the people were well satisfied with. I then gave a lengthy exhortation by way of remarking upon the day called Christmas, and the proper mode of observing the day. The people were all attention. and very still. I believe great good has been done to-day. The Lord has highly favored us with his presence. Hundreds felt their hearts and souls affected, and I have no doubt but that the fruits of this day will appear in days yet to come. One gentleman came to me, as soon as meeting closed, with tenderness of heart, and addressed me thus: "My dear sir, there never was such a Christmas spent in the County of Essex. O! this is the very way to spend the anniversary of our Lord's birth." *

After this visit to Marblehead Mr. Cooper returned to Lynn, where he spent the closing days of the old year, 1793, and the first half of January, 1794. In a sermon on the subject of the New Year a review of the past year was made, and, as during that period a number of persons had died—about fifty in that small town —the congregation was most warmly urged to prepare for eternity by a more devoted and earnest life of faith and godliness. The new year opened here with a development of some uneasiness among the Methodists as to the question of the place where their preacher should board ; some being desirous that he should continue where he was, others that he should remove. Both parties applied to Mr. Cooper to learn what was his preference, whether to board at Captain Johnson's or

* Cooper's Diary.

13

Mr. Newhall's. He declined to enter into the matter with them, and the Society, being convened, determined by a vote on Thursday night, January 9, to remove the preacher to Mr. Newhall's. By reason of this state of anxiety he took board at neither of the places mentioned for two weeks, but visited the friends through town, breakfasting in one house, dining in another, and supping in another. The movement was very popular, and in its execution the families of E. Burrill, Mr. Blaney, Mr. Fuller, Captain Ramsdell, Mrs. Farrington, D. Newhall, Dr. Gardner, and others, were visited, and, as a result, the class-meetings were more fully enjoyed, the prayer-meetings more largely attended, and the spirit of brotherly love more powerfully made manifest. Such was the value of this movement that Mr. Cooper adopted it in the other parts of his district, and in every charge made it a point to " visit from house to house." Thus he moved in Marblehead, where at the class-meeting held seven offered to join on probation, and were received; in Salem, where on Saturday, February 1, at night, he preached, and, in speaking of the outlook there, says:

At night I preached in Salem to a small and attentive company. I live in expectation that there will yet be an opening in this town for Methodism. For Methodism! What is that? Why, most generally, the doctrine of *free will* and of *free grace* to and for all who will accept the offers of mercy, together with the doctrine of *faith* and *good works*, that is, practical and experimental religion, by a perseverance in holiness of heart and life to the end, is now called Methodism. May the Lord prosper it every-where, is my prayer.*

A brief review of the history of the work on the district over which Mr. Cooper presided from the 1st of January, 1794, to the session of the New England Conference for that year is now presented to the

* Cooper's Diary.

reader.   Boston, in the early part of February, seemed
to be much " at a stand," with her small Society ; and
the members were derided with charges of association
with Beverly Allen, who, two years previously, had
been expelled from the Church for misconduct, and
was now guilty of the added crime of killing the sheriff
sent to arrest him for his criminal conduct.   The enemies of the Methodists in Boston so used this event
to the injury of the Society that Mr. Cooper was
led to the following course.   Said he, under date of
March 8, 1794:

To-day I had published in the newspaper a certificate showing that
B. Allen, of Georgia, has not been a preacher among us for more
than two years. He, poor man, has, it is said, been guilty of mur-
dering a Federal marshal, and this is published as being the conduct of a Methodist preacher. I believe the certificate which I have
published to-day will give satisfaction, so far as to prevent the Methodist Connection from being reproached for the crime of that poor
apostate man.*

The growth of the Society was small, only eight
persons having been added thereto during the Conference year.

Needham Circuit comprised the appointments of
Weston, Waltham, Framingham, Needham, East Sud-
bury, and Lincoln.   The circuit was cared for by
Messrs. Mansfield, Brown, and Bowgles, of Needham;
Herrington and Cobb, of Weston; Bemis, of Waltham;
and Stone, of Framingham, together with others whose
names will appear below.   On Saturday, February 8,
was held at Weston a quarterly meeting for Needham
Circuit, of which the following account is given by
Mr. Cooper:

Saturday, February 8.   I dined at Mr. Bowgles', and then rode to
Mr. Herrington's, in Weston, where quarterly meeting began after

* Cooper's Diary.

two o'clock. We had a comfortable season. Here I met Brother Hill, who had lately returned from his north-west tour. He gave good tidings of a prospect up in several towns which he had visited sixty or seventy miles off, and wants to visit them again very much, which I hope he will find it convenient to do.

Sunday, 9. Love-feast began at nine o'clock. We had not so refreshing a time as I have often seen, though numbers professed to be very happy. At eleven o'clock public preaching began. We held meeting in the Baptist meeting-house, and administered the sacrament there also. I believe very few, if any, made any objection. Upon the whole, I hope this quarterly meeting is profitable, though not so powerful as the last in this circuit. We, the preachers, lodged at Mr. Cobb's, who lives nigh the meeting-house, upon the Hon. Moses Gill's country-seat.

The preaching services at Weston, as seen above, were in the Baptist church; at East Sudbury they were held at Mr. Underwood's; at Framingham, at Mr. Hill's; in Waltham, at the town school-house. Here there seemed to be a decided religious development among the people; they were much wrought upon, and eagerly listened to the word as delivered by the Methodists. Mr. Gale and his lady were devoted friends to the cause. The Society at Lincoln held its meetings at Mr. Parks's. We give the following from Mr. Cooper's diary:

Wednesday, April 16. At three o'clock I preached in Lincoln, at Mr. Parks's, to a crowded congregation of attentive hearers. After preaching, Esquire Adams came and spoke to me, and gave me an affectionate invitation to come and see him, which I promised to do when convenient. He pressed a piece of money into my hands to help me along in bearing my expenses through the world as I travel on from place to place.

The increase of membership on the circuit, for the year, had been from fifty to seventy-six.

The third circuit, Lynn, was composed of the following places for preaching: Lynn, Marblehead, Salem,

New Mills, Manchester, and Ipswich Hamlet. In the Annual Minutes for 1793 the number of members of the Church on the circuit was reported to be one hundred and sixty-six. In 1794 they were given in as being one hundred and forty-nine, a decrease of seventeen. As seen above, Lynn is set forth in the said Minutes twice—first as the appointment of Rev. Jordan Rexford, and then, as connected with the province of Maine, under Rev. Jesse Lee, though the number of members is given only once, and, therefore, includes both the town itself and the adjacent charges connected with it in constituting the circuit. We have also shown that the Methodist Episcopal Church in the town of Lynn was, for the Conference year of 1793, 1794, under the pastoral charge of the Rev. Ezekiel Cooper, who boarded there, and was also the presiding elder of the district, while Mr. Rexford boarded at Marblehead, and was pastor of the other part of the circuit.

At Lynn Mr. Cooper had, by the selection of the Society, his home at Mr. D. Newhall's for the year 1794, they having met on Thursday night, January 9, and by a vote determined that the preacher should remove from Captain Johnson's to Mr. Newhall's. Here also was boarded the preacher who had charge of the Society while Mr. Cooper was engaged in ministerial duty in other parts of the district. The ecclesiastical management of this church, however, was in the hands of Mr. Cooper solely. Though the Minutes of 1794 give the name of Rev. Jesse Lee as the pastor, yet he had no ecclesiastical authority over them, nor did he attempt its exercise. Such is the importance of the period now passing under review that the writer has determined to set forth to the reader the outline of the early history of Methodism in the town of Lynn, before giving that of the district.

As may be seen, by reference to *Lee's History of the Methodists*, the first Methodist sermon was preached in Lynn on the 14th day of December, 1790. On the 20th of February, 1791, the first class was formed, consisting of eight persons. The first Methodist meeting-house built in Massachusetts was begun at Lynn, on June 14th, 1791, raised on the 21st, and dedicated on the 26th of said month and year.* The Annual Conference for New England was held also here for the years 1792, 1793, and 1794.†

Among those who supported the cause of Methodism in Lynn, during the year 1794, were: E. Burrill, Mr. Fuller, Captain Randall, Mr. Farrington, D. Newhall, Dr. Gardner, Mr. Blaney, Mr. Bustard, Mrs. Ingalls, Mr. Bartlett, John Philips, Mrs. Lewis, Captain Williams, Mr. Costin, Theophilus Breed, Captain Mansfield, and Mr. Johnson.

The second session of the New England Annual Conference, held in Lynn in August, 1793, has been described in the earlier part of this chapter. The third session of that body was also holden in this town. Of this Conference Dr. Stevens says, "we have scarcely any information," and then intimates that the session was inharmonious, and its termination "grateful to Bishop Asbury's wounded feelings." The following extract, from Mr. Cooper's diary, will be read with interest by those who would have the business of the Conference made known to them more fully. Says he, under date of Wednesday, July 23 :

This afternoon the bishop and two or three of our elders and three other preachers, in all eight, came to town ready for Conference. At night Brother Roberts preached. This day I examined the steward's book, and discovered a mistake or two, which I had rectified.

Thursday, April 24. We began Conference to-day. Though all the

---

* See Lee's *History of the Methodists,* p. 165.   † Ibid.

preachers were not present, yet we could go on with the business. At night the bishop preached.

Friday, 25. All the preachers of the district being present, we entered fully into the business of the Conference. Although some things in this Conference were disagreeable, it was much better than that of last year. At night Brother Spry preached a very thundering sermon, which offended some people, who cannot bear any thing but smooth things.

Saturday, 26. There were a number of country friends at Conference to whom the time was profitable. This day was appointed for fasting and prayer in all the Society. At five o'clock in the morning there was prayer-meeting. At eleven o'clock, according to the appointment of Conference, it fell on me to preach a sermon on fasting, which I did, showing the purposes and the manner of holding a fast. The Lord gave me some freedom, and we had a solemn time. To-day we finished Conference, excepting the ordinations, and the preachers prepared for their several stations.

During the time of Conference three or four of the preachers rode down to Nahant, a kind of island, connected to the mainland by a beach nearly two miles long, and like a mill-dam, over which the tide at high water sometimes flows. We rode upon the high part, and spent some time in viewing creation's wonderful form. The bishop withdrew some distance from us, and sat down upon a rock alone, as if in deep reflection upon the stupendous works of God. 'Tis difficult to describe the extraordinary situation of this place, but it is one of the curiosities of nature. Lord, 'tis the work of thy hand!

Sunday, 27. In the forenoon the bishop preached an ordination sermon. We had a vastly crowded assembly. Soon as sermon was finished an elder and a deacon were ordained, then the sacrament was administered. Two sermons were preached in the afternoon. This has been a fine day, particularly its love-feast, which was held at eight o'clock A. M. We had a joyful season.

Monday, 28. The bishop and the greater part of the preachers left town.*

For several months during the year a malignant fever had prevailed, and death had entered several homesteads. Among those called to their eternal reward were Mrs. Ingalls and Mrs. Lewis, choice spirits, loved

* Cooper's Diary.

by the Church, and honored and respected by the whole community.

Measures were adopted prior to the session of the New England Conference in Lynn, in 1794, for the finishing of the church, which had been erected three years previously.   Says Mr. Cooper, under date of Monday, July 21, 1794:

To-day we held a Society parish meeting, to conclude upon finishing the meeting-house, and upon raising £30 as our part toward building a school-house in the east ward of the town. . . .

Tuesday, 22.   To-day friend Johnson began to procure plank to finish the meeting-house.*

In addition to the information given in regard to the " meeting-house," the reader's attention is probably arrested by the unusual expression, in Methodist circles, of a "Society parish meeting."   It seems to the writer to refer not only to the society in Lynn, but also to that of the Methodists in the adjoining towns of Woodend, Gravesend, Swampscott, and other places contiguous, as may be shown in the following extract from Mr. Cooper's Journal:

Monday, July 14.   I set out upon visiting the friends, and propose visiting all the week, so that I may get through the Society this week. Met class at five o'clock P. M.   Lodged at Mr. Eben Burrill's, about two miles from my boarding-place.

Tuesday, 15.   This forenoon I crossed the hills to the Farms, and then returned over the hills by Swampscott, where I visited four families.   Then I returned to Woodend; met a class at five, and another at eight o'clock P. M.; lodged at Mrs. Sye's, where I met the classes.

Wednesday, July 16, 1794.   To-day I visited at Gravesend, from house to house, for seven or eight families.   As I returned went round by Deacon Farrington's, where I drank tea in company with a number of ladies who were upon a visit at the Deacon's, two of whom I never had the pleasure of knowing before.   We spent an agreeable

---

* Cooper's Diary.

afternoon, though, in the midst of so sociable a company, and while I was considerably cheerful and free in conversation, I felt an anguish in my poor heart which none of them, I suppose, apprehended. There is such a thing as to sorrow and be cheerful, too, when among friends. At night I met class at friend Johnson's. We had a lively time. I felt some comfort among them. I don't know that I have been more happy for a long time.

Thursday, 17. I still pursued my visiting. Met class in the chapel at three o'clock, and preached at night.

Friday, 18. I walked and visited the people so much that I was quite tired before night. At five o'clock I attended a funeral, and afterward paid a short visit to three families, the last of which was at friend Pratt's, where I stayed all night.

Saturday, 19. I went on visiting. I called upon ten or twelve before four o'clock, at which hour I met the children. Afterward I called at two or three places, and then retired home. This has been a fatiguing week to my body and mind.

It will be seen, by reference to the *Minutes of the Several Annual Conferences* for the year 1794, that Mr. Cooper was appointed to take his station in New York; but, for some reason, he did not engage in the work there for several months, but continued in New England, and exercised pastoral authority over the Church in Lynn and vicinity. In referring to it in his diary, under date of August 8, he says:

I am appointed to New York, where I am to go in September or October.

He retained his pastorate over the Society in Lynn until the 6th day of October, when, he says:

Monday, October 6. I took my leave of Lynn. I have been preaching, off and on, in that town for more than a year and a half.*

There is given us, by reason of this unusual course of procedure on the part of the appointing authority of the

* Cooper's Diary.

Church, additional information as respects the state of the Methodists of this town.

The Rev. Jesse Lee having taken charge of the district over which he had formerly presided, Mr. Cooper, on Tuesday evening, July 29, held a meeting of the leaders and stewards of the Lynn Society, and conversed at length with them " upon points of moment relative to their conduct, and the Society in general." On Tuesday, August 19, he met two classes, and turned out of Society four members who, for some time, had habitually neglected their class-meeting. On Thursday, the 28th of said month, he says :

To day brother Thompson came to town and preached for me at night. Through the day I passed among the friends as usual, met one class, etc. There is more than a class for every day, besides visiting and preaching and other duties which take up a preacher's time pretty constantly.

The Methodists of Lynn about this time were sought after by the Episcopalians, as the following will show. Says Mr. Cooper, under date of September 4 :

Friend Johnson this evening showed me a copy of the letter of invitation from the minister and church of the old parish, inviting our people to come and join them, which friend Johnson quite smiles at, and has some thought of returning the compliment, were it not that the greater part of that Church we would not have unless they first reformed from what they are. So that we could not invite them sincerely in their present condition.

The " compliment " was not returned, but Mr. Cooper found, on visiting his members, that the committee of invitation had personally visited his members, but found only two in the charge willing to separate from the Methodist Episcopal Church in Lynn and return to their first love.

In addition to this opposition, Mr. Cooper had given

offense to a deist who had heard him preach, and who threatened him with a letter of reproof for the views he had set forth in the sermon. The theme of the discourse was "The Excellency of the Scriptures," which Mr. Cooper discussed,

1. As a book of information, being (*a*), the most ancient and rational account of the origin of the universe; (*b*) of the creation of man; (*c*) of the perfections and properties of Deity; (*d*) of man's fall by sin, and rise by grace; (*e*) of the duties of man in moral and religious life; (*f*) of immortality, future rewards and punishments; (*g*) of judgment, etc.

2. Their great benefit to human society. For where the Scriptures are, we find, (*a*) the greater light and knowledge; (*b*) the greater improvement in art and science. We see also, (*c*) their effect upon the judgment, conscience, and conduct of those who read and believe them.

3. Directions and application given.

The deist, after hearing the sermon, said the speaker was "a fluent, tonguy person, but like others was mistaken."

Mr. Cooper requested his informant to encourage the deist to write as he threatened. He did it not.

While there was opposition both ecclesiastical and personal, other Churches also were affected by internal strifes, which led to separations, and in some instances to an indorsement of the Methodist movement. For instance, at Waltham, on Monday afternoon, a town meeting was held in the church of the "standing order," to determine upon the question of raising the preacher's salary. The opposition was so great that the salary was voted to be increased only by a majority of one vote. Mr. Cooper was passing by the church just as the meeting was "breaking up." A gentleman coming out requested to have a little talk with him. It was granted. Whereupon he informed him concerning the meeting; accused his pastor of preaching for money; said that he would pay no more money, but would come and hear the Methodists, and would give $100 to aid in building a church for them. There was much murmuring among the people, and the next day they attended in large numbers the services of the Methodists, held in the school-house, and ministered by Mr. Cooper. Many of them heretofore had refused to hear a Methodist preacher.

The time was now drawing near when Mr. Cooper was to leave the district over which he had presided, and to take a station in New York. This had been determined in the session of the Lynn Conference held July 24–27, where it was also arranged that he should remain in charge of the district until September or October. He was now, for the most part, making his last tour through his district, accompanied, in several instances, by Rev. Jesse Lee, who had been appointed to be his successor. Though there had been in the past some estrangement between these two ministers, they were now in unity and harmony with each other. Of this Mr. Cooper speaks as follows:

Thursday, October 2. I returned to Lynn, where I met Brother Lee, who had got back from his western tour. He and I were quite comfortable together. Although there was a great trial between us some time ago, yet now we are as friendly as ever, having made up our difference. I think he is as near to me as ever he was. All things are passed over and laid aside.

While preparing for his departure to New York Mr. Cooper received the following valuable letter from Bishop Asbury:

Lord's Day, September 28, 1794. New York.

MY VERY DEAR BROTHER: I am now satisfied that you should take your stand here till further orders. It is my wish that you should keep a conference with the preachers in this city, stationed and supernumeraries. It is my desire that once in five or six weeks each one of you should spend a Sabbath in Brooklyn. Brother Phoebus has heard my mind. I want quarterly-meetings to be held at each of the three houses, first at one and then at another. Meet the first day, and the following day call the leaders and stewards in conference—close conference about the work of God and their souls, the order and harmony of the Societies, and their temporal supplies. Have a love-feast for all of the Societies. Let me hear from you, and you shall hear from me. I have been greatly employed preaching three times this day ; am going off early to-morrow morning.

Thine in love,   FRANCIS ASBURY.

I give it as my real opinion, that you should have no open love-feast. Attend to this.   F. ASBURY.

This letter was written a few days after the session of the New York Annual Conference, which was begun in New York, September 22, 1794. It was an appointment of Mr. Cooper to the charge of New York and Brooklyn as chief pastor, and as we shall subsequently find, to the presiding eldership of this circuit, and of Croton and New Rochelle, and Long Island. By order of that Conference, Sylvester Hutchinson and Robert Hutchinson, the former being in charge of Croton and New Rochelle, and the latter in charge of Long Island Circuit, were to change with Lawrence McCombs every three months.*

Mr. Cooper, though separating from the dearest friends of his ministerial life, to one of whom he had become affianced, obeyed the summons, and in a few weeks after receiving the above letter took his station in New York, according to appointment.

* Minutes, 1794, 1st edition.

CHAPTER X.

METHODISM IN NEW YORK AND VICINITY, 1794, 1795.

As in the preceding chapter there were given, so in this are given, historical facts which throw light upon matters that have been occult, supplying some of the broken links that are apparent in the recitals of our most eminent Church historians, and correcting some statements made by them by reason of their want of exact knowledge of that age of the Church. Of these misstatements one demands correction now because of the facts given in the letter of Bishop Asbury and of the Conference Minutes of that date. Both Bishop Simpson and Dr. Abel Stevens, in their highly valuable, and, for the most part, accurate sketches of Methodism in its ecclesiastical and personal development, give to the reader of their biography of Ezekiel Cooper the impression that Brooklyn and New York was the field of his labor, after he left New England. It will be seen, however, that Brooklyn was to be visited by the New York pastors only once on the Sabbath day in five or six weeks; while the two churches in the city were to have a sermon twice every Sabbath. New York was Mr. Cooper's special field of labor, and not Brooklyn. Besides the effective ministers appointed to this charge in 1794, there were supernumerary or located preachers, resident in New York or the village of Brooklyn, Jacob Brush, David P. Candall, and William Phoebus, M.D. These, we shall see, were co-workers with the stationed preachers in preaching the Gospel and upbuilding the Church.

Mr. Cooper arrived in the city of New York on the 29th of October, and entered at once upon his pastoral duties, though his heart was overwhelmed with grief on account of the death of his mother, the tidings of which sad event had reached him that day. To show the state of the Society in New York at this time, the following extracts are given from his Journal:

This evening (October 29) I attended prayer-meeting in the city among our friends. My old acquaintances appeared glad to see me, and I was glad to see them. Though in the midst of sorrow, I can yet feel some gladness of heart. Here I fell in with the preachers, with whom I feel friendship and love.

Thursday, 30. I visited a few friends. At night we had a meeting of the stewards and leaders to consult upon the best method of carrying out our religious economy for the preservation and promotion of piety among us, and the enforcing of discipline. We had some debates, which I did not like so well; there appeared too great an inclination to opposition by some, and not enough inquiry after the most eligible methods. When men seem inclined to oppose each other more than to give or receive information. it makes me feel disagreeable; and when any betray an air of self importance it hurts me. A childlike humility should attend us in all our counsels.

Friday, 31. At night I preached to a large congregation in the old church; felt some considerable liberty and many hearts were touched ; a little more and we would have had a shout—some did lift up their voice aloud. The Lord moved upon us.

Saturday, November 1. To-day I dined with a large company at Mr. McKenness's, a British agent, in this city. Here I was in company with three or four gentlemen who were opposed to the French in their present contest with England. We, in consequence, had some opposition to each other in the company. The Rev. Mr. Pilmore was among us, and this is the first time I ever saw him. He is a celebrated preacher, but not so agreeable in company; there is in him an assuming, overbearing manner which renders him rather disagreeable. Two other of our preachers were in company, and several ladies. After politics were dwelt upon awhile, we turned the subject upon religion, on which we continued till we parted. It was laid upon me to pray, so we joined in fellowship and prayer and parted.

Sunday, November 2. I preached in the old church in the forenoon, and administered the sacrament to three or four hundred people. In the afternoon I preached in the new church. In the evening, after preaching in the old church by Brother McCombs, there broke out a powerful work among the people; a shout lasted till near eleven o'clock. O may this be the beginning of a great and glorious work. All this week I spent in York. I was looking around and seeing how matters were in Society. The Society is large, and, for some time past, has been dull in religion. The last year, it seems, they have lost more than a hundred members; but they appear to be encouraged that a revival will take place.

The membership in the two churches in New York, as reported in the Minutes of 1794, numbered, " whites, 575; blacks, 135. The previous year they were reported to be: whites, 639; blacks, 154, showing, as by the Minutes, a loss of 83. This, according to Mr. Cooper's showing, was increased after the close of the Conference session. During the Conference year of 1794–95, the number was again increased, and the report for that year was: whites, 600; blacks, 155, showing an increase of 55. The number of members in Brooklyn was not reported separately until 1795; and though they had built a church, to which Bishop Asbury referred in the letter given in the last chapter, saying that he wanted "quarterly meeting to be held in each of the three houses," namely, two in New York and one in Brooklyn, the membership was numerically small, having, in the Minutes of 1795, the number of whites, 23; blacks, 12. We continue Mr. Cooper's Journal:

Tuesday, November 4. I preached at night to a large congregation.

Wednesday, 5. I rode out with Mr. Ellis a few miles in his carriage. Dined at Mr. Fosbrooks. At night had prayer-meeting.

Thursday, 6. I accompanied Brother Garrettson through town. We dined at Mr. Vanderliff's; then visited lawyer Livingston, with whom we stayed awhile; went to Mr. John Livingston's and drank tea. Although it may be deemed honorable and be pleasing to some to move in so high a circle as those great men, yet I can say there is more happiness where there is more simplicity, in a lower circle.

Sunday, 9.　In the forenoon I preached in the new church; we gave the sacrament to two or three hundred.　We had a lively time. I dined at friend Bleecker's.　At night I preached to a crowded concourse of people in the old church.

Having gained a knowledge of the state of his charge, Mr. Cooper left New York on the 10th of November, and visited his bereaved relatives in Maryland, where, on the 1st day of December, he, with his brothers, sisters, and other relatives, attended the funeral of his mother.

He returned to New York on the 21st day of December.　It was Sunday; and, not having time to take breakfast, he hastened to church and preached the morning sermon.　After dinner he preached again, and in the evening "had a comfortable time in meeting the Society."　The three months' appointment of Rev. Lawrence McCombs having expired, he had now gone to his appointment on New Rochelle Circuit, and the Rev. Sylvester Hutchinson, late of that circuit, had become his successor in New York.　With his new colleague pastoral work was resumed by Mr. Cooper, and thus an introduction given to all under their ministrations.

As Dr. Wakeley has beautifully shown in his *Lost Chapters,* etc., the New York Methodists were, in the early days of the Church, noted for their generosity to and filial regard for the Methodist preachers; and he has, in his recital of the story, brought forth the names and Christian characters of laymen who otherwise would have been unknown to succeeding generations.　It is the privilege of the writer to add to that list.　Read the following from Mr. Cooper's Journal:

Wednesday, December 24.　I attended the funeral of Mrs. Gray, an old widow lady of this place.　She has left the principal part of her

14

fortune to be distributed among the Methodist preachers. There were four ministers who attended. Among the ministers, doctors, and pall-bearers, there were fourteen scarfs, three and a half yards of linen in each pall, which made forty-nine yards of fine linen, besides gloves, distributed. In the evening I preached a funeral sermon on the occasion of her death.

To show how the Methodists observed Christmas day in New York at this time, we have the following :

Thursday, 25, was Christmas. Another anniversary of our Lord's birth I have lived to see. We had the sacrament in both churches, and three sermons preached in each. I lament that men so generally make Christmas a day of frolicking instead of worship. We, however, had a comfortable day in our churches.

Friday, 26. I visited several friends. In the evening, after sermon, we had a friend tried before the leaders and stewards; but he was acquitted of the charge, yet was found deserving of reproof, which I gave him.

On the following day the child of Mr. Craft, one of the representative members of Methodism in the city, was buried. The next day, after evening preaching, a Mr. Vanskirke came to Mr. Cooper, with tears in his eyes, telling him that he lived above Albany, in the Mohawk wilderness, where they had but little of the Gospel, and implored an interest in his prayers. On Monday evening the "select bands" were met; on Tuesday Mr. Hutchinson preached his first sermon; and on Wednesday, the last day of the year 1794, a watchnight service was held, beginning at eight o'clock P. M., and closing at half-past twelve A. M. Mr. Cooper says of it :

Thus ended the old year, and began the new one in public worship. I preached from 1 Thess. v, 6; Brothers Phoebus, Hutchinson, Smith, Valleau, and Brush exhorted. We had a comfortable time; the Lord was gracious unto us. Nearly five hundred people stayed till after midnight.

On the 1st day of January, 1795, Mr. Cooper preached a New Year's sermon in the old church, and in the afternoon went over to Brooklyn and delivered a New Year's discourse in their new church. On the return trip the boat in which he had taken passage was crowded, he says: "as thick as we could stand." Describing the crossing he says:

As we passed some sailors in a boat they cried out, "The devil will have a fine haul if he gets that boat," meaning us. Somebody in our company replied to them, that they would stand the worst chance, for the devil would get all of them were he to come, but could only get a part in our boat. This introduced a very serious discourse among us. In the evening we had a precious time in the old church. While I was in the closing prayer it seemed as if the glory of the Lord filled the house. Brothers Phoebus, Humbert, and I spoke to the people; Brother Hutchinson prayed once.

Another instance of Christian liberality is here presented to the reader. Under date of January 2, 1795, Mr. Cooper says:

Mr. McKenniss called to see me one day and gave me forty shillings to distribute to the poor. He is the British agent here, who has charge of the packet; he receives and forwards all the dispatches to and from the British Government and the United States.

On the day following he began the distribution, the first being made to Mr. Crum and family, where God met the pastor and the family in a gracious manner while they were at prayer. Among the members of the Methodist Society in New York at that time were, in addition to those already mentioned: Messrs. Young, Jones, Mitchell, Coddington, Anderson, Valleau, Bowen, Miller, Dunnevan, Kip, Campbell, West, John Brower, Bull, Fosbrook, Staples, Dr. Wainwright, Sharock, Vanderbilt.

It had been arranged by the Society in the city for the holding of the sacrament of the Lord's supper on

the first Sabbath in each month, in the morning at the
old church and in the afternoon at the new church;
and in the evening of the same day was "a meeting of
the Society at large," where those who could not attend the sacrament either in the morning or afternoon
were privileged to receive it at the close of the Society
meeting.

On Tuesday, January 6, says Mr. Cooper:

This is a day set apart by the various denominations to hold what
they call a concert of prayer; namely, for all who will join of every
denomination to unite in prayer for the outpouring of the Spirit of
the Lord upon the world. They propose setting apart four
days in the year for the purpose, and begin with the first Tuesday
in January, and to continue it the first Tuesday in each quarter
of the year. We have joined them. At two o'clock we assembled
in each church for prayer. At night I preached upon the subject of
prayer; the Lord assisted me. We had a comfortable time.

In order to do his pastoral work the more efficiently,
it was a custom with Mr. Cooper to be with his members daily at their family table one after another, as
the following will show. Says he, under date of
February 1:

I have not been regular with my diary for two weeks and more.
Those two weeks past I have visited many of our friends; have
breakfasted, dined, or drank tea with upwards of twenty different
families, besides other visiting, the poor, the sick, etc. I generally
take breakfast, dinner, or tea from home every day, excepting Sabbath, and sometimes all three from home. A preacher's charge, in
York, is great.

During the week through which he was now passing
he received a letter from Bishop Asbury, which, he says,
gave him "great and trying exercises of mind." The
letter will explain itself. It is as follows:

CHARLESTON, *January* 2, 1795.

MY DEAR BROTHER: I am, by the good and always kind providence of God, brought safe to this city in peace, but a little unwell by

hard traveling and changes. Serious things have taken place here. Brother Hughes is dead, Captain Darrall and William Adams drowned. We creep along, with an increase of hearers and members. Some wandering stars appear and shine a little in the new Trinity. We pay our debts, and go on fair and easy. I must say, every time I visit Charleston my feelings are better, and I hope there is some fruit of my toil.

I should be much obliged to you to favor me with your former kindness in letters. Any thing that is of moment for me to know, especially from the eastward, that comes to your knowledge. Charleston, Holston, Baltimore, Philadelphia, and Boston or Hartford, are good points to meet me at with letters.

I am in hopes that something valuable will take place in York in the year 1795. Your attention ought to be paid to Discipline, and visiting from house to house, but not to eat and drink. I am pointedly against that. You have a house to eat in; you need not go to feast with the Church of God. We ought to visit as doctors, or as persons to plead the cause of their souls; not as guests, to eat and drink, but as divines for souls. I am convinced it is and will be an evil. We have had few city preachers but what have been spoiled for a poor man's preacher. That is a truth we can awfully substantiate. What persons and times are past and gone, let them go. I trust your soul is more engaged with God than ever, and you will send me good news of the spiritual affairs of the Society; as to the temporal matters, these grow fast enough.

Cokesbury is out of blast, and let it go; we were great too soon. My ten years' dread is over; I shall leave the world and my charge shortly. Excuse my not writing a longer letter. I have many to write.

I am thine as ever,   F. ASBURY.

It was a custom with the New York Methodists to have a care for the spiritual interests of the prisoners in the City Jail. They had preaching regularly, once a month, on Friday, and such other spiritual counsel as is connected with a faithful pastorate. To give one of the many instances recorded by Mr. Cooper, take the following from his journal:

Friday, February 6. I visited the prisoners, carried a Bible and hymn-books with me, which I gave to such as I thought would use them to advantage. I went to see the poor criminals; there are three under sentence of death; they were much affected while Brother Hutchinson and I talked and prayed with them, and desired that we would come again.

The following is given to illustrate the interest taken by the Methodists of the city in national thanksgiving. Under date of February 19, Mr. Cooper says:

This was Thanksgiving Day throughout the United States, appointed by the president. We had public worship, the same as on the Sabbath, three times. In the forenoon I preached upon the occasion, showing the many signal mercies which the Lord had bestowed upon us as a people which called for our thanksgiving, and wherein an acceptable thanksgiving doth consist. The Lord favored us with much of his presence; great power rested upon us, which was melting to our hearts; and, I believe, the congregation felt grateful to the Lord for the benefits of providence toward them as individuals, and to the land in which we live in general. One person wrote me a letter, disapproving of my preaching at all on politics, which I touched upon considerably. But I feel a clear conscience; I did no more than my duty upon such an occasion. Surely to repeat our preservation from war, our constitutions of government, internal tranquillity, the prosperity and growing condition of our country, together with the grounds of all those mercies under God, cannot be amiss on a day appointed for thanksgiving. Nay, I should hardly have done my duty to have neglected them. But I cannot learn that more than one was dissatisfied. Many wanted the sermon printed, to which I almost agreed.

Mr. Cooper was now but thirty-two years old; yet such was the reputation he had won by strict adherence to the Discipline of his Church and devotion to the pastorate in its varied forms of labor that he was regarded as a safe adviser by his bishop, a father by the younger clergy of his Church, and an able minister of the Gospel by those even who rejected its truths. Though quotations from the record of his personal history have been elaborate, it is due to the Church of his

choice and the descendants of his family line still further to make known the personal history of one of the
most excellent of our ecclesiastical fathers, about whom
little is really known. On the 22d day of February,
1795, then being thirty-two years old, he received an
invitation from a company of New York deists to
preach for them a sermon. They gave the text; it
was: "But of that day and hour knoweth no man, no,
not the angels which are in heaven, neither the Son, but
the Father." Mark xiii, 32. The letter asking the
favor was so civil and candid in its tone and manner,
that Mr. Cooper consented to grant their request. He
thus speaks of it:

I agreed to take the text, and found an unexpected liberty while
preaching. I am informed that good was done; the faith of numbers
strengthened. But I do not hear that one deist was convinced.
However, I received a letter of thanks from the deists acknowledging. "that my arguments upon the subject were equal to any they
had heard advanced by any one, and superior to any they had seen
among the writers against Thomas Paine's *Age of Reason*." I thought,
though, that I had been quite successful in so far gaining upon them
(more so than I really expected), but still they were not convinced.

As Thanksgiving Day was observed by preaching—
morning, afternoon and evening—so also was the general fast day throughout the Methodist Connection
observed in the New York churches of that denomination on Friday, February 27.

The three months' service of Rev. S. Hutchinson was
now drawing near its close, and Rev. Lawrence
McCombs, his predecessor, was by appointment to return to the city churches for another three months'
term of ministerial duty. He desired, if admissible, to
remain in the country, and wrote to that effect to Mr.
Cooper. Mr. McCombs's future prominence in the
Church demands that this letter be presented to the

reader. It has not before this appeared in the public
print. It is as follows:

WHITE PLAINS, *March* 2, 1795.

VERY DEAR BROTHER: I have wanted to open my mind to you for
some time, and did send to you by Brother Hutchinson to the same
purport, but now undertake to inform you by letter. Since I have
been traveling I have sustained considerable loss; therefore I am
resolute to take care of what little I have, unless taking care should
interfere with my appointment. But I would sustain considerable
loss before I would neglect my regular appointment, given me by the
bishop. But I suppose I ought to attend as much to the appointment in the country as in the city; and as considerable difficulty
presents itself to view, I think it not expedient for me to come and
stay in the city until the expiration of three months more, unless
those difficulties can be removed. I believe I have no choice with
regard to any appointment to preach given me by the bishop. I will
state the matter:

1. The bishop has given me my appointment both in town and
country; and unless you will stand between me and the bishop at
Conference, I think I ought to fulfill my appointment and stand for
myself.

2. My creature [horse] cannot be kept without considerable expense, therefore I do not think it fair play for me to be at such expense, when it is not my turn in town; but if the brethren in
York are willing to pay for its keeping, I will come to York as
freely as I would go anywhere. If not, I would rather stay in the
country. But to be obedient to you I will as far as is consistent with
the nature of things.

I would not have you to think I am in the least worried, from the
manner in which I have written; it is only because of my wish to
do right. I shall expect to receive a line from you on the subject at
the first opportunity. My soul is in some degree engaged with my
God, and I want it to be entirely my meat and drink to do his will.
I feel some oppositions, from different quarters, to prevent my progress in religion; but I feel resolute to do the will of God as far as I
am able; yet I find that I am short in my conceptions, and extensive
in my ideas, and my understanding wants much clearing; and I
know that to God I must go for all that I lack; but O! the slowness
of my movements in things of a religious nature. Remember me to
inquiring friends. I am still, as ever, your son in the undivided
Gospel of Jesus Christ.   LAWRENCE MCCOMBS.

Mr. McCombs did not succeed in his petition, but, as will be seen, was again employed with Mr. Cooper in serving the churches in New York and Brooklyn. The election of trustees for the church in New York occurred soon after this, as will appear from the following extract from Mr. Cooper's journal:

Monday, March 16. This day we had our election for trustees in the church. Assembled at eleven and finished at one o'clock. There was the greatest election ever known upon the occasion at any time whatever before. There was a perfect party piece of work, one for putting out the old members, and the other for keeping them in. The contention rose so high that I was much grieved. I thought that some were quite out of a religious line of conduct. The election caused great uneasiness in the Society; unfriendly things were said of each other, which I feared would be a means of getting some of them out of the Society. However, we settled matters tolerably well. The old trustees were continued in office.

On Sunday, March 22, Mr. Cooper, after preaching in the morning in the city, went to Brooklyn, where he spent the afternoon and evening, preaching on both occasions. In the afternoon he, with Dr. Phoebus, held a love-feast that was enjoyed by many of the New York Methodists who had accompanied them. The evening being rainy, but few attended church. Of Brooklyn's inhabitants he thus speaks:

The people in this village appear very careless about religion, though they have had much preaching. We have a clever preaching-house built and a small Society.

It will give pleasure and instruction to the reader to have the contents of a letter from Dr. Thomas Coke now set before him. Though it is long, yet its matter is too valuable to permit us to lose a sentence. Its style is different from that used by educated men of the present generation, but it is presented as a true copy of the original from the bishop's pen. We read:

IRELAND, *April* 23, 1795.

MY DEAR BROTHER: I embrace an opportunity of writing to you a few lines. Though a multiplicity of business in respect to the Churches and the press engrosses the greatest part of my time, I do not forget my American brethren, but frequently have them before me in meditation and prayer; frequently your pine-trees, and oaks, and dogwood, and red-flower, etc., are before my eyes, and the congregations in your forests, among whom I have been so much blessed.

Blessed be God, I am not without my great comforts, in ministerial respects, in these kingdoms. The last year was the greatest Methodism has ever known in Europe. The flame does not burn so strong the present year in some particular parts, but it is far more extensive in its operations, so that I have good hopes that the increase of vital religion will, on the whole, be as great the present year as the last.

In the West Indies we go on rapidly, blessed be God, in spite of war and pestilence; about nine thousand of the Negroes are members of our Society, and much in earnest. But the yellow fever has swept off four of our most useful preachers in about twelve months. Six missionaries have been sent over in that time, and the work goes on. We have missions in nine of the islands; and no outward attack or inward insurrection has been known in any one of them since the establishment of our missions. So wonderfully are we protected by the providence of God. At Sierra Leone, in Africa, four hundred of the Nova Scotia Negroes are members of our Society, and one of the natives. We are going to plant a colony of Methodists in the interior parts of Africa, about five hundred miles from the coast, among a people lately discovered, who are mild, peaceable, and when compared to the Africans on the coast tolerably civilized. The Lord has not yet been pleased to open our way to the East Indies; but we wait his good time.

O my brother, labor to stir up our dear American brethren who are children of God to go on to perfection. Let them expect and pray for the universal reign of Christ; the time is hastening on when all the world shall bow the knee to Jesus; great, very great, are the calamities which Europe now suffers; but all is intended by the governor of the Church to pull Anti-christ from his throne, and to usher in the great millennium.

I am just beginning my tour through Ireland. As far as I have gone the Lord has been with his feeble servant, and has favored us with times of refreshing. Let me hear from you by the first opportunity, directing to me at the New Chapel, City Road, London.

We should, my dear brother, be exceedingly zealous for the preservation of all parts of our Discipline; all that is carnal militates against it; but it is the blessed hedge which, in the hand of God, is the means of preserving the divine life among us.

I intend, with the help of God, to be in Baltimore by the 20th of October, in the next year, to meet Brother Asbury and the rest of the brethren in General Conference; in the meantime remember me in your prayers, and don't forget to pray for your European brethren in general.

I am writing a comment on the Bible, and shall begin to print, God willing, about October next. Whether it will be satisfactory, others must judge. But I would fain do something for my Lord in that way.

It gives me great satisfaction that my dear respected Brother Asbury enjoys good health. You have need to pray much for the continuance of his life.

I am glad to hear that your district schools are going on prosperously; may the Lord increase the number of them, and give his constant blessing to them for the sake of the rising generation.

My dear brother, have great compassion for the poor Negroes, and do all you can to convert them. If they have religious liberty their temporal slavery will be comparatively but a small thing. But even in respect to this latter point I do long for the time when the Lord will turn their captivity like the rivers of the South, and he will appear for them; he is winding up the sacred ball; he is sweeping off the wicked with the besom of destruction, with pestilence, famine, and war, and will never withdraw his hand till civil and religious liberty be established all over the earth.

I have no doubt that if the body of Methodist preachers keep close to God they will be the chief instruments of bringing about this most desirable state of things. Let us be a praying, preaching, self-denying, mortified, crucified, zealous set of men (as, blessed be God, is the case with most of the preachers, more or less, at present), and we shall carry the world before us. God, even our own God, will give us his blessing. We shall be polished shafts in his quiver. He will use us as the ready writer does his pen, and open doors to us for the salvation of souls which will astonish us.

May the Lord bless you, my dear brother; may he fill you with faith and the Holy Ghost, and be your exceeding great reward for ever and ever !

I am your very affectionate friend and brother,   T. COKE.

It will at once be seen that the above letter is valuable in historic matter and affectionate in brotherly counsel. Bishop Coke was a scholar, a clear and correct writer of his native language. The paragraph relative to missions, if read by Bishop Taylor, will be a spur to him to lay broad and deep the foundation of the Gospel in the continent of Africa, where his predecessor, almost a hundred years ago, superintended the raising of the Gospel banner over Methodist missionaries who carried the light of sacred truth to that benighted land.

Another scene is now presented which, though not ecclesiastical, nor exclusively associated with the Methodist Society of New York, was regarded by the pastors of the Methodist Episcopal Church with great interest. It is a description of "moving-day" in the city ninety-one years ago. We are indebted to Mr. Cooper for its development. Says he:

May 1, 1795. This is moving-day in the city of York. Every May day is a general moving among the tenants. It appears that near, or quite, one fourth of the people move. If so (and some think more), well on or upon ten thousand move, taking them little and big; but I do not think quite so many move. However, it is wonderful to see the people moving; the streets all day swarmed with them. And many, I understand, cannot get houses to enter. Poor creatures! I do not know what they will do. Rents are at an amazing height. Small rooms rent for £20 or £30, and indifferent houses from £60 to £100, such as formerly were only £20 or £30. And, after all, numbers cannot get them, there are so many people in the city. People from the country have come down, and from France, West Indies, Nova Scotia, England, Ireland, etc., have crowded this city wonderfully. Hundreds of new buildings are up, or going up. What were fields look like a new city.

We now enter into a field of which there has been but little historical account as to its early connection

with the Methodist movement in that region; namely,
Long Island Circuit.   It first appeared in the Conference
Minutes of 1785, with Ezekiel Cooper as the preacher.
A year after the number of members on the circuit was
reported as: whites, 146; blacks, 8.   It then included
Brooklyn.   We have before stated that Mr. Cooper,
according to the Minutes of 1794, was stationed in New
York and Brooklyn, but that he was the presiding elder,
also, of the district in which New York was included.
We shall now follow him in his excursion through Long
Island Circuit, for the performance of the duties of that
office.   See the following, from his diary:

Wednesday, May 13.   I left the city upon a visit to Long Island,
to go around the circuit, attend quarterly meetings, and see my old
friends.   Friend John Brower and his wife, and old Mrs. Kipp and
Brother McCombs went over to Brooklyn with me.   We dined at Mr.
Dayrell's.   He and his lady are very kind indeed.   He is a cousin
of William Pitt, the Prime Minister of England.   He came over to
America during the last war, and married here, sold his commission,
and has stayed in this country ever since.   But I find he is warmly
attached to Britain yet.   In the evening I preached in Brooklyn,
about a mile from the ferry.

Thursday, 14.   I rode to Jamaica in company with Brother Van
Nostrand and Dr. Anderson—members in New York.   I preached in
the evening with some degree of liberty to a considerable congregation.   Here I began to find some who had heard me nine years ago,
and profess to have then been stirred up to seek after the Lord.

Friday, 15.   The Doctor, Bro. Van Nostrand, and I, set out in company, all being bound to quarterly meeting.   We rode to Serring-
town, and dined at Jacob Serring's.   This is the first house in this
town that was opened to the Methodist preachers.   I preached here
about ten years ago, and formed the first Society.   We have now a
church built, in which I preached at four o'clock this afternoon.   It
gave me satisfaction to see so many of my old friends.   Drank tea at
John Serring's, and lodged at Coe Serring's.

Saturday, 16.   We rose early, got breakfast, and started about six
o'clock for Comack.   We rode about twenty-four miles or more by
twelve o'clock.   Here, at Comack, quarterly meeting began.   I

preached from Romans viii, 24. Here I saw many of my old friends, among whom I labored nine or ten years ago. Many are gone from time, some are moved to other parts, and others have turned back from the Lord since then. It was melancholy to think of, that some who were eminent for piety had turned aside into open sin. The dear people were glad to see me. In the afternoon I visited several families, Samuel Brush's and friend Combs's particularly. I put up at James Hubbs's. In the evening we walked over to see Judge Smith, at his request. He pressed me to stay all night with him, but my previous engagement with friend Hubbs prevented.

On his journey to Comack, Mr. Cooper visited a place that had taken its name from the Indian religion, Manitou, the name of one of their gods. It was a very high hill on the Brushy Plains. Though the hill is quite sandy, yet on the western end thereof he found "a natural well of water." He tells us:

This well is, at times, so full that a man may dip the water out with his hand. It is seldom known to fail, and the water is very good. The Indians handed down to the white people the following tradition concerning the well: "On a certain time, in the days of their forefathers, a number of hunters were in those woods, and no water could be found. At length, when the hunters were nearly famished with thirst and could find no water anywhere, one of them shot up an arrow, and said, 'Where the arrow fell there would be water.' When the arrow fell it struck in the top of this sandy hill, and, when they pulled it up, water gushed out at the place, and ever since there has been a well of fine water."

Says Mr. Cooper:

It is well known that there are no natural ponds, springs, brooks, or streams of any kind near this place; and it is with great difficulty that the people around can dig wells so as to have water. There is a well within less than a half mile of this place, and down in the valley, too, that is seventy or eighty feet deep; so that I view this to be a curiosity indeed, and hard to be accounted for.

On Sunday, the 17th, the quarterly meeting exercises were continued; at half-past eight o'clock love-feast began; at ten o'clock the Lord's supper was celebrated;

and at eleven o'clock public preaching began.   The
congregation to which Mr. Cooper preached at this
hour was said to be the largest ever known at a quarterly meeting on Long Island up to that time.   It was
a season of refreshment to all.   At the close of the sermon the quarterly collection was taken, when the following scene occurred.   Says Mr. Cooper:

There is one thing which I could but remark as singular in the
congregation to-day; namely, a Dr. Blatchley, who is also an officer
in the militia, was at meeting in his full regimental dress, tassels upon
his shoulders, etc.   When we made the public collection for the use
of the Gospel he was one who stepped forward and went among his
acquaintances collecting.   It is uncommon to see a man of his appearance collecting in a large congregation for the benefit of the Gospel and Methodists, especially in a place where the Methodists have
been so little thought of.   We made the greatest collection that has
ever been made on this circuit, it is said.   The night was spent at
John Weeks's.

The next day Mr. Cooper and his companions left
Comack for the southern part of the island.   To him
the road was familiar.   They visited Mr. Conkling, a
home of Mr. Cooper's nine years before.   Then husband,
wife, and daughter were members of the Church, but
they had now greatly declined in religion.   At four
o'clock P. M. Mr. Cooper preached at Mr. Chichester's,
in South Huntington, near the bay.   The dwelling-
house being too small to hold the congregation, the
service was held in the barn.   Again he was greeted by
old acquaintances.   The day following he preached at
Mr. Raynor's, in South Hempstead.   Says he: "I put
them in mind of the old paths, and pressed them to
walk therein, holding the promise: 'And ye shall find
rest to your souls.'"   On Wednesday Rockaway was
visited, and after dining with "friend Demott" the
party rode to "the meeting-house," where Mr. Cooper

preached. Then they rode two miles farther toward
Jamaica. The next day they dined in Jamaica, and
Mr. Cooper was urgently pressed to stay and preach for
them that evening ; but, having an appointment at
Newtown at four o'clock P. M., he was obliged to move
forward. The appointment was filled. This night
was spent with Mr. Dean, of whom Mr. Cooper thus
speaks:

> We put up at Mr. Dean's, a gentleman who is very friendly to the
> Methodists. Two of his sisters are in Society in York. Mr. Dean's
> place is one of the prettiest and most agreeable seats I have seen
> upon the island.

On Friday, May 22, the company started before
breakfast for New York, breakfasted in Brooklyn at
Captain Dayrell's, and entered the city about noon.
Thus ended his first excursion as presiding elder. It
would have been made three months earlier, but he was
detained in the city on account of sickness.

The following Sabbath being Whitsunday, the New
York Methodists observed it, and the day following,
after the manner of the Church of England, from which
we had, as a Christian denomination, separated. To
show this, read the following from Mr. Cooper's
journal:

> *Sunday*, May 24. This being Whitsunday, I preached from Acts
> ii, 4, in the new church, and we gave the sacraments. A powerful
> time we had; the Lord was with us, of a truth. Several were so
> wrought upon that for some time they could not walk nor stand. We
> had a small shout of joy and gladness at the entrance of the ark into
> the camp.
>
> *Monday*, 24. Being Whitsuntide, we had preaching three times—
> Brother Brush in the morning, at the old church ; I at three o'clock
> P. M., at the new church ; and Brother McCombs at six o'clock P. M.,
> in the fields. We had a large company in the fields, and, generally,
> they behaved well. In the close we had considerable power attend-
> ing the word. I hope good was done. Field preaching is not liked

by all, but it is calculated to do much good; thereby those hear the word who go to no church.

We now call attention to the custom, observed by the early Methodist Episcopal Church, of distinctly celebrating a Sabbath, especially in the cities, once a quarter, as an important period. Says Mr. Cooper:

Sunday, May 31. This was quarter day, on which the public collection was made. We collected upward of £80; but I am told some of our friends think I begged too hard. I preached from Prov. xi, 23–25. The other preachers in their sermons said something upon the subject. Only myself it was that said too much. This week we begin our quarter visitation in Society: the classes to visit, tickets to renew, and sundry things that will keep us very busy.

On Wednesday and Thursday, June 3 and 4, Mr. Cooper, accompanied by two of his members, Mr. and Mrs. Fosbrook, was in Elizabethtown, N. J., visiting, among others, Rev. Thomas Morrell, who was very unwell. A very pretty "preaching house" had been erected by the Methodists in that town. Mr. Cooper preached in it, though it was not entirely finished, and was the instrument in God's hands of bringing comfort to many of his hearers. He visited also the Crowell and Robertson families, with whom the history of the past was recalled. Returning to the city, quarterly visitation was resumed, which for the most part consisted in preaching, meeting the classes, and giving tickets for the quarterly love-feast. The love-feast was held on Wednesday evening, June 17. Mr. Cooper thus speaks of it:

This evening we held our quarterly love-feast; the Lord was powerfully present. I have not seen so good a time for a great while past. We were strict to our rules in admitting no person whatever, excepting members, who had been in more than twice. Some were much hurt, but we find that it is best to go by rule. One was set at liberty in love-feast, and many strengthened.

15

The remainder of the month was devoted to preaching, administering the ordinances, Christian conversation with the disciples of the Master, among whom were " old Brother Staples, Sister Staples, Dr. Wainwright, and others " of that class which believed in the sanctification of body, soul, and spirit to God.

On the 29th of June Bishop Asbury visited the city, and gave to the Church the privilege of enjoying his ministrations and social intercourse for about ten days. There were also at this time in the city, besides Messrs. Cooper and McCombs, the pastors, the Revs. Freeborn Garrettson, Kendall, Ware, and Roberts. As Mr. Cooper has left an account of the bishop's method of movement when visiting the pastoral charges, and as its perusal will give delight to his successors in the episcopacy should they peruse the recital, I here quote the following:

Monday, 29. Bishop Asbury came to town in company with Brother Ware. He proposes staying with us a week. The bishop does not bring us any particular account of the work southward. He began this afternoon to meet the classes, intending to meet them all before he leaves the city.

On Tuesday the 30th, the bishop and Mr. Cooper were visited by the Rev. Uzal Ogden, who brought with him the first volume of his *Answer to Paine's Age of Reason*, and left it with them for perusal. He also brought a few sheets of the second volume, which was then going through the press. In the evening the bishop preached to a very large congregation in John Street Church. We now give a description of the manner of celebrating the Fourth of July in New York in 1795. Says Mr. Cooper:

Saturday, July 4. This is the day of Independence, kept with great pomp in this town. The wickedness of the citizens is truly great on this day. Instead of reverencing the name of God for his providential delivering of our country, the people seem disposed to spend their time in licentiousness. Surely the sins of the people are enough to provoke the Lord to enter into judgment with us !

At three o'clock the bishop, the other preachers, the trustees, stewards, and leaders, had a meeting together to spend a few hours in religious exercises, and conversing upon the state of the Society with regard to temporal and spiritual affairs. We had a solemn time, and, I hope, profitable to us all.

Sunday, 5.   We had a comfortable day.

Monday, 6.   The bishop met three classes at ten o'clock, five at three o'clock, and four at eight o'clock. At three o'clock we had a powerful time ; the Lord was with us of a truth; every heart seemed filled with joy.

The next day the bishop left the city, and in the afternoon Mr. Cooper himself began his route to the quarterly meeting at New Windsor, being accompanied by his brother Sharock. The seat of the quarterly meeting was within the bounds of the district over which the Rev. Thomas Ware was presiding elder. It was about sixty miles above New York, a short distance from West Point, and was connected with the circuit which Mr. Cooper had traveled seven or eight years before. To reach the town he sailed up the Hudson in a vessel commanded by a Captain Brown. There were many passengers, and more than could be supplied with berths or bedding, some having to lie by night on chests or the floor to obtain any rest. The result was that some were disorderly, and disturbed those who otherwise could have slept. The wind being unfavorable, they were two days and nights on the trip; but these servants of God did not forget their duty in publicly confessing Christ; on the contrary, they had evening and morning prayer, and all on board were called to attendance upon this means of grace. By this course the respectful carriage of the thirty passengers was secured, and resulted in gentle Christian conversation, whereby

the minds of many of them were enlightened and good
was done.

On the 9th of July they landed at New Windsor, and
were received by Mr. William Ellison, and afterward
by his relatives Mr. John Ellison and lady, who were
all earnest supporters of Methodism, and had a warm
affection for Methodist preachers.

On Saturday, the 11th, quarterly meeting began at
one o'clock. There were five preachers present, a large
assemblage of laymen, many of whom greeted, for the
first time for eight or nine years, their old pastor and
spiritual father. Mr. Cooper preached, also, the next
morning at eleven o'clock. The Sunday service was
opened by a love-feast, beginning at nine o'clock; then
came the sermon, and at its close the sacrament was
administered to "a large body" of communicants. In
the afternoon Mr. Cooper preached at Mr. Fowler's,
about eight miles from New Windsor. On Monday,
after visiting "a few old acquaintances" in the morning, he rode in the afternoon to Newburg, where, in
the evening, he preached in the Presbyterian Church
to the largest congregation that had ever been known
to assemble in that "meeting-house." Here he was the
guest of his old friend Foster. On Tuesday he returned
to New Windsor, and at night set sail for New York,
where he was landed on Thursday morning before
breakfast.

The remaining weeks of Mr. Cooper's pastorate in
New York for this term were spent in the routine work
of the Church. In August there appeared to be a contagious fever spreading through the city that alarmed
the people greatly. In the midst of its prevalence
Dr. Anderson, one of the members of the old church
in John Street, and physician in charge at Bellevue
Hospital, was taken also with the fever, and dispatched

one of the Health Committee, an alderman, to Mr.
Cooper, requesting him to visit him. Bellevue (at that
time retaining the original French name, *Belle Vue*)
was about three miles outside of the town limits, and
was the place to which the Board of Health sent all
those who were stricken with malignant or contagious
fevers. Risking the danger of exposure he, accompanied by the doctor's father and mother, rode out to the
hospital, and was gratified to find him much better.
The mortality in the city and vicinity, however, was
great.

On the 26th of August Rev. Wilson Lee, who had
been designated at the session of his Annual Conference, held the previous July, to succeed Mr. Cooper in
New York at the end of his conference year, arrived
in the city and gave aid to him in his ministerial labors. Besides him were also Revs. William Jessup,
from Nova Scotia, and John Kingston, from the West
Indies. With these to help him, Mr. Cooper attended
the quarterly meeting on Long Island Circuit, which
was held on the 29th and 30th days of the month.
Here he was privileged to greet more of his friends of
former years—the Furmans, Coe Searing, the Harpers,
and the Edsalls.

Returning to New York, he received, September 2,
a letter announcing the severe and probably fatal illness of his brother Richard. He resolved to go home
as soon as he could get ready, and at once began "to
fix matters to leave the city." While making his preparations he was called upon, on Thursday evening, September 3, to open and close with prayer a meeting of
a new organization, to be held in Wesley Chapel in
John Street. The society's name was "The New York
Society for Suppressing Vice," and was composed of
the various religious denominations organized for the

suppression of vice, Sabbath breaking, tippling houses, etc. It was making a successful beginning. Within two weeks two hundred respectable citizens had joined it.

On Sunday, September 6, Mr. Cooper preached his farewell sermon in each church and gave the Society his last lecture; and, having closed up all his business, on Wednesday, September 9, 1795, bade them adieu as their pastor.

CHAPTER XI. •

METHODISM IN PHILADELPHIA AND VICINITY, 1796.

THE Annual Minutes of 1795 report Mr. Cooper as supernumerary, and, as all supernumeraries at that period of our Church life were assigned to a charge as such, he was assigned to Philadelphia, with John McClaskey as elder in charge. The historical account of this period being very meager, the records of Mr. Cooper are highly valuable, and will be set forth in such detail as time and circumstances will permit.

An interval of a month elapsed between his adieu to the Methodists of New York and the session of the Philadelphia Annual Conference where he was made supernumerary. It was spent mostly in Delaware and Eastern Maryland among his relatives. The Conference, held in the city of Philadelphia, began its session October 5, and closed by final adjournment on Saturday, October 10, 1795.

On the following day, in the forenoon, Bishop Asbury, accompanied by Mr. Cooper, preached in the African church, and administered the holy communion. Says Mr. Cooper:

This African Church is a congregation of black people, who have procured for themselves a house of public worship and put themselves under our charge. There is another African congregation in the city, under the care of the Protestant Episcopal Church.

The Methodists had in the city at this time two other houses of worship — St. George's and Ebenezer — and the membership was: whites, 311; blacks, 121; total, 432.

A small portion of the conference year, 1795–96, was spent by Mr. Cooper in Philadelphia. On the adjournment of the Conference he returned to the Peninsula, and held no pastoral relations with the Church in Philadelphia for three months. These months were spent among his relations on the Peninsula, in Annapolis, and Baltimore.

On the 15th of January, 1796, he returned to Philadelphia for the purpose of occupying the place of assistant to Rev. John McClaskey, for three months. Under that date he says:

We reached the city about six o'clock in the evening. I put up at Captain Manley's, where I am to stay three months if I stay in the city. He and his wife are very kind to me indeed. This house has been my home these many years, when in Philadelphia.

Sunday, 17. I preached a sacramental sermon in the new church at eleven o'clock, and heard Brother McClaskey preach in the old church at three, where I preached at night. We are likely to have large congregations, and I feel a hope and expectation that the Lord will revive his work more or less. Brother McClaskey and I are to be colleagues this winter. He is a faithful soldier of the Lord.

A clear and impressive account of his pulpit ministrations has been left to us by Mr. Cooper, showing that on the Sabbath and during the days intervening he rendered those services to constantly increasing congregations; but we must be content with only an occasional quotation from his journal. Among these the following is given under the date of January 24:

In the evening I attended the new church. The Lord was with us in his blessed word, and I hear that several were powerfully wrought upon, and some renewed their covenants. When I closed my sermon old Father Abbott, though very weak in his body, felt a desire to speak a few words; but he was so feeble that he could not say much or speak with any degree of power.

Again:

Sunday, February 14. I had to preach in the evening a charity sermon for the relief of the poor. When done preaching I came out of the pulpit, and four preachers of us collected more than £50 for the poor, which is to be distributed according to their necessities.

Sunday, May 22. I preached a charity sermon for the African Society at half-past six P. M.

While Father Abbott was in the city Mr. Cooper aided him in preparing the manuscripts for publication of the journal of his life and experience.

The month of March, 1796, was devoted by Mr. Cooper to a tour through some of the circuits in New Jersey, and in attendance upon their quarterly meetings. During this tour he visited Mount Holly, where he was the guest of Esquire Shiras; New Mills, at Isaac Budd's; Francis Bodine's, near Egg Harbor; Hawkin, where a quarterly meeting was held March 5, 6, under the charge of Rev. Richard Swain, assisted by Rev. Joseph Lovell. Eight years before Mr. Cooper had preached on this circuit, and every-where was greeted by old friends. During this meeting he was entertained by Esquires Conklin and Randolph. From thence he went to Wiertown, preached in the school-house, and visited Mrs. Headly and Mr. Chamberlain; thence to Goodluck, preached there at Mr. Woodmansee's, not in the "meeting-house;" thence to Tom's River, where was a "small Society at friend Irons's. This Society had been formed within a few years. Having closed his visit to Burlington Circuit, his next excursion was through Freehold Circuit, where Anthony Turk and Daniel Crouch were appointed to labor for that year.

Mr. Cooper thus describes a part of the country within the bounds of this circuit, known as the Salt Meadows:

It is truly desolate and dreary to travel this piney and unsettled country. Nothing but solid woods for many miles together, as though a traveler were banished from all human kind, and gone from all settlements. Once in awhile we come to a small place cleared, with some one living on it.

He had been misdirected, and was so led to pass through most desolate parts of the circuit. At night, however, he arrived at Mr. Allen's, with whose father he had had Christian fellowship when, nine years before, he traveled this section, then a part of Jersey Circuit. Here he preached on the 11th of March, and then, with Daniel Crouch, rode to Mr. Chamberlain's, within nine miles of Monmouth Court-house, where he was greeted by Anthony Turk, the other circuit preacher.

The Society in that neighborhood held their meetings at Mr. Burgh's. He preached for them on Saturday, March 12, taking for his text the words, "Comfort ye, comfort ye my people, saith your God." It was a timely discourse, producing most important results, which Mr. Cooper thus pictures:

We had a powerful time. I have not seen so powerful and lively a meeting for a long time. The people were ready to take wings and fly away. Many of them praised the Lord aloud. Every heart seemed tendered into love and humility. There had existed a very disagreeable dispute between some of the members of this Society, which was feared would make a rent or division, and that some would be turned out, among whom was the principal leader and a public speaker who had been the most useful member in the whole Society. But providentially we this day settled the matter, and compromised the affair, so that peace is restored in an amicable manner. I baptized two of the principal acting members, both leaders. This is a good society, upon the whole, and there appears to be much religion among them. I believe my coming here has been of great use in settling the dispute, which had well-nigh murdered the souls of several. I am ready to think the Lord sent me for this very purpose, for only a few days ago I had no intention of coming, but by providentia direction I have been conducted.

The next day he preached again at ten o'clock A. M. at Mr. Burgh's with great success, and in the afternoon at Freehold meeting-house, where they had " a melting season," and thence went to Mr. Garrett Morford's, where again he had the company of the preachers of the circuit. On Monday morning, at the request of the preacher in charge, Rev. Mr. Turk, he met the Public Bands "at friend Morford's." Then he visited Mr. Rice, one of his members eight years before, and in the afternoon rode to Mr. Pyle's, who meeting him in the piazza embraced him in his arms. Here, eight years before, he was at home with " old brother Leonard," who had gone to the mansions of the blessed. Mr. Pyle had taken the place of his father-in-law, and it was to Mr. Cooper the same old home. He enjoyed the brotherly care of the family for two days. From thence he went to Tinton Falls and preached at Mr. Morris's, then rode to Esquire Little's, where the night was spent. He next visited and preached at Red Bank, where a good Society had been raised within a few years. There was no preaching in that neighborhood when he was one of their circuit preachers.

Friday, March 18, was fast day. Mr. Cooper met the Public Bands at two o'clock P. M., and in the evening they had watch-night services, he preaching till half-past nine, and being followed by speeches by four of the local brethren. The remainder of the night was spent with brother Turk at friend Chandler's.

On Saturday they rode to Long Branch, where the quarterly meeting began. The presiding elder, Rev. John Merrick, preached, and Mr. Cooper delivered an exhortation. The Sabbath exercises were of the usual order. Love-feast at 9 o'clock A. M., followed by the Eucharist; preaching at 12 M. Mr. Cooper preached, after which an exhortation was given by Mr. Pyle, and

Mr. Merrick closed the services. Among the families that supported the Society at Long Branch were the Drummonds and Kings.

Retracing his steps, Mr. Cooper again went to Red Bank, where he preached, and with Mr. Shadwick, his host, visited from house to house, gained an entrance into Mr. Pintard's house, and was instrumental in breaking down the violent opposition of Mr. Pintard to the Methodists. He next visited Mr. Throgmorton in Colt's Neck, preached at Mr. Pyle's, and on the 23d of March, after breakfasting at Mr. Grandine's, preached at eleven o'clock A. M. in Monmouth Court-house, at Freehold. After dinner at Mr. Lloyd's, then Sheriff of that county, he called to see Esquire Dennie where, with tears, old recollections were recalled, and hopes of a future union quickened. From thence he journeyed to Philadelphia.

Resuming his labors in Philadelphia, he preached twice on Sunday, April 3, and assisted in administering the sacrament. He was, however, in feeble health, and thought much of "taking a horse and traveling to and fro through the country." On Sunday, April 10, he preached at eleven o'clock A. M. in the African Church, and administered the sacrament. In the evening, as he was going into the old church to preach, a letter was put into his hands bearing a request from sundry persons that he should preach from Rev. xii, 1. He did so, and gave great satisfaction. Other denominations sought also to secure his services. On Monday Dr. Van Pelt called upon him with an invitation "to hold meeting for the St. Paul's Church Society," and a Mr. Ellison called with an invitation for him "to hold meeting in the Presbyterian Society." He agreed to do so for each. In the evening he was solicited to preach again for the African Society on the following evening. This was also done. On Wednesday, the 13th,

he preached for the Presbyterians, having Dr. Chandler
to assist in the services, and on Friday evening, after
tea with the Rev. Mr. Turner and the Rev. Dr.
Rodgers, Episcopal clergymen, he preached in the St.
Paul's Church.

On Sunday, April 24, the presiding elder, Rev.
John Merrick, being in the city, Mr. Cooper preached
once with great liberty, and in the afternoon at Rev.
John Dickins's, with Mr. Merrick, had "a profitable
conversation upon the deep things of religious experience." All three engaged in the discussion.

Mr. Cooper visited Germantown on Saturday, May
7, 1796. Here, on the next day in the afternoon, he
preached to them in the Academy. Two weeks after
he was here again, and thus began an organization which
has now become an important factor in the Methodist
Episcopal Church. The state of Mr. Cooper's health
was now such that he did comparatively little work in
the churches in Philadelphia for the remainder of the
conference year. On the 2d of May he left the city
for a visit to Baltimore and the eastern shore of Maryland, and was absent for five weeks. Returning on the
28th of June, he remained until July 4th, when he again
departed, going into New Jersey, to Shrewsbury and
other places, and did not return for two months. Under date of October 7, 1796, he says:

Since September 4 I have been constantly in the city, preaching
four or five times a week, and attending to other duties of my station.
At Brother McClaskey's request I transcribed the Articles of Association entered into for the incorporation of our African Church. Last
week Brothers Haskins, Dickins, McClaskey and myself fully considered and agreed upon the principles of incorporation for a Chartered
Fund for the better support of our itinerant ministry; and Brother
Haskins has accordingly drawn up an instrument for the charter, and
if approved of by the General Conference, it is to be established as an
Incorporated Fund for the uses and purposes therein mentioned.

This account of the origin of the Chartered Fund appears for the first time in public print, and will be a guide to the future historian of our Church.

On the 10th of October, 1796, was opened in Philadelphia the Annual Conference for that year, known then as the District Conference; it continued in session until Friday the 14th. The membership in the city had increased: whites, 52; blacks, 60; total, 112. Mr. Cooper's relation in the ministry had been changed from supernumerary to effective, and he was continued in the pastorate in the city. This was not, however, the original arrangement, as may be seen by the following extract from his journal. Under date of November 22, he writes:

I took the stage and rode to Philadelphia. This afternoon I met Brother Lee,* who will be my colleague for the ensuing year in this city. At Conference here, in October, I somewhat expected to have gone westward, to Pittsburg, Little York, and Carlisle for my station, Esquire Shiras at Pittsburg, had applied in so pressing a manner to the Bishop, and also to myself, to have me stationed there, that the appointment was made; but the trustees of the Society in this city united in a petition so strong to the Bishop for my continuance here, that after we got to Baltimore (at the General Conference), the appointment was altered for me to stay here.

Feeling the pressure that was upon him to continue his pastorate in Philadelphia, and the other stationed itinerants having gone to the General Conference, Mr. Cooper remained with them until he had made out a plan for the local preachers to supply the pulpit until their return. Having done this he left the city, and in two days arrived at Baltimore, to take his seat with his brethren in General Conference. The body had now been in session for eight days, having begun the proceedings on the 20th ultimo, and was through with

* Wilson Lee, Minutes, 1796, p. 71.

the principal business of the session. It adjourned finally on November 3, 1796.

Before returning to Philadelphia, Mr. Cooper made an excursion through a part of the Peninsula, during which time, on Sunday, Novembr 20, he preached in the morning at Dover, Delaware, in the State House, and in the afternoon preached a funeral sermon in the Protestant Episcopal Church, over the remains of Mrs. Coleman.

Having resumed the labors of his station with Wilson Lee, between whom and the church over which they were associate pastors were the strongest bonds of Christian union, the congregation began to increase, and the cause of the Master to flourish. New places for preaching were opened outside of the city limits, as, for instance, at the house of Captain Decatur, thirteen miles out; and whatever would lead to the establishing of the Methodist Episcopal Church was religiously, prudently, and hopefully undertaken. Philadelphia was at this period in many respects the most, important city on the American continent. Here the United States Congress held it sessions; here the President of the United States delivered his biennial address; here, besides the Mayor's Court and the Court of Common Pleas or Quarter Sessions, the State Legislature convened. Both clergymen and laymen had abundant opportunity for reflection upon the subject of making and executing laws, the causes and necessities thereof, and for learning lessons of wisdom from the wise men of the nation. Nor was the city behind other cities in providing for the various forms of literature, of science, and of art. The sympathy of the citizens with these may be seen by the following testimony of Mr. Cooper in regard to one of the Departments. Under date of Saturday, December 17, 1796, he says:

The Philosophical Society having honored me with a card requesting me to attend the delivery of a " Eulogium on their late President,
Dr. David Rittenhouse," to be pronounced before them this day at
twelve o'clock by Dr. Rush, I attended, and was highly pleased with
the principal part of the eulogy—and particularly with the vindication of the Christian religion, and the principles of liberty which
were urged clearly and boldly before a large assembly of the first
citizens of the United States and many respectable foreigners. The
President of the United States, both houses of Congress, the State
Legislature, Select and Common Councils, all the clergy, etc., besides
a large concourse of other citizens, were there; not less, I judge,
than a thousand or twelve hundred people. The Presbyterian
meeting-house in High Street was well filled.

Mr. Cooper had, during the previous conference year,
been boarding with Captain Manley, where he was
most kindly entertained ; but for greater convenience
to him in his work he was called upon to bid adieu to
this Christian home, and took board with Colonel North
and his family. The colonel was a member of the Select City Council and a trustee in St. George's Methodist Episcopal Church. The family was equally as
kind as the one he had left.

The old year was closed with a watch-night service
in St. George's Church. Mr. Cooper preached with
much freedom from 1 Peter iv, 7, 8. John Dickins, William Haskins, Mr. Jolliff, Richard Swain, and
William Chandler exhorted in order, one after the
other, and the meeting was closed by Rev. Wilson Lee.

The year 1797 was to the citizens of Philadelphia in
some respects a year of sadness. One of the first and
most painful of these scenes of sorrowful sympathy was
the affliction brought to the family and friends of a Mr.
Brown, a wealthy manufacturer, who lost by the burning of his residence on the night of the 27th of January
his wife and three children. Himself and a servant
girl also subsequently died, by reason of the burns they

had received during the conflagration. The burial of
the mother and her three children is thus pictured by
Mr. Cooper. He says :

Saturday, January 28. At four o'clock in the afternoon I attended
the funeral of Mrs. Brown and her three children, who perished by
the fire yesterday morning. There were about a dozen clergy, and I
believe, at the lowest calculation, not less than five thousand people.
The streets were crowded from side to side so full that it took two or
three, with the sexton, to clear a passage for the procession to the
church. It was truly an awful sight to see a mother and three children borne to the grave at once, who were all well and cheerful two
days ago. How suddenly do things change! Two days ago, going
through the city in health and gayety; now carried, mournfully and
solemnly, to the grave amid thousands of melancholy spectators.
How awful is the reflection! how sorrowful the scene! Every thing
looks gloomy, and the thousands of faces appear sad !

This affecting circumstance has filled the city with more melancholy than any one occurrence that has been known before for a long
time, if ever.

Where people at one time moved about with broken
hearts, the scene was within a month changed into that
of joyful hilarity, respectful congratulations, and animated discourse. Such was witnessed on the anniversary of President Washington's birth, February 22,
1797. In ten days he was to lay aside the magisterial
robe of State, and take his place as a private citizen
among his countrymen. Because of his position before
the country, and in view of these facts, great ado was
made throughout the city on the return of the anniversary of his natal day. Public bodies called to pay last
respects to him as President of the United States, and
national airs were sung to the praise of him who was
truly styled the father of his country. On the last day
of his official life as President, namely, March 3, 1797,
he received a visit from the clergymen of the city, of
which Mr. Cooper thus speaks:
16

Friday, March 3, 1797. This day at three o'clock the ministers of different denominations met at the college, and from thence waited on the President of the United States at his house, and presented him with an address, and received his answer. There were more than twenty of us, of different communities, who put our names to the same address, and went in harmony together to the house of the President. We sat a little while with the old gentleman, who conversed with us on the subject of his retirement. This is the last day of his political life as the chief magistrate of the States.

The next day at twelve o'clock General Washington's successor, John Adams, was sworn into office by the Chief Justice in the House of Representatives. This was another scene of thrilling interest, the house being densely crowded with spectators. When General Washington entered he was saluted with a general plaudit which rang through the house in loud acclaim. Soon after, on the entrance of John Adams, the President elect, the house again echoed with applause. Silence having been obtained, he arose and delivered a stirring address, and then going to the table where the judges were seated took the oath of office; he then withdrew, followed by Thomas Jefferson, the new Vice President, and the assembly separated.

During the earlier part of April Mr. Cooper attended a quarterly meeting held on Bethel Circuit, New Jersey. He was the guest of Mr. Bates for a few days, and rode with the family to the quarterly meeting on Saturday, April 8, where he preached, and also on the Sabbath ensuing. Here he was the guest of Mr. Dilks, who also entertained, with him, the preachers on that charge— Revs. John McClaskey, presiding elder, and John Regan and Anthony Turk, circuit preachers. The season was one of religious power. On his return to Philadelphia the next day he was accompanied, he tells us, by Brother McClaskey, Brother Regan, and five or six other friends. "As we traveled I found my mind comfortable. Our conversation was principally upon divine things. We sang parts of several hymns on the road."

Having returned to the city on Good Friday, which occurred that week, and which he always observed religiously, he preached a sermon " suited to the day;" and on Sunday, April 16, Easter Sunday, his discourses were concerning the resurrection of our Lord.

After the close of the Easter services Mr. Cooper began to make preparations for leaving Philadelphia, in order that he might take his station on Pittsburg Circuit, to which he had been appointed at the beginning of the conference year (see above). His description of matters is so graphic that the reader is asked to read it, because it reflects materially on the state of Methodism in the city at that time. He says:

This week I was preparing to leave the city with an intention of going home first, and then to cross the Chesapeake Bay to Annapolis; so on by Alexandria and through the north part of Virginia to Pittsburg, and not to return to Philadelphia till Conference. I bought a horse, and was almost prepared to start, when the society rose almost in arms against my leaving them. There were such solicitations for me to stay, that I found there was danger of injury being the consequence of my going, inasmuch as great and grievous trials had begun to seize fast hold on many minds among our principal and influential friends. Their temptations were strong, and they so fully showed by word and action how they felt, that I judged, in counsel with some of the most judicious, that it would be best for me to stay. It was believed that two or three of the preachers wished me away, and not from proper motives. Whether this was the case or not, it was so believed from appearances, etc.; and this laid the great foundation of the trials which took place. And had I gone, it is yet thought, the consequences would have been bad. There appeared to be general dissatisfaction at the move for my going. This hint stands for my apology for staying. Soon as I agreed to stay things began to calm away, and I hope will subside. Hence my journey to Pittsburg is frustrated once more. The circumstances which have taken place relative to my leaving the city have filled my mind with deep reflection. First, it has given evidence to me and others of the friendship of the people toward me. Secondly, it has also given an opportunity to discover the minds of a few who might, probably, wish me away. Thirdly, it has led me to pray and to watch, particularly on some occasions which, otherwise, I might have neglected more. And I hope with humility and gratitude that I may be led and drawn nearer to the Lord. O may I fulfill the expectation of friends in the discharge of my ministerial duty!

Resuming his work in his old field, he discharged the duties of a pastor in a manner so worthy as to bind the affections of the people to him in bonds that the century now closing has not broken. This will fully appear as we proceed with our narrative.

As stated above, Mr. Cooper introduced Methodism into Germantown, Pa. On Sunday, June 4, 1796, he preached twice to its citizens; and at the close of his discourse organized the first Methodist Society established in that town. He thus speaks of it: "After preaching, at three o'clock, I joined eleven in Society. O may this be a foundation for a large Society in that town!" A week thereafter, attended by his brother, Foxall, he preached at the quarterly meeting at Bristol; then they rode to Morrisville, and thence went to Trenton. After giving an account of his previous movements on that day, he says:

Sunday, June 11. I crossed over to Trenton and preached there by candle-light to an attentive congregation. I opened James i, 25. It has been about nine years since I traveled this circuit or have been in this city. Great changes have taken place since then; but numbers of the old standards are yet here and standing fast in the Lord.

Monday, 12. I took a walk with old friend Coots to see how Trenton had improved since I was here. We went to the Academy and visited each room, and heard the scholars in each department in their exercises. There appears to be good order in the school, and I think it promises well, so far as I can see or understand its objects and regulations. Trenton has improved; the State-house is a considerable addition to the place.

In July Mr. Cooper's colleague, Rev. Wilson Lee, was prostrated by sickness, and the burden of the charge fell wholly upon Mr. Cooper. From that time to the close of the conference year, he made no excursions within the bounds of other charges; for though his colleague was restored to health, the yellow fever made its appearance in August, and the services of both were demanded in care for the dead and dying. The account left by Mr. Cooper of this terrible scourge, and of his own sacrifices and those of his brethren, is so thrilling that it is for the most part now laid before the reader of these pages in the words penned by Mr. Cooper in his journal. He begins thus:

Sunday. August 13. Brother **Regan** preached for me in the morning, and assisted me with the sacrament. He and I this afternoon attended the funeral of young Mr. Wild, who died with the fever which is beginning to take place in this city. We both visited him while he was ill. This week the people begin to be much alarmed about the contagious fever, which appears threatening. The doctors are divided in opinion, and are writing in opposition to each other; and the fears of the people are wrought upon amazingly.

Sunday. 20. I preached to-day, seriously, upon the subject of the sickness; warning the people to prepare. The terror through this week caused the people very much to flock out of town: by the last of the month it is believed that one third of the people had moved to the country.

The beginning of September the fever increased, and the people kept flying, and by the middle of the month about half the population had removed—some believe two thirds. The city seemed depopulated. Colonel North's family, where I lived, stayed until Thursday, the 14th of September; and some of our friends advised me to go also, as the family where I lived had gone; but my mind was not so free to go. The deaths are now between twenty and thirty a day—more than thirty died one day. But as I was stationed here as a preacher I resolved to put my trust in the Lord and stand by the dear people in the days of adversity and distress. Truly things appear gloomy and melancholy, but the Lord he is God. He saved Daniel in the lion's den; he saved the three Hebrew children in the fiery fur-

nace; and he is able to save in the midst of a raging fever. Through
mercy I am very little afraid, and cannot say that I am any alarmed
or terrified.

I concluded to stay in Colonel North's house. Miss Fanny Wolf,
one of our friends, stays also to take care of the house, so that, with
the assistance of a little girl of one of the neighbors, she keeps house,
cooks, etc. 'Tis a solemn time for prayer and meditation. I have
ventured to go among the sick, and, two or three days, I felt very
poorly myself; but I took medicine for three successive days and
found relief.

Saturday, September 16. Brother Lee, Brother Dickins, and myself came to a resolution to publish in the public prints that our Conference [the Philadelphia Annual—P.] would be held at Duck Creek
Cross Roads [Smyrna, Del.], instead of this city. I called upon three
printers, all of whom promised to publish it on Monday. So I furnished them with a copy. We also wrote circular letters to the different districts to the same purpose.

We have accounts that Brother Regan is dead; that he took the
fever while in town and died some days ago. Thus his course is
run and his work is done. We have no doubt that he rests with
his Lord in heaven. When he was leaving the city I accompanied
him to the boat, where we conversed some time upon the very awful calamity, and the uncertainty of life and every thing in this world.
We then parted with clasped hands, commending each other to God
and divine protection. We hoped to meet again in time, but death has
cut him off, and we shall meet no more till we appear before the Lord.
O may I be prepared to reign with him in glory, with all the saints
above! By grace I may be saved, and by grace through faith only.
My trust is in the Lord, my Saviour.

It is my intention, if the Lord spare me, to stay in town until I
go off to Conference. The people are dying fast; between twenty
and thirty die a day; and in my ministerial calling I have to go
from end to end and from side to side of the city. It may naturally
be supposed that I feel at times apprehensions of danger; but I reason thus: if the people ever want the visits and counsel of a minister, it is in time of affliction and distress. Shall I leave them now?
No; it would be like a shepherd flying from his flock in time of danger! Although I risk my health and life, yet my duty is to feed and
comfort the flock of Christ, and not flee until called by the duties
of my profession to take charge elsewhere, or attend Conference, or
something of a passing nature. Truly it is affecting to see the

sorrows and woes of the afflicted and distressed. Sometimes the
nearest friends fly from the sick, and leave them in their anguish
and misery. How melancholy to see parents leave their children,
and children their parents! and sometimes fear preys so powerfully
that a husband or wife cannot have resolution to stay with the
companion of his or her life. To attempt a full description of
the various scenes of distress would be in vain; imagination can
scarcely figure out the miseries of many. Even among the well
the distresses were truly great; business being so stagnated that
the poor were out of employ, many were, consequently, deprived of
the means that brought them daily the necessaries of life. Had
not the public, by legislative authority, made an appropriation of
$10.000, the poor might, many of them, have been entirely desti-
tute of a mouthful of bread. O to think! a family, a mother and
house full of children, with tears and sorrow, lamenting their fate—
not being able to leave the place, nor to procure a piece of bread
to satisfy their hunger. But by the public moneys there was a small
relief; however, the $10.000 were soon distributed to the hundreds
of poor and needy. The Commissioners let this be known, and
begged the voluntary contributions of the citizens who were able.
The feelings and sympathy of the people, in and out of the city,
soon drew their contributions forward, by which means we hope the
sufferings of the poor will be alleviated.

The Conference year had now drawn to its close, and
on the 7th day of October, 1797, Mr. Cooper left Philadelphia *en route* to the seat of the Conference, Smyrna,
Del. On that day he arrived at Wilmington, Del., and
the day following, Sunday, Oct. 8, he preached to that
congregation at eleven o'clock A. M., and was followed
by Bishop Asbury, who preached at three o'clock P. M.,
and Jesse Lee, who preached at night. On the 9th
they, with other preachers in company, arrived at
Smyrna, and on Tuesday, the 10th, the Conference session began.

Early on Tuesday morning Bishop Asbury sent a
message to Mr. Cooper requesting him to act as Conference secretary, but he had become so enfeebled by
the duties devolved upon him through the past two

months, that he sought to be released therefrom, and was excused. The Conference was six days in session, and, says Mr. Cooper:

We had a glorious time. The Lord was with us, indeed. Peace, unity, and love reigned among the preachers, and great power attended their ministry. A number were converted. Almost every day and evening we had a shout among the people.

Friday, 13. Was the day of ordination; ten or eleven elders and three or four deacons were set apart to those offices, and solemnly ordained.

Sunday, 15. We had a happy time in love-feast. The Bishop preached at eleven o'clock, I at three o'clock, and Jesse Lee in the evening.

During the year now closed the church in Philadelphia, notwithstanding the scourge of the yellow fever, had increased in membership among the whites, though the decrease was considerable among the blacks. The gain of the former was eighteen; the loss of the latter was eighteen.

Mr. Cooper's station for the ensuing Conference year was at Wilmington, Del., which included also the adjoining village of Newport. Besides this, the Conference had put him in charge of a great duty in connection with the book business of the Church, as may be seen by the following extract from the Conference Minutes of 1797. On pages 19 and 20 of the Minutes we read:

Quest. 14. What regulations have been made in respect to the printing business and the publication of books?

Ans. The Philadelphia Conference, in whom the management of these affairs was invested by the General Conference, and who have not time during their annual sittings to complete this business, have, by the advice and consent of Bishop Asbury, unanimously appointed the following persons to be a Standing Committee, namely, Ezekiel Cooper, Chairman; Thomas Ware, John McClaskey, Christopher Spry, Presiding Elders; William McLenahan, Richard Swain, Solomon Sharp, and Charles Cavender, Elders.

The above Committee are to meet at Philadelphia on the 2d of January, 1798, and once a quarter afterward, or oftener if necessary, to consider and determine upon what manuscripts, books, or pamphlets shall be printed.

Four of said committee, when met as above, shall proceed to business, provided that the chairman and one of the presiding elders be present. And the General Book-Steward shall lay before the Committee all manuscripts, books, and pamphlets which are designed for publication, except such as the General Conference has authorized him to publish.

CHAPTER XII.

THE METHODIST EPISCOPAL CHURCH IN WILMINGTON, DELAWARE, AND VICINITY, 1797, 1798.

AFTER spending two weeks in visiting his friends in Delaware and Maryland, Mr. Cooper entered upon the duties of his pastorate at Wilmington and Newport. He had earnestly desired the Bishop not to give him the charge of a circuit or station for that year. He says:

I wanted to be as one that serveth, and not to have rule or authority in discipline or government. Power and authority I never coveted, but wish others to exercise it who like it better than I. Once I thought that I would be relieved from having the care and charge; but as the Bishop requests it, I, merely in compliance with his desire, submit.

He found the Church in Wilmington to be in a state of disorder and confusion: "Scarcely any regularity at all, and rather a general anarchy in the affairs of the Society, and a disunity and murmuring, one with another, prevails." The number of members had been reported to the Annual Conference, held the month previously, to be: whites, sixty-one; blacks, thirty-seven. He found, after a careful survey of the whole field in Wilmington, "forty-nine whites, thirty-two blacks." He addressed himself at once to the work of seeking to restore in them the spirit of union and brotherly love.

As stated in the preceding chapter, Mr. Cooper was appointed to be chairman of the Committee on "Printing and the Publication of Books." To this responsible duty the following letter from Bishop Asbury refers:

MY VERY DEAR BROTHER: All things are well with us here. I am absent from Conference by weakness of body. I am full of infirmities, but the will of the Lord be done.

I hope the Standing Committee will magnify their office, and show their taste and spirituality also. I wish to print nothing but sterling sense and sentiments. There appears a harmony in the whole body of Conference. I am teaching and training them to do without me. My grief is, I am Bishop alone; my honor and office I cannot give to another; if I could, I judge it would be soon done.

If you ever supposed alienation of affection in me to you in my refusing to write, you are mistaken. But the best of men are men at the best.

I have a wish that a few letters I wrote upward of thirty years ago, copied and preserved by my friend Andrews, might be put into the magazine. I am sure I am right in my desire of printing the Notes on the Discipline. You, in your annual distant station, can hardly conceive the mischief and abuse we meet with from unchristian and illiberal minds. In many parts they raise a dust and escape in the clouds.

Next Sabbath I hope to preach in the new building. Last Lord's day I had to speak on the death of Martha Fonerdon, from John's Gospel, eleventh chapter, 24–27 verses. O, my dear Cooper, be wholly for God. This will be a year of judgment and mercy.

I am ever thine, in Jesus,   FRANCIS ASBURY.

As to the Notes on the Discipline, I wish them to be printed in January. By all means leave out the letters. Put the Deed at the end, and place the different branches of the Minutes of the last General Conference in the sections where they belong. And about Brother Dickins's allowance, put it all to death; it is no article of faith nor discipline.

Do your best; take time; expect no thanks from men, but do all you can. Angels can do no more. I shall be very free in giving my opinion on any subject the Committee shall think proper, through you, to consult me.

I write to you from Baltimore, October 24, 1797. Bear this in mind.

The above deeply interesting letter — valuable on account of its historical significance—will serve to correct a mistake made in the edition of Asbury's *Journal*, vol. ii, p. 353, where the name of Martha Fonerdon, as given in the letter to Mr. Cooper, and also in the *Journal*, vol. ii, p. 354, is recorded as Martha F. Allison. The correction of the error is due to the descendants of so noble and worthy a character as this lady established in the early annals of Baltimore Methodism.

Within a few days after the receipt of Bishop Asbury's letter, Mr. Cooper was called upon to perform an act of brotherly regard for another member of the Society at Baltimore. Having secured the services of his brother, Thomas Bell, for a week, in Wilmington, he took passage with Captain Foudray for Philadelphia. Here he did the work for which he had mainly embarked. He says:

Saturday, November 18. I attended the Register's Court, at the request of Mrs. Wright, from Baltimore, who had applied for the administration on the estate of her sister, who died in the fever in this city. A *caveat* was entered against her by a set of vile and wicked men who sought to keep her from her sister's estate; and such another scene of villainy I never saw in any trial as appeared in this business. However, Mrs. Wright easily cast them, and obtained a decree in her favor. It was proposed to prosecute the wretched creatures for perjury and design to defraud.

Returning to Wilmington, he took board with Captain Michael Dawson, where, in a quiet home, with a small family in easy circumstances, he spent many happy days. His pulpit labors for the Sabbath were preaching, morning and evening, in Wilmington, and in the afternoon at Newport. In addition to this he also preached during the week, generally on Thursday night. Soon the congregations began to increase, and clergymen of other denominations waited on his ministry, which act of brotherly fellowship he cordially reciprocated. Thus

Episcopal, Presbyterian, and Methodist clergymen gave countenance to each other and mingled with the members of the several denominations in social intercourse. Among the laity, those in the highest circles were led to regard the hitherto despised Methodists with favor, an illustration of which is given in the following extract. Says Mr. Cooper:

Thursday, November 8. In the evening I preached with much liberty from Rev. xxi, 7. Had a large congregation, among whom were three ministers; and, for the first time, the judge of the Federal Court for this district and his lady were at our church.

Dr. Coke, who had unexpectedly arrived from England in November, and who had had his sympathies wrought upon to a great degree by reason of the location of so many of the itinerant preachers, "through weakness of body or family concerns"—the number at this time was forty-three—wrote to Mr. Cooper a letter, which certainly demands of the ministry and membership of the Methodist Episcopal Church in America of the present generation our grateful recognition of the brotherly spirit of that noble man. The letter is given below, and is now first published. Let the recollection of its author's kindliness dwell in our memories. He says:

NEW YORK, *December* 6, 1797.

MY DEAR BROTHER: I have long groaned in spirit over the loss we have suffered by the withdrawing of our married ministers on this continent from the general work for want of support. The evil sustained by this is unmeasurable. I therefore wish to devote £60 per annum sterling ($266 64) toward the help of our married ministers, till there be a regular and sufficient supply for them, on the following plan, namely:

If you find out by personal interview, or by correspondence, that any preacher who is a valuable man in the work is going to sit down, or has sat down, because he is going to be married, or is married, and because he has not sufficient support for himself and family, and you have reason to believe that the want of support is the true reason of his going to withdraw from the itinerant plan, or of his having withdrawn; I beg of you, in such case, to offer to him, in my name, £20 a year sterling ($88 88) till such time as a regular and sufficient support be provided, if he will continue on the itinerant plan. And if he accept of the offer, I beg of you to give him a draft or bill of exchange, signed by yourself, on me, at Mr. John Bebbington's, umbrella maker, City Road, London, for £20 sterling; and if any thing prevent my return till the General Conference, and the second year commences before my return, I beg of you to draw upon me a second time for £20. I choose to put confidence in the brethren concerned, and, therefore, would have the whole year's allowance made to them at the commencement of it. You may, therefore, go as far as to assist three ministers on this plan, so as to make up the £60 per annum. And I desire you will inform the brethren thus assisted that I expect they will take exactly the same pains in their circuits to get the salaries, both for themselves and their wives, as if I had given them no assistance; this I insist upon. Tell them, also, that I expect them to keep this a secret, as the discovery of it might prevent my friends assisting me to bear my traveling expenses; but if it be discovered by the means of drawing bills on me, let it be discovered in such case; let not the good be lost on that account. Be pleased to draw upon me sixty days after sight. I shall give my agent in London sufficient directions on this subject, and shall be prepared for you; and I will take care that if a bill or bills to the amount of £60 sterling come to London while I am on my voyage returning, there shall be money enough left behind in the hands or at the command of my agent to answer such bill or bills. And I shall consider your assisting me in this business as a great favor conferred upon myself; as you will thereby afford me an opportunity of glorifying God, I believe, in the most useful manner with my little substance.

Your faithful friend,   T. COKE.

To EZEKIEL COOPER.

P. S. If in any case you judge that £20 or £24 Pennsylvania currency will be sufficient, you may fix the allowance, that is to say, my additional assistance, accordingly.

That the matter of a competent support for our married ministry lay very near the heart of Bishop Coke will be seen, also, by an extract from a letter addressed to Mr.

Cooper by him a year after the foregoing epistle, dated New Chapel, City Road, London, December 18, 1798. In this he says:

The work of God in America lies exceedingly near my heart. I long to hear of those great outpourings of the Spirit with which you were blessed some years ago. But you may depend upon it, my dear brother, that the work will never flourish as extensively and permanently as we could wish till you have further provision for a married ministry; and this will never be the case till the traveling preachers take that business up in a way they never hitherto have done. It is contrary to the word of God and the reason of things to suffer the married preachers to drop off as they do for want of food for themselves and families. It is a most crying evil, and will ruin the work of God in America if some remedy be not devised. I could weep tears of blood about it. And this is not an opinion precipitately formed, but has been the firm sentiment of my mind ever since I knew America.

So deep was Dr. Coke's interest in this matter, that in less than a month after writing the letter from which the above extract is taken, he wrote a third to Mr. Cooper, which, though antedating our history of the work under Mr. Cooper's charge, is here given. It is as follows:

ISLAND OF JERSEY. *January* 12, 1799.

MY VERY DEAR BROTHER: Having an opportunity of sending you a letter by the pious captain of an American ship, who will soon sail from Guernsey (a neighboring island to this), I embrace it in order to write to you once more before I have the pleasure, God willing, of seeing you. I bless God, he has wonderfully restored my health. I am quite renewed, and with some allowances feel the vigor of youth. This is the Lord's doing, and it is truly marvelous in my eyes. I can bless God also that I am enabled to walk with him, but I am very weak in spiritual things, and want your prayers and those of all the brethren. I am now on this Island, and have been endeavoring to put an end to a very dreadful persecution of our people here, which was carried on for six years; and the Lord has given me the hearts of the King and his Council, and has enabled me to bring this business to a happy conclusion. Since I had the pleasure of being with you, I have spent a considerable time in Ireland. You have, undoubtedly, received accounts of the dreadful rebellion in that country. I was in Ireland at the height of it, and was obliged to employ much of my time in gaining the protection and interference of the government in that kingdom in behalf of our suffering preachers, and God was pleased to give me success, without which (humanly speaking) they would not have held their Conference, nor would many of them have traveled. I shall visit Ireland again, God willing, next spring, and return to the English Conference in July, and set off in the Packet for New York in the beginning of September. And I can truly say, Brother, that I anticipate the pleasure of seeing you again. My soul is always refreshed among you, but I continually bemoan that great deficiency among you—the want of support for a married ministry. I have known America for fourteen years; and when I consider what a number of holy, experienced, zealous, able men have been laid aside, and rendered comparatively useless through this great evil, I am sometimes grieved above measure. It makes me go sometimes heavily along, not deserted of God (glory to his Name), but oppressed in spirit. I recount to myself the names of numbers who have answered the above description, and then consider what they are now in the Church of God—holy men, it is true, but almost useless. I pass an hour in praying over this awful subject, and then another hour, and then I cast myself before God, crying out: O Lord, what a glorious number of able men should we have had jointly with those who now labor in the work if this great evil had not existed; and then, methinks, I could weep tears of blood! But I know, Brother, that it is in the power of the General Conference to remedy this evil for the future. I am sure you will bear with my weakness, as it flows from the purest love to the cause of God in America.

The schism which took place in England is confirmed. We have lost, our enemies say, five thousand; but I am sure we have added in the balance of England alone, since the schism, seven thousand and upward, and have got rid of as troublesome a set of people as ever, I think, plagued a church of Christ. Their head, who was the great, active man among them in speaking, travelling, and writing (Alexander Kilham), died the other day by swallowing a little bone in a mutton chop. It was extracted, but had so lacerated the wind-pipe that he expired within a few hours.

The raising of money for the work in the West Indies has wholly lain upon me, in consequence of there being so many chapels built this year to supply for the chapels which were lost by the schism. Twelve able missionaries have been sent over within eleven months, three of whom have families. The expense of that work will be this year about £2.400 ($10.665 60). But God has given us about eleven thousand souls in those islands, besides those which have been safely lodged in Abraham's bosom. O what is money compared to immortal souls, for which Christ died?

May the God of Love, the Father of our Lord Jesus Christ, and our Father in Him, fill you with every grace and gift of his Spirit necessary for your own salvation and the salvation of thousands. Give my kindest love to all the preachers, traveling and local, in your neighborhood, and also to all the private members to whom I am personally known, and don't forget to pray for

Your truly affectionate friend and brother,   T. COKE.

EZEKIEL COOPER, Presiding Elder of the Methodist Episcopal Church: care of the resident Elder of the Methodist Church, John Street, New York.

These important letters will furnish the reader with data to guide to a proper estimate of our honored Bishop Coke, who introduced, advocated, and succeeded in securing the passage of a rule by the General Conference of 1800, by which the salaries of the "distressed" preachers were increased, and therefore locations in the ministry became less frequent, and many of those who had previously taken that course returned to the effective ranks of the Methodist itinerancy. Having in this digression placed on record the above facts, we resume the narrative, drawn from Mr. Cooper's papers, after the reception of Dr. Coke's letter from New York.

On the 16th of December, 1797, Dr. Coke visited Mr. Cooper at Wilmington, Del., and as the Publishing Committee were soon to have a session in Philadelphia, Rev. James Moore came to take Mr. Cooper's place for a few weeks during his absence. These, with Judge Bassett and others, had a social gathering

17

at Mr. Cooper's boarding-house, which continued until about nine o'clock P. M. The hours were spent in the discussion of several important points of doctrine and opinion, the chief of which was concerning the millennium, and whether Christ's reign during the thousand years will be personal or spiritual. Says Mr. Cooper:

This brought on a considerable dispute in a Christian and friendly way. Doctor Coke and Judge Bassett were both of the opinion that Christ will reign personally the thousand years. I rather favored a spiritual reign. It was argued, on their side, that the primitive Fathers held with the personal reign, and that the Scriptures held out that idea. I opposed,

1. That the first Fathers of the Church did not hold it; and that none of the Fathers during the first century ever advanced the idea. Ignatius of Antioch, Dionysius the Areopagite of Athens, Clemens Romanus, Polycarp of Smyrna, and their contemporaries, held no such doctrine. And that according to Eusebius of Cesarea, in his Bibliotheca Patrum, one Papius was the first who introduced that doctrine. True, after him, others of the Fathers held it, and it has been called by some the "Dotage of antiquity," according to Dupin's History of the Fathers. I argued,

2. That it appeared to me, where the Scriptures spoke of Christ's personal coming, it referred to his coming at the day of judgment, which is understood to be after the thousand years spoken of are expired; and that when his reigning a thousand years was mentioned it did not appear to be expressed that he then was to come personally. Further, if he then came personally, and is also to come personally at the day of judgment, then there are two comings yet to be expected, which will make three comings in all, and, of course, after he comes the first of those two last times, he will return again, for which I see no Scriptural authority. And thus we left the subject.

The Sabbath following was observed by a love-feast at nine o'clock A. M., preaching at eleven o'clock, by Dr. Coke; then followed the Lord's supper; at three o'clock P. M. by Mr. Cooper at Newport, and in the evening by Dr. Coke at Wilmington, who afterward met the Society.

On Monday the 18th of December, Dr. Coke, Rev.

Christopher Spry, presiding elder, and Mr. Cooper went to Philadelphia to sit with the other members of the Book Committee. They opened the session on Wednesday, December the 20th, nearly two weeks earlier than the time ordered by the Philadelphia Conference. This was, probably, because Dr. Coke could then meet with them, but could not later because of his return to Europe. The members present were, besides Dr. Coke, Christopher Spry and John McClaskey, presiding elders; Richard Swain, Solomon Sharp, Charles Cavender, elders; and Ezekiel Cooper, chairman.

The session lasted eight days, during which time the Committee prepared for the press—being mindful of Bishop Asbury's instructions in the letter to Mr. Cooper, given above—The Form of Discipline, with Explanatory Notes, and four sermons on The Duty of the Gospel Ministry, by Dr. Coke, "on sundry other publications," and passed certain resolutions, besides making "a few regulations respecting the Book Concern."

On Friday, December 29, Dr. Coke and Mr. Cooper took the stage from Philadelphia to New York, where they arrived the next night at about nine o'clock. The passage across North River was difficult, because of the ice ; and the ferriage, which was commonly twelve and a half cents, was raised to seventy-five cents.

The packet in which Dr. Coke took passage not being ready to sail, he was delayed in New York for a week. Mr. Cooper remained with him. The time was devoted to the work of the ministry, and to social Christian communion with the Methodists of New York, then under the pastoral care of Revs. George Roberts, Joshua Wells, and William Beauchamp. Mr. Cooper has left the following record of the Doctor's embarcation. He says:

Saturday, January 6, 1798. The doctor sailed about twelve o'clock. I went on board with him, and stayed till the packet began to move. Then I, together with Brothers Roberts, Wells, and others who were on board to see him sail, took our leave of our dear friend and bishop, wishing him a safe and comfortable voyage to Europe, and a useful visit there. I felt solemn on this occasion in parting with the Doctor, in whose company I have been from the 16th of last month—more than twenty days.

As will be seen, Mr. Cooper spent at this time several weeks in New York and the surrounding villages. The record left by him is of such historic value that the reader is again privileged to read it in its original language. Mr. Cooper says:

Sunday, January 7, 1798. I preached a sacramental discourse for Brother Roberts at eleven o'clock; and, by request, I preached at three o'clock a charity sermon for the benefit of schooling poor children. In the evening I preached at the Two Mile Stone, in a small preaching-house lately built there. Our Society has four preaching-houses now in New York. The one on the North River side of the city [Duane Street] is an elegant house, the best we have in the United States.

I spent several weeks in York and on Long Island together, in visiting and preaching among my old friends and acquaintances. I have been the longest acquainted with the New York Society of any of our traveling preachers who are now traveling, Bishop Asbury excepted. I feel my heart much united with them, and my visit I feel to be comfortable to my soul.

Friday, 12. I visited and preached in Brooklyn. There appears some prospect in this place, which has been a hard place to work upon.

Friday, 19. I visited Newtown, and stayed four days, principally at my good friends', Dr. Wainwright and Mr. Staples; preached twice on Sabbath, with some degree of satisfaction and freedom, to an attentive and considerably large congregation. I was filled with joy and sorrow upon this visit. Some are fallen away who used to be faithful.

Sunday, 28. I preached three times in York with much satisfaction. I have now preached eighteen times in the city, and three times on the island, in all, twenty one times since I came to York, and now I am to depart, not knowing that we shall meet again.

Monday, 29.   Dr. Johnson and I took our leave of York, and our friends there, in order to return to the South.   We both stayed at Mr. John Mills's, one of the kindest families I ever knew, and with whom I am very much united.   I feel myself under great obligations to this family for their long, many, and continued favors to me.

On the 2d of February Mr. Cooper returned to Wilmington, and was warmly greeted by the members of the charge.   He soon was at home again with Captain Dawson, who during his absence had changed his residence, and was delighted with his room, where from the window he could, by the aid of a glass, " see all the shipping and vessels passing up or down the Delaware, fourteen or fifteen sail often in view at once."   His pastoral work was at once resumed, and his congregations, both on the Sabbath and on Thursday night, were large and growingly interested in the word of life. Under date of February 11, he gives an account of the Society at Newport, which is the first we know of.   He tells us:

I dined to-day at Mr. Lattimore's, in Newport.   Our Society here is small, but I am very much pleased with it.   Mrs. Lattimore, Mrs. Robertson, and Mrs. Miller are three excellent souls.   There is but one white man in Society, that is Mr. Miller.   After preaching and class I returned to Wilmington, and preached again in the evening. Preaching three times a day, and class, and general society meeting is rather too much for me.

It was the custom at this time for the Society in Wilmington to hold a weekly prayer-meeting on Tuesday night, and after the service was ended a singing-meeting, to practice on Methodist tunes, was begun, dating from February 13, 1798.   The spirit of revival began to manifest itself in March, and as the closing days of the month drew near several were united to the church—the gay and worldly having thrown off their splendid attire and put on garments of such plainness that " some hardly knew them." As Mr. Cooper was a strict observer of the old rule to set apart Easter Sunday for special service, he advised the friends on that day, which occurred on April 8, 1798, to bring their children to church to be baptized. After the sermon ten persons were publicly baptized, mostly children.

As the time for holding the Philadelphia Annual Conference had been changed, Mr. Cooper met his brethren in the Conference held in Philadelphia June 5, 1798, having served his charge in Wilmington about five months, and reporting an increase of members—of whites eight, blacks eleven. The Conference continued in session four days. Mr. Cooper was reappointed to Wilmington and Newport, "six months" [see Conference Minutes, 1798, p. 18.—P.]; and after ten days' visiting among his friends in Philadelphia resumed his labors, taking his lodging, as before, with Captain Dawson and family. There was no change in the plan of his ministrations, except that in Newport preaching was arranged for once in two weeks, with which was connected three days of pastoral visitation in that neighborhood.

On Sunday, July 8, after preaching in the morning in Wilmington, he went to Newport and preached in the afternoon. At the close of the sermon a violent storm of wind, rain, thunder and lightning arose, detaining the congregation in the church while it lasted. The people were intensely alarmed; and as the windows were not glazed, the rain drove through the house, forcing the people to huddle together in different places, in the corners, in the pulpit, under the pulpit. When the storm abated he rode to Wilmington, and preached again at eight o'clock P. M. The day following he returned to Newport to engage in the three days' visiting, according to his plan. This method resulted in breaking down the opposition which some had to Methodism, for he visited friend and foe alike.

Toward the last of August the yellow fever began to spread in Wilmington, which so alarmed the people that as many as could do so prepared to move away from the town. It had also reappeared in Philadelphia in a worse form than in the previous years, 1793 and 1797, and in New York and Boston. In September it continued to increase so rapidly in Wilmington that, by the middle of the month, Mr. Cooper tells us:

The place seems almost desolated, the people have so moved out. We [the Methodists—P.] have only about twenty white friends left in town. I have still to be alone in friend Dawson's house. Here I read, write, pray, meditate, and sleep; but have to go among the few remainng friends to get refreshments, etc.

The congregations were greatly reduced, and these were sometimes led to bewail the solemn state into which the whole population had entered. Of this the following will give an illustration. Under date of September 16, Mr. Cooper says:

To-day, while we were in church, there came three corpses in one cart to our church-yard, and all of them the daughters of Mr. Osburn. It very much affected me to see the old parents attending their three children to the grave. Two of them were married women, the other not quite a woman grown. They died last night within about one hour of each other, and certain I am that they are much lamented. The old people have lost four children with this fever: their only son died some days ago. There have ten persons died' in this little town during the last twenty-four hours. I was glad to see friend Osburn and his wife bear their great affliction with so much fortitude of mind—for, surely, without considerable fortitude, patience, and resignation they would be overwhelmed by such troubles, especially as the disease is of such a nature that their nearest friends are generally afraid to go near them. While I was with them my heart overflowed, and I was constrained to vent my emotions of soul by weeping and mourning with those who wept under the great and almost unspeakable distress.

The Society and friends at Newport, realizing the great danger to which Mr. Cooper was exposed, joined in an invitation to him to make his home with them, and would accept no denial. To show how devotedly true that honorable and distinguished servant of God was to the flock over whom he had pastoral charge, he consented, with this proviso, which is given in his own words. He says:

I told them, provided they would agree for me to come into Wilmington and preach every week, I would agree to stay principally with them, as so many of our friends were now there. They wanted me to give up the idea of coming to Wilmington at all while the pestilence continued, but I told them I could not; I had a charge here, and could not relinquish it in time of their distress; it would not do to forsake the flock in time of their affliction and danger. However, they agreed to my proposition, and I came out to spend the week with them. I lodge at Major Robeson's. He and his wife and children are so kind to me that I consider myself under the greatest obligations of gratitude. This is much more comfortable than to live as I did in Wilmington. I was obliged there to live all alone, as there was no house and family which I could conveniently be in. Now I have three miles to ride in, and then return here to lodge and live. The solicitude of these dear friends, about my safety and comfort, particularly Mrs. Robeson and Mrs. Latimer, has made deep impressions on my heart. May the Lord bless them and theirs for life and for eternity!

The fever continued in its violence through the months of September and October. During the prevalence of this disease, in the early part of September, Mr. Cooper attended the Cecil Quarterly Meeting. He was conveyed thither by Mr. John Miller, of Newport. When they arrived, Saturday, September 8, Rev. Thomas Ware, the presiding elder of that district, was preaching. Mr. Ware, discovering Mr. Cooper in the congregation, soon finished his discourse, and then he and the other preachers requested their honored brother " to come up and speak to the people." He did so, and preached a sermon to them, taking for his text 1 Corinthians xiii, 13, "Now abideth faith, hope, charity." Thus there were two sermons delivered during one session of the congregation.

In the afternoon and evening the Quarterly Conference sat upon a very unpleasant matter, it being the investigation of charges of immorality against "sundry of our preachers and members." The accusants failed to appear, but the matter was investigated as far as the inquiries of the body could go. All the accused were acquitted, and pronounced innocent. These charges had created great "noise and confusion," says Mr. Cooper, "through all the country round." The Sabbath services were such as were usual at that period of our Church-life. Mr. Cooper preached with great success at eleven o'clock A. M. While attending the Quarterly Meeting he was, with the other preachers, the guest of Mr. Carnan.

At the close of the service on Sunday morning Mr. Cooper visited Mrs. Cowden, the widow of an eminent clergyman of the Church of England, "a pious, devoted woman, and a great friend to religion and to the Methodists." After dinner they went to Elkton, where at five o'clock P. M. Mr. Cooper preached in the Court-house. Thence returning, he, with Rev. Mr. Bonham, a Methodist preacher, spent the night at Mrs. Cowden's.

On Friday, the 28th of September, Mr. Cooper received intelligence of the death of Rev. John Dickins, of Philadelphia, and his daughter Betsy, both of whom died of yellow fever September 26, 1798. Though memoirs of this distinguished Christian minister have been given in most of our Church histories, the following tribute is due both to his memory and to that of his successor in the book-publishing department of our

Church. Says Mr. Cooper, after mentioning the fact of his death:

These tidings affected me much. In him his family have sustained an irreparable loss as a husband and a parent. The Church, also, will sensibly feel his loss as a minister; and the whole Connection will have cause to lament his death, as he superintended all our Book Concern in printing, etc. I am very doubtful whether we shall be able to supply his place with one so well qualified for that station; so that in many points of view his death will be greatly felt. However, our loss is his infinite gain. "The Lord gave, and the Lord hath taken away: blessed be the name of the Lord." May I be as prepared to leave the world, when called away, as I believe he was.

Before closing this chapter it will be pleasing to the reader to peruse a letter addressed by Rev. Richard Allen, colored, then a local preacher in the African Methodist Episcopal Church in Philadelphia, and "the leader" * in erecting the first African Church in America; it was built in Philadelphia in 1793. The letter was prepared under the direction of the official Board of the Bethel African Methodist Episcopal Church, and intended for Bishop Asbury, but, not knowing his address, was sent to Mr. Cooper at Wilmington. It is as follows:

Philadelphia, *February* 22, 1798.

Reverend Sir: Knowing it to be our duty to write to you, and [that we] ought to have done it before now but knew not how to convey it to you, we take the present opportunity to inform you that there has a very great revival taken place in our Churches, and is still increasing and spreading. Our evening meetings mostly continue until 10 or 12 o'clock, and from four to eight persons are convinced and converted of a night, whites and blacks. Our Churches are crowded, particularly Bethel. We are now making more seats, and think shortly we must enlarge the house. It is at Bethel the work is most general. At prayer-meetings the house is crowded, and persons under conviction for weeks go there to get converted. The Lord meets them in the means, and they return to their houses rejoicing.

---

* See Simpson's *Cyclopedia*, pp. 26, 27.

Such a revival has never taken place in this city before. Many backsliders are reclaimed, and old believers are getting more zeal for the glory of God and the salvation of souls. At our love-feast on the 16th instant, the house was crowded, and continued until after 12 o'clock. Such a time of the power of the Almighty has not been seen these twenty years here: he has greatly blessed the labors of his servants. Our class-meetings are crowded and remarkably lively; in short, we have no barren meetings.

We have the pleasure of informing you that there is a great revival in all the churches in the city; many are convinced and converted, and many added to the number of the whites. May the glory redound to His great name who is the author of it! Mr. Moore's appointment among us has proved a great blessing. We have great reason to believe the appointment to be of God, although he has been afflicted in health for some time, and unable to preach; but we know this also was permitted by Him who orders all things well. Mr. Lee is very well in health, and has cause to rejoice exceedingly that his labors are not in vain in the Lord. Almost all the people that labor amongst us, and the preachers, are nearly worn out, the work is so great and the meetings so frequent. And what is very singular in such a case, we have no opposition or persecution, the enemies of the work look on with wonder. The Lord restrains them. Our congregations nearly consist of as many whites as blacks: many that never attended any place of worship before come; some through curiosity, and many of them are awakened and join the Society, so that nearly as many whites as blacks are convinced and converted to the Lord. We desire to continue in the bands of love, and as of all the fold of Jesus to strive for the furtherance of the Gospel: and we hope in the strength of the Lord to be humble and obedient to those that shall from time to time have the rule over us in the Lord.

All through the winter, and of darkest nights, and the way being so muddy for want of pavement, all these things did not hinder the house from being crowded, the people so thirsted for salvation. Many of the official members are very useful in our prayer-meetings: in particular Henry Manley; his labors and pleadings with the Lord at such times are indefatigable, for when the meetings are almost broken up he often renews them when there are souls in distress, and at his pleadings the Lord often sends the blessing down.

We must conclude our imperfect account of the work amongst us, trusting that He who has begun the work will carry it on to perfection; and that you, reverend sir, may often have the happiness of hearing good news from Zion, and that your hands may be often strengthened in seeing the work flourish on the right and on the left.

Your unworthy servants in Jesus,   RICHARD ALLEN,
                                     JUPITER GIBSON.
Signed by order of the Board.

N. B.—We humbly hope you will excuse the liberty we take in sending you this letter, as we intended sending it to the Bishop; but we found the direction was not right, and we believe you will be glad to hear of the work of God among us.

The foregoing is a faithful copy of the original, with the exception that the words misspelled and the grammar in some cases have been corrected, in order that the reader might understand the meaning designed to be conveyed. The number of colored members in the Methodist Society at Philadelphia was, in 1798, one hundred and eighty-four. They were all under the pastoral supervision of Revs. Wilson Lee and James Moore, the preachers assigned to the charge of the station in Philadelphia.

By reason of the vacancy in the office of Book Steward made by the death of Rev. John Dickins, announced above, Bishop Asbury wrote the following letter to Mr. Cooper:

GERMANTOWN, *October* 4, 1798.

MY VERY DEAR BROTHER: What I have greatly feared for years hath now taken place. Dickins, the generous, the just, the faithful, skillful Dickins, is dead! I have had but one day to deliberate; duty, necessity, calleth me to be precipitant. You will anticipate what I am going to write. It is to you, and you only, I can look at present, in the recess of the Philadelphia Conference, to assist Asbury Dickins in the conducting our work as heretofore. You will correct the press? You will superintend the state and entries of the various accounts, that the Connection and the family suffer no material injury? The Magazine must be continued; five or ten thousand hymn-books will be wanting immediately, and sundry other books. Brother Lee [Jesse.—P.] will, if he is furnished with proper papers, collect what money can be obtained southward. We have done what we could eastward. My dear brother, I need say but little; you will now have it in your power to render the Connection and family such extensive service as your heart, I hope, desires. I can only appoint at present, that the cause and family may not suffer. What the Philadelphia Conference will do, is with them. I hope to be at Isaac Hersay's upon Friday evening: at North East on Sabbath-day. My horse is worn down. My health is greatly repaired, but ah! what is life? We have had great prospects eastward. As soon as the city is accessible you will go in. We shall send the Minutes for the present year. My long-lost manuscript journal I left with Betsy Dickins; I must read it over before any thing can be done. I am afraid to have it sent but by a sure hand, by land. I feel resolved, if the Conference pleaseth, to publish my scraps of journals as my all to the Connection, and answer to those that trouble me. In this sickly state of things I must make haste.

Some letters written by Mr. O'Kelly, now in Philadelphia, to Mr. Wesley and the Doctor, I wanted to confront that wonderful man. Brother Lee and some others, with myself, premeditate to attend the Republican Conference to demand the author of the book entitled *Christicola,* and controvert the charges as false.

I am, as ever, thine, FRANCIS ASBURY.

Mr. Cooper received the above letter about three weeks after it was written. With great reluctance he submitted to the appointment of the Bishop, and began at once to prepare for the duties thus given him. On Sunday, October 28, he preached his last sermons in Wilmington and Newport as the pastor for that Conference year.

CHAPTER XIII.

THE METHODIST BOOK CONCERN, 1792–1808.

THE circulation of religious books began with the rise of Methodism in America, the followers of Wesley being inspired by the counsel of that godly man, who said to his preachers: "See that every Society is supplied with books, some of which ought to be in every house." Owing to the difficulty of obtaining a supply of Mr. Wesley's publications for a field then so distant as America was from England, a reprint of some of them was made in this country before the organization of the first American Methodist Conference in 1773. At the session of that body the first query was, "Ought not the authority of Mr. Wesley, and that Conference, [the British Wesleyan.—P.] to extend to the preachers and people in America, as well as in Great Britain and Ireland?"

The answer was, "Yes."

Of the six rules agreed upon by the Conference were the following:

Rule 4. None of the preachers in America to reprint any of Mr. Wesley's books without his authority (when it can be gotten) and the consent of their brethren.

5. Robert Williams to sell the books he has already printed, but to print no more, unless under the above restrictions.*

Nine years elapsed before any further mention was made in the Annual Conference Minutes of the book interest of the societies, yet it had so grown that a rev-

* Methodist Conferences, vol. i, 1813.

enue was obtained by the sale of books which was devoted to the support of the itinerant preachers. The writer has before him a manuscript copy of the Minutes of 1782, issued before any Conference Minutes had been printed, and, though remarkably preserved, one hundred and four years old. The difference between the item about to be quoted from that copy and the printed edition of the Minutes of 1813 is such that a comparison should be made by a close student of our early history. From the MSS. we have:

Quest. 11. What shall be done to get a regular and impartial supply for the maintenance of the preachers?

Ans. Let every thing they receive, either in money or clothing, be valued by the stewards at quarter meeting, and an account of the preacher's deficiencies given in to bring to conference, that he may be supplied from the profits arising from the books and the conference collections.

It will thus be seen that some systematic method had already been adopted by the Societies and Conference regulating the sale of books and the disposition of the percentage raised thereby.

No further mention is made, in the Conference Minutes, of the book interest until the session of the General Conference in December, 1784, at which the Methodist Episcopal Church was organized, and "A Form of Discipline" adopted "for the Ministers, Preachers, and other Members of the Methodist Episcopal Church in America." In the deliberations of that body the questions and answers, to which they agreed, were framed by Mr. Wesley himself. The fiftieth and fifty-first questions, with the answers, are thus given:

Quest. 50. Why is it that the people under our care are not better?

Ans. Other reasons may concur, but the chief is because *we* are not more *knowing* and more *holy.*

Quest. 51. But why are not we more knowing?

Ans. Because we are idle. We forget our very first Rule, "Be diligent. Never be unemployed. Never be triflingly employed. Never while away time; neither spend any more time at any place than is strictly necessary."

I fear there is altogether a fault in this matter, and that few of us are clear. Which of you spends as many hours a day in God's work as you did formerly in man's work? We talk, talk, or read history, or what next comes to hand. We must, absolutely must, cure this evil, or betray the cause of God.

But how? 1. Read the most useful books, and that regularly and constantly. Steadily spend all the morning in this employ, or at least five hours in four-and-twenty.

"But I have no taste for reading." Contract a taste for it by use, or return to your trade.

"But I have no books." We desire the assistants will take care that all the large Societies provide Mr. Wesley's Works for the use of the preachers.

But what shall we do for the rising generation? Who will labor for them? Let him who is zealous for God and the souls of men begin now.

1. Where there are ten children whose parents are in Society meet them at least an hour every week.

2. Talk with them every time you see any at home.

3. Pray in earnest for them.

4. Diligently instruct and vehemently exhort all parents at their own houses.

5. Preach expressly on education. "But I have no gift for this." Gift or no gift, you are to do it, else you are not called to be a Methodist preacher. Do it as you can, till you can do it as you would. Pray earnestly for the gift, and use the means for it.

The tendency of such pointed legislation was to increase the demand for books as the Church grew in numbers, territorial extent, and power; and every minister who had been admitted into holy orders was expected to secure such a supply as was needed.

The work had become now so important that in 1789 Philip Cox and John Dickins were appointed "book stewards," the former for that half of the Conference territory which extended from Washington to

Gloucester, embracing forty-eight circuits and stations; and Mr. Dickins for that half which extended from Calvert Circuit, Md., to Cumberland, in Tennessee, embracing forty-nine circuits and stations. In 1790 the whole work was committed to John Dickins, and the title of his office was changed from that of Book Steward to that of "Superintendent of the Printing and Book-business." This was also retained the years following. By the action of the Conferences of 1791 the surplusage of the Preachers' Fund was deposited "in the Book Fund." *

In 1792 the title Book Concern first appears in the Conference Minutes; it is in connection with the following question :

> *Quest.* 16. What is the sum total for which the Book Concern is now accountable to the Preachers' Fund ?
> *Ans.* £182 16s. 3d.

The quotation is taken from the " Minutes taken at the several Conferences of the Methodist Episcopal Church in America for the year 1792. Price, one-sixteenth of a dollar. Philadelphia: printed by Parry Hall, No. 149, in Chestnut Street; and sold by John Dickins, No. 182 Race Street. M,DCC,XCII."

The edition of the Minutes as issued in 1813 has no mention of the above historic fact.

In 1793 the Book Concern was, by the Minutes of that year, declared to be accountable to the Preachers' Fund for £301 17s. 2d. In 1794 it was £415 7s. 8d. In 1795 it was £400 17s. 9d. ; in 1796, £419 0s. 1½d. The money account herein set forth in pounds, shillings, and pence, was in Pennsylvania currency, according to the Minutes of the Conference of 1791, as published in the edition of 1813, entitled, " Methodist Conferences."

* See Minutes, 1791, edition 1813.

18

The publishers, Daniel Hitt and Thomas Ware, thus represent it:

Quest. 13. What is contributed toward the fund for the superannuated preachers and the widows and orphans of preachers?

Ans. £61, 11s. 2d., P. C.

Quest. 14. How was this applied?

Ans. Some part of it is lodged in the respective districts, and the remainder deposited in the book fund.

The original Minutes, as published from year to year, do not mention the class of currency on which the reckoning was based. After the General Conference of 1796 the Chartered Fund, which was established in the place of the Preachers' Fund, held the indebtedness of the Book Concern to the Preachers' Fund by its transfer to that organization. From that time no mention is made, in the original or compiled Minutes of the Annual Conferences, of the amount of indebtedness by the Book Concern to that fund.

It has been generally held by all our Church historians that John Dickins, who was stationed in New York from 1783 to 1789, with the exception of one year—1785, when he was appointed to Bertie Circuit in Virginia— was continued in that charge for five years in order that he might superintend and direct the book business. Such, we think, is not the case. Mr. Dickins throughout the course of his ministerial career in America was so situated that he was not subject to the changes of his co-laborers. He was admitted on trial in 1777, and appointed to North Carolina as his circuit. He was admitted into full connection and classified among the "assistants" in 1778, and appointed to Brunswick, Va. In 1779, '80 his appointment was at Roanoke, two years. In 1781, '82 he desisted from traveling. In 1783 he re-entered the traveling connection and was stationed with Samuel Spragg in New York, where he remained until 1785. Being returned to New York in 1786, he continued there also the year following; but, having in 1787 been ordained to the eldership in the Methodist Episcopal Church, he, with Henry Willis, also an elder, had charge of New York, New Rochelle, and Long Island Circuits. In 1788 he had charge solely of the Society in New York. To this statement must be added the stronger facts: that no publications, after the order to print such documents as the Conferences might agree upon, bear the imprint of his supervision. The Minutes of the Christmas Conference of 1784 were printed by Charles Cist; those of the Annual Conference of 1785, in Baltimore, by John Haynes; of 1786, in Baltimore, by William Goddard; of 1787, in Baltimore, by John Haynes; and of 1789, in New York, by William Ross. Not until he had opened the book business in Philadelphia, in 1790, did he have the supervision of the printing.

When stationed in Philadelphia, in 1789, he was the only traveling preacher appointed to that charge, and, to show his relation to the ministerial work therein, he is set forth as elder; and then follows his designation as "Book Steward." He was not as yet general superintendent. Philip Cox, stationed at Gloucester, was also set forth as "elder and book steward." Each of these held the same official relation to the Church.*

In 1790 the official title of "Superintendent of the Printing and Book Business," as above stated, was given to John Dickins, located in Philadelphia, while Philip Cox and William Thomas, elders, were appointed to be "Traveling Book Stewards," the former for the southern part of the Methodist field; the latter for the peninsula. It was during this year, therefore, that the Book Concern was definitely opened, under the individ-

* See Minutes for 1789. Printed by William Ross, New York, pp. 7, 8.

ual supervision of one man. The appointment of traveling book stewards was continued until 1798. In this service Philip Cox was employed four years. Of him is given the following from the Minutes of the Conferences of 1794, under

Quest. 11. Who have died this year?
Ans. Philip Cox.

His last services were great in circulating so many hundred books of religious instruction. On his return from a visit to the westward he was attacked with a disease in his bowels, accompanied with a fever and delirium. He observed on Sunday, the 1st of September, that it was such a day of peace and comfort to his soul as he had seldom seen. Tuesday he reached home, after which he continued delirious till, on Sunday, the 8th, he departed in peace.

Besides him William Thomas served in the same work one year; John Hutt, three years; Salathiel Weeks, four years; John Baldwin, four years; Thomas Bowen, one year; and Solomon Covington, two years. From this it will be seen that during the first six years of the existence of the Book Concern, from 1790 to 1796, there were seven sub-agents of Mr. Dickins, the superintendent, sent out into the field by regular appointment of the Church authorities at Conference to aid in the circulation of books and the upbuilding of the book interests of the Methodist Episcopal Church in America. The publication of Methodist and other religious works went forward also in 1790, and during the year a room was secured by Mr. Dickins for the deposit and sale of books. The house was situated at No. 43 Fourth Street. In 1792 the house was on Race Street, No. 182. In 1794 Mr. Dickins removed his stock to No. 44 North Second Street, near Arch; in 1795 to No. 50 North Second Street, where the business was conducted until after Mr. Dickins's death in 1798. The printing was done in separate houses: first by Prichard & Hall, in Market

Street; then by Parry & Hall, in Chestnut Street; then
by Henry Tuckniss, Church Alley; then by William
W. Woodward, Chestnut Street, near Front; and finally,
during the continuance of the Concern in Philadelphia, by Solomon W. Conrad, Pewter-Platter Alley,
No. 22.

The first publication issued by Mr. Dickins was *The
Arminian Magazine*, Vol. I., at 12*s.* a volume. Then,
from 1790 to 1794, books were issued in the following
order:

1. Rev. Mr. Wesley's *Notes on the New Testament*, in 3 volumes,
well bound, 1790, 1791, at 17*s.*

2. *Thomas à Kempis*, bound, 2*s.*

3. *Primitive Physic*, bound, 3*s.*

4. *The Form of Discipline for the Methodist Church*, with treatises on
Predestination, Perseverance, Christian Perfection, Baptism, etc., all
bound together, 3*s.* 6*d.*

5. The Experiences of about twenty *British Methodist Preachers*,well
bound and lettered, 5*s.* 7½*d.*

6. *The Experience and Travels of Mr. Freeborn Garretlson*, well
bound.

7. A pocket *Hymn Book*, containing three hundred hymns, well
bound and lettered, 3*s.* 9*d.*

8. The excellent Works of the Rev. Mr. John Fletcher, published
one volume at a time; the whole will contain about six volumes; the
1st, 2d, and 3d volumes now published, well bound and lettered, at
5*s.* 7½*d.* per volume.

9. An Extract on *Infant Baptism*, stitched, 9*d.*

10. An Abridgment of *Mrs. Rowe's Devout Thoughts*, bound, 1*s.* 10½*d.*

11. *Children's Instructions*, stitched, 6*d.*

12. *A Funeral Discourse on the Death of that great Divine, the Rev.
John Wesley*, stitched, 11*d.*

13. *The Saint's Everlasting Rest*, well bound, 5*s.* 7½*d.*

14. *Minutes of the Methodist Conferences*, 4*d.*

15. The distinguishing marks of a work of the *Spirit of God*,
stitched, 8*d.*

16. The first volume of *Mr. Asbury's Journal*, containing three hundred and fifty-six pages duodecimo, well bound and lettered, 5*s.* 7½*d.*

17. *The Solemn Warnings of the Dead; or, An Admonition to Un-*

converted Sinners, by Joseph Alleine. Also, Baxter's *Call to the Unconverted,* bound together, 3*s.*

18. *The Life of Mr. Thomas Walsh and the Journal of Mr. John Nelson,* bound together and lettered, 5*s.* 7½*d.*

Note.—The price of the books in the foregoing catalogue is Pennsylvania currency.

The list of books above presented was issued by John Dickins, and published at the close of the volume indicated above as No. 18. There is bound with this volume, not noticed, however, by Mr. Dickins, as the final tract, *A Race for Eternal Life,* by the Rev. Mr. Fletcher, published, as the title page informs us, by John Dickins, in Philadelphia, in 1792. I have also before me the third volume of Mr. Wesley's *Explanatory Notes,* issued in Philadelphia, and "sold by John Dickins, No. 43 Fourth Street, near the corner of Race Street, 1791." During this period volume ii of the *Arminian Magazine* was also issued.

As seen in the preceding chapter, Mr. Dickins died from yellow fever in September, and Bishop Asbury appointed Mr. Cooper to fill the vacancy occasioned by that death. As the pestilence was still raging, the duties of the office were not assumed until the fever was abated. Mr. Cooper spent the interval in a visit to his relatives and friends in Delaware, East Maryland, and Annapolis, Md.

On the 1st of December he arrived at Philadelphia, as he tells us, "in order to see about our book business." The next day, being the Sabbath, he preached once. On Monday, the 3d, he began to acquaint himself with the affairs of the Book Concern; the result was as follows. He says:

Through this week and the week following I was engaged in looking into the affairs of the book business. And I find it in such a situation that I am not inclined to engage in it, as agent, this winter. There is a considerable incumbrance on it, which I am not willing to take upon myself; and the executors of Brother Dickins's estate will not give me the property on hand unless I will first assume the payment of the debt due from the Concern, which is more than $4,500. I proposed that I would be accountable for as much as the amount of property put into my hands, or that I would be accountable for all the property which I received either in books or money, in the payment by the different persons in debt to the Concern; but that I should not engage to pay a large debt upon the credit of debts due to the Concern—scattered abroad from New Hampshire to Georgia—and some of it in very doubtful hands and of many years' standing. So I, of course, do not engage in the business till further instructions, and a suitable stipulation between me and the Conference, or between the Bishop and me. However, at the request of friends, I agree to stay in the city this winter and serve the Church in the line of the ministry. The book business will be at a stand for awhile; yet I do not know that any great injury will be sustained thereby, as the accounts can be settled and the moneys due collected, after which it may start again.

Mr. Cooper immediately advised Bishop Asbury of his determination. His letter was received by the Bishop while at Charleston, South Carolina, and a reply was immediately made. It is as follows:

JANUARY 8, 1799.

MY VERY DEAR FRIEND: I anticipated the difficulties that would come in your way of conducting the Book Concern. It was not in my power to stipulate with you for what sum, and for what time, you should have the management. We feel ourselves under doubts with respect to remitting money without special assurances of the application and proper security for our property. We cannot desire any person to do our work for nothing; yet we want it punctually done. Brother Haskins's and Asbury Dickins's letters came while the Conference was sitting in this city. Conference voted, hit or miss, to carry on the work forthwith, and nominated several books to be printed immediately. Conference agreed that a committee should consider the contents of your letter, received this day. We feel our doubts concerning the printing of more books at present. We have some scruples upon our minds if it will be possible to carry on the work in Philadelphia in future. The collecting of money will be attended to by Brother Lee, with the greatest activity and punctuality. If you stay in town, I wish you would see books sent to orders, that we may sell off with great speed. I judge it will not be improper for you, upon the side and safety of the Connection, to keep a list of money paid to the executors, and how it is applied; and you may keep an account of all the books you send out, and receive the cash for them; and what you shall have for your service you must leave to the Conference. How to talk at the distance of seven hundred miles is not easy. My infirmity, and the general abuse I have had from men that have risen up against us, and the great suspicions raised in the minds of some of the ministry still with us, maketh me very cautious in my movements.

If I should not write to Brother Haskins, you may show him this letter and welcome.

I am, with respect and heartfelt concern, thy brother in Jesus,

FRANCIS ASBURY.

On the same sheet are also the following:

CHARLESTON, *January* 9, 1799.

MY VERY DEAR FRIEND: You see how large a letter I have written with my own hand upon a broken sheet of paper. When I began I had no thought of writing so long a letter. I have been employed in dictating near three hundred pages, in answer to Mr. O'Kelly's spite and) malice. Conference time we have had but six boarders in our house, and frequently in my room, and great part of the Conference visiting. We have had great peace. I wish, if a vessel should offer, my letters in packet may be sent to me at Norfolk or Newbern. I shall be at the former in March. The work of God is under a pleasing growth in the South.

I am, with continued respect to thee, F. ASBURY.

CHARLESTON, *January* 9, 1799.

DEAR BROTHER: I have liberty from Mr. Asbury to write to you, and request you to have the Minutes of the last year's Conferences printed, from one to two thousand copies—any number you please, not exceeding two thousand; and, if the Philadelphia Conference should disapprove of it, I will engage to pay you the money that shall be expended, and take the whole concern on myself. If you are unwilling to have them printed, please to let me know of it against I get to Baltimore, and, I expect, I shall have them printed at Baltimore. I think it is quite likely the book business will be removed to Baltimore. Asbury Dickins had the copy of the Minutes.

 I remain yours in love,   JESSE LEE.

P. S. I expect to collect a good deal of book money, but shall feel unwilling to send it forward till I can hear that some Methodist *man* is willing to receive it and answer for it. If you undertake that part of the business I will gladly remit the money to you as soon as possible. I expect to be in Newbern by the middle of February, and in Norfolk the last of March.

I expect to have $400 or $500 in my hands for the Book Concern in a few days.   J. L.

The Minutes were printed, as desired, by "William W. Woodward, No. 17 Chestnut Street."

Mr. Cooper, taking his residence with Mr. Doughty, No. 352 Front Street, engaged in ministerial labors, and, on Sunday, January 6, 1799, preached a funeral sermon on the life and character of the Rev. John Dickins (which was taken down in short-hand by a Mr. Carpenter, who took down the debates in Congress), and afterward consented to its publication, giving the copy to Mrs. Dickins and her children, to be printed for their benefit. Asbury Dickins determined to put it through the press at once.

On Thursday, May 2, 1799, Mr. Cooper was with his brethren, about forty in number, in the Baltimore Annual Conference. During the session Bishop Asbury requested him to agree to engage in the book business for the Connection, and proposed to have the Conference called at an early hour (though the body had formally closed its session previously) that they might indorse the appointment of the bishop. Mr. Cooper says:

I told him it was not worth while to call the Conference, for I could not agree to engage at all; at any rate, I could not at present. So he declined calling the Conference.

On Thursday, June 6, the Philadelphia Conference was opened, and remained in session until the following Tuesday. It took action in regard to the Book Concern, of which Mr. Cooper thus speaks:

During the Conference the brethren proceeded to choose an agent for the Connection, to carry on the book business in the place of our late friend, J. Dickins. The vote, which was taken by ballot, was almost unanimous for myself—but two dissenting votes, and one of them I gave myself. Thus I was the choice of the brethren. But, ah, how I felt in agreeing to the appointment! I submitted to the desire of my brethren with much reluctance, and take it as my cross. I only engage for one year at a time.

Before the close of the Conference session the newly elected agent prepared an address "To the Preachers and Friends of the Methodist Episcopal Church," which received the indorsement of the Conference, and was circulated throughout the Church by being published in the Conference Minutes for the year 1799. It abounds in utterances of such wisdom and appositeness to the work assumed, that it is here reproduced.* It is as follows:

DEAR BRETHREN: Bishop Asbury and the Philadelphia Conference have made choice of me, as agent for the Connection, to superintend our Book Concern, as editor and general book steward; and as I have been prevailed upon, though with reluctance, to accept the appointment, I consider it my duty to address you upon the subject.

It is well understood that the book business among us is designed for the excellent purpose of spreading and cultivating moral and religious knowledge; hence we confine ourselves to the publication of books and pamphlets upon subjects of morality and divinity, more especially such as treat on experimental and practical religion. It is also known that the pecuniary profits arising from the business are appropriated to the exclusive benefit of the Connection, as an auxiliary to us in the important work of spreading the gospel of our salvation the more extensively through the world. From these considerations it must appear to be the duty of all our friends to promote

---

* See *Conference Minutes*, 12mo edit., 1799, pp. 22-24.

the Book Concern by all convenient means and religious endeavors. What can an agent do in this business without the mutual endeavors of preachers and members in selling, buying, and circulating the books? Also, it is indispensably necessary that punctuality be observed in making remittances, that the agent may be able to make his payments to the paper-makers, printers, bookbinders, etc. Every one who has money in hands due to the Connection should forward it without delay. And I hope that orders for books will be sent on; which I will endeavor to answer as soon and so far as the returns I receive will enable me to do.

In consequence of numerous drafts formerly made upon the Concern for different purposes, and the great neglect in making remittances, the business is considerably in debt, and somewhat embarrassed. When I engaged in the business I had not one dollar of cash in hand belonging to the Concern, and have received but few remittances since. There are large sums due, and I most earnestly solicit the brethren to diligence and punctuality. The business may answer a noble purpose to the Connection, provided the brethren are spirited and industrious in promoting of it. Some of our brethren have acted laudably and praiseworthily in this business. I wish the same could be said of them all.

It is my deliberate opinion that no other drafts whatever should be made on the Concern until its debts are paid, and the capital be sufficient to carry on the business without further embarrassments. O, brethren, help this important work! I also advise, in all cases of transfer of books, debts, etc., from one to another, that the brethren be regular and particular in the same; and that they give correct notice thereof to the agent here, with a receipt or certificate from the person to whom a transfer may be made. If a transfer be made at any time to an improper person, it ought to be considered that the agent here may refuse releasing the one and holding the other. In cases where it can be done, the brethren, in all exchanges of books or transfers, should settle them among themselves, and not trouble the agent with them. There have been inconveniences arising from want of attention in this matter. If one preacher leave a circuit with books in it, he should have them collected at one place, and make out an exact inventory of them; and the preacher who succeeds him should, in duty, take charge of the books, as per inventory, and advise the agent accordingly.

I have opened my accounts, and expect to make out bills, etc., in dollars and cents. This will be easier to the brethren throughout the United States; for dollars and cents are every-where the same, but pounds, shillings, and pence vary in the different States.

In brotherly love, dear brethren, I am yours affectionately,

EZEKIEL COOPER.

PHILADELPHIA, *July* 10, 1799.

On the day following the reading of the above address the Conference adjourned, and the preachers repaired to their different stations. In a few days Mr. Cooper rented a book-room, and entered upon the work assigned him. He says:

But, ah, the trouble I have in closing up and settling the old concern, and commencing the new! Were the fatigue and labor to continue as it now is, I would not carry it on for any consideration: but I hope it will be easier by and by.

In two months' time, however, another embarrassment was thrown upon him. The former tenant of the property leased by him had moved out without having paid the rent; and, as the law of the city corporation was such that any person's property found in the house abandoned under such conditions was liable for the rent, the Connection property was in danger of being seized for back rent on the house. To avoid this the agent, on Tuesday, August 13, at one o'clock P. M., "called a cart, and got a few friends to assist" him, and moved all the books and papers to another place, thereby securing them.

The interests of the Book Concern were now carried forward with earnest zeal, the editor and superintendent regarding it as his own business, to which all other ecclesiastical duties were subordinate. In September the yellow fever had again appeared in Philadelphia. "All business was stopped, and about half, or more than half, of the people were moved out." Under this condition of things there was a suspension of the printing and sale of books, etc., in the city for several weeks; the work, however, was resumed in the latter part of October, and pressed forward.

On the 6th of May, 1800, the General Conference began its session in Baltimore, Md. There were one hundred and fifteen preachers who were members thereof. The session lasted until May 20. Ezekiel Cooper was continued as superintendent of the Book Concern, and its interests were placed under the supervision of the Philadelphia Annual Conference, as before. After the adjournment of the General Conference, the Philadelphia Annual Conference was held at Smyrna, Del., beginning June 2. From thence Mr. Cooper began to visit the several Annual Conferences accessible to him, year by year, in behalf of the Book Concern. Thus having, at the close of the Philadelphia Conference, returned to Philadelphia, and spent, says he, "better than a week fixing and arranging the Connection business, during which time I got the Minutes of the General Conference printed, Wednesday, June 18, I took stage for New York Annual Conference." He remained there several days, and then came back, July 1, to Philadelphia, and engaged in forwarding "the Connection printing and book business."

During this year a serious and ugly dispute arose in the society of Methodists in Philadelphia, which also much affected Mr. Cooper, and opened up a course of opposition that finally led to the removal of the Book Concern from that city. It is here alluded to solely for the purpose of putting the reader in possession of points that will enable him to understand the import of some letters that are introduced. The first of these is from Bishop Asbury, followed by a note from Bishop Whatcoat on the same sheet of paper.

My dear Cooper: Grace and peace be with thy spirit. I have meditated a letter to you for some months. We have had a gracious season in Conference for five days. Brother Blanton is located. Stith (Meade—P.) is to preside in the State of Georgia, James Jenkins in South Carolina. Brother Blanton showed me an answer of $1,000, by John Harper. William M'Kendree, you perhaps know by this, commands in the West. John Kobler was appointed to the Richmond District, but I fear he hath failed. I heard that P. Bruce was at his father's in North Carolina. I desired him, upon his return, to see if J. Kobler was upon his station; if not, to take it himself; if Brother Kobler was in place, I desired Brother Bruce to go to Norfolk. We will do what little we can to collect for you; but we might as well climb to the moon as attempt to get some of those debts.

I thank you for the advice **given** of the middle ground. We have some time to consider upon it between this and the Yearly Conference, when it will probably be brought before the Yearly Conference; at least, we may suppose, the Presiding Elder and Elder will implead each other at the Conference.

I had no doubt but you would feel like wishing to be out of the business of book-making; but, my dear, it is not so easily done. You will have many a shot. I say in all company, when I speak, that you are deeply concerned for the interest of the Connection, and go very near the wind in all your movements for our good. You are easy of access, I have found; readily pacified by a word or a line; you are not a man of intrigue, but open, and therefore I love you. The very thought that I gave you a nomination to your appointment is enough; those that dislike me will disapprove of you. I advise you, as a friend, to retire into your own business as much as possible. I only wish that those who think hardly of you or me could, if it were right, be punished with our places they so much envy; but many would. God forbid! and we also will oppose it.

I think our Scripture Catechism is one of the best in the world, but it could be mended by you, and laid before the next Conference in the amendment. I gave the outlines to John Dickins. I think now if you propound in your own language questions such as these, What is the duty of parents? What is the duty of husbands, wives, children, ministers, rulers, subjects, masters, servants? What is the duty of Christians one to another? and so on, and answer them wholly in Scripture, it would, in my view, be most excellent. We could enforce catechising if we had a complete guide.

Thine,   F. ASBURY.

CAMDEN, January 7, 1801.

Bishop Whatcoat's note was:

MY VERY DEAR BROTHER: We spoke to the Conference about the ten dollars you reminded us of, but, do not come at it. You must set it down to the Sinking Fund. The books were spoiled and scattered. We are concerned for the peace of the Church; much prayer, patience, and forbearance, with great moderation, appear to be needed at this time. What need have we to "stand like an iron pillar strong." May the good Lord bless you, and all the Lord's people.

Thine in love,   R. WHATCOAT.

In March another letter was written to Mr. Cooper by Bishop Asbury, and illustrates the great care that servant of God exercised in his movements in regard to the Church over which he presided, and her interests. Thus he wrote:

MY VERY DEAR BROTHER: If we do for you, in return you will serve us. We wish to take the following, or a better plan, if it can be found, through Jersey:

Monday, June 8, to leave Philadelphia and preach at Clonmell, three o'clock P. M.

Tuesday, June 9, to preach at Salem, two o'clock.

Wednesday, June 10, to preach at Bethel, two o'clock.

Thursday, June 11, to preach at New Mills, three o'clock.

Friday, June 12, to preach at Emley's, two o'clock; but I must be at Joseph Hutchinson's that night.

Saturday, June 13, to preach at Brunswick, twelve o'clock; Drake's, five o'clock.

Sunday, June 14, to preach at Elizabethtown all the Sabbath.

You will consult Brother Sharp, and do the best you can. I am not able to say what places ought to be in the vacancies, but we must be at Joseph Hutchinson's and Brunswick, and Drake's and Elizabethtown, that we may come in time to the York Conference.

We could not collect any money from Thomas Bowen. According to his settlement with Jesse Lee, he holds the Connection in debt to him. Brother Whatcoat hath received but very little of your money as yet, but he has sent you one hundred and twenty dollars. Forty-nine you will be pleased to pay Sister Dickins from Henry Bradford, as a part of payment he hath obtained for land sold in North Carolina; the remnant you will enter to Brother Whatcoat's credit, as he expecteth to receive money of yours at the Virginia Conference.

100 dollars United States Bank, No. 129.

20 dollars Bank of New York, No. 334.

This small sum will be of use to you, but the money Brother Whatcoat will collect, of yours, will be of no use to him, only a burden. I am, with respect. yours, FRANCIS ASBURY.

PORTSMOUTH, *March* 27, 1801.

$100
  20
——
 120
  49 to E. Dickins.
——
  71 to R. Whatcoat.

I have enclosed the twenty dollar bill in a letter to T. Haskins for you, F. ASBURY.

The Annual Conference held in Philadelphia June 1, 1801, was brought to face the difficulty which had arisen among the Methodists in that city, and sought to compose it. The effort was not successful, however, and soon after the adjournment of the Conference a number of members withdrew in a body, and set up their worship in the old City Academy. Both preachers and members were held to be separates from the Methodist Episcopal Church. Mr. Cooper now opposed the separates, and used all his influence in upbuilding the Society at St. George's and Ebenezer. The opposition to him by reason of this became more violent, and, as they regarded him as "the leader, the counsellor, and the mainspring or organ of those they were opposing," every method that could be devised was undertaken to have him and the Book Concern removed from that city to another.

Mr. Cooper, notwithstanding the opposition, applied himself diligently to the duties before him, and kept up a correspondence with Bishop Asbury, thereby availing himself of his counsel, and keeping the Bishop in full information concerning things transpiring around him.

A third letter from the Bishop will show this.   Read the following:

CAMDEN, SOUTH CAROLINA. *December* 31, 1801.

MY VERY DEAR BROTHER: I have received your letters, for which I thank you, and for other attentions.   When we were told that the debt was paid [that is, due by the Church in Philadelphia—P.] I wondered by what mint or magic you had collected $4,000 in four months; but when we had chapter and verse the wonder ceased.   O zeal! zeal! what will it not do when made elastic by opposition!   I hope the next thing will be to purchase, as perhaps you may at a low price. or build, a house for the preachers, after more than thirty years.

I find that the book market is good in the South, and the presiding elders and preachers are very diligent.   I believe *we* need say but little.   As to Bowen and Weeks, I doubt if any settlement to purpose will ever be made.   I do not wish to meddle much in the Book Concern; we have so many cooks, and some very unskillful.   I pushed three books into the press. and I shall expect reflections as long as they are in circulation, if I am in circulation.   As a friend, I would advise you (as I am one that has eyes and ears every-where) to keep close to Fletcher's and Wesley's most excellent parts.   As to my Journals, I feel my delicacies about having them printed at all in my *lifetime;* it may only put it into the power of my enemies to abuse me, as Mr. O'Kelley has so often done; while at the same time my hands will be bound by inability or some local influences.

I am sorry to be a burden to my friends or the Connection.   I do not wish to crowd myself or the Connection with more services than they call for.   I was willing. at the request of some of my special friends. to submit an impression of the Journal to the press; 'tis true the General Conference approved it. and it was my wish it should go out in numbers; but it appeared to me that the general mind of the General Conference was that it should come out in a volume.   I have been taught to understand that a printer should point; and if he could not point he could not print.   I do not chose to print any man's Journal but my own.   My language in preaching and writing is my own—good or bad.   If you choose to send out the number, upon good paper, I shall submit; but I have been making up my mind closely to inspect, and strike out what, upon close thinking, I shall disapprove, and lay them by to be printed after my death. or to let them die with me.   About twenty pages in four months' traveling will not be a great burden to the press.   My first part was transcribed by one that did not understand my writing.

19

As to the Hymn Book, I can only say we have such a republic of critics and pointers, they will do as they please; but, I presume, if you had a thousand more to send into every district than you have sent, they would soon be sold; only let the work be done well, and there is no doubt of the sale of our books. The Presbyterians and others will purchase our books.

To the Trustees of St. George's Church in Philadelphia:

RESPECTED BRETHREN: I thank you for the attention you have manifested to me in your address, and account of payments. I rejoice exceedingly that we are just; may we also be generous, and do nothing through strife and vainglory. I hope your zeal and charity will provide a house for your preachers, and prevent a moth-eating rent. Let us pray much, and love the more; then we shall live holy and die happy. Farewell!

Since I began this letter Brother Whatcoat arrived with your letter, an apology for paper. Your pardon is granted. See, thou art made whole. It is generally granted our books are the best, intrinsically and extrinsically. Only let us keep them so.

    Yours, for Christ's sake,   FRANCIS ASBURY.

The account of the payment of the debt due by the Society in Philadelphia, which had been created under the financial administration of those who now had withdrawn, is briefly given here for the reason that the book agent, Mr. Cooper, was largely instrumental in securing the money needed therefor, though he thereby added to the growing spirit of opposition to his carrying forward the book business in that city. The separatists, during the year, bought a part of the "Old Academy" for a church, and organized a society which afterward became one of the most important and valuable of the Philadelphia Methodist Episcopal Churches—the Union Methodist Episcopal Church.

At the Philadelphia Annual Conference held in May, 1802, they became connected again with the Methodist Episcopal Church, received a preacher from the Con-

ference for their pastor, and gradually a spirit of harmony brought the two Societies into the relation of
ecclesiastical fellowship and brotherly union.

The interests of the Book Concern were still pressed
forward by Mr. Cooper, and much to his satisfaction
and that of his friend, Bishop Asbury, improvements
were made in every department. Prior to 1802 no
distinctive and separate Annual Conferences, though so
called in general parlance, existed, but the whole
Methodist territory was divided up into districts. Mr.
Cooper's power of reducing things to system now was
made manifest, and thenceforth, from 1802, the Minutes
represented the Conferences by name, and designated
the districts within the bounds of each Annual Conference. The number of Conferences was seven. 1. Western: embracing Kentucky and Holston Districts.
2. South Carolina: Georgia, Seleuda, and Camden Districts. 3. Virginia: Salisbury, Newbern, Norfolk, and
Richmond Districts. 4. Baltimore: Alexandria, Pitts-
burgh, and Baltimore Districts. 5. Philadelphia: Delaware and Eastern Shore, Philadelphia, New Jersey,
and Albany Districts. 6. New York: New York,
Pittsfield, New London, Vershire, and Canada Districts.
7. New England: Boston and Maine Districts.

Among the appointments in the Philadelphia Conference, we have the following :

Philadelphia District, Thomas Ware, Presiding Elder. Ezekiel
Cooper, Superintendent of the Printing and Book Concern. The
preachers stationed in Philadelphia and the presiding elder of the
district are appointed the book committee.

That committee was composed of Thomas Ware,
John McClaskey, and George Roberts. The following
paragraphs, apparently extracted from some report of
the Superintendent of the Book Concern, are here in-

serted as belonging to this sketch of Mr. Cooper's work
as such superintendent and editor:

The editor would suggest to the bishops and Conferences the
propriety in future of entering the return of members under the head
of each district respectively, as in the case of the stations, that
the circuits and numbers of each district may stand together. It is
morally impossible to ascertain the number in the respective States;
in sundry instances the circuits take in a part of two States, part of the
numbers being in one and part in the other. Not only so, but the returns this year, in manuscript, were so entered that the editor could not
in all cases ascertain to which of the States the circuits belonged,
and consequently he has thought it proper to print the names of the
circuits and the numbers without mentioning the States.*

It is hoped that our preachers and brethren will continue their
laudable endeavors to promote the interests of our Book Concern. It
is well known that our principal design in this business is to promote the spiritual welfare of our fellow creatures by disseminating
among them religious knowledge, that thereby they may become wiser,
and better grounded in the knowledge and love of God. And as the
pecuniary profits arising from the Book Concern are to be applied to
the support of the ministry, who are engaged night and day in
spreading the Gospel, it may be truly said our whole design in this
business is the salvation of men, for whom Christ died. O brethren! who would not endeavor to promote such a cause?

The Book Concern is in a prosperous way at present, and promises
fair to be useful to the Connection. We hope by the next General
Conference that all its debts will be discharged, and a sufficient capital established to carry it on, and to allow a handsome annuity
toward the support of the poor itinerant ministers, their wives, and
children. Your Agent in this business has paid better than $2,000
of the old debts since last General Conference, and the Concern is
very little in debt on account of any contracts made since that time;
however, we may safely say, it is now $2,000 less in debt than it
was then, so that the prospect is encouraging.

Our Hymn Book has been revised and improved, and the copy-
right secured, agreeably to the concurrent resolve of the Baltimore,
Philadelphia, and New York Conferences. We hope our friends will
particularly attend to the request of the Bishops in the preface to the
Hymn Book, and remember that the title of our Hymn Book, in

---

* Minutes taken at the several Annual Conferences, etc., 1802.

future, is to be, " The Methodist Pocket Hymn Book, revised and improved," etc. It appears that some persons attempted to take au ungenerous advantage of us in the publication of our old Hymn Book, but we hope our friends will guard against being imposed on by such publications of our books. It has been in contemplation to publish a Methodist Repository, consisting of experiences, accounts of revivals of religion, remarkable deaths, etc. It might be well for our brethren and friends to write or collect such accounts as they have knowledge of, and forward them to furnish matter for such a publication. There have been great and glorious revivals in many places, also various remarkable and interesting occurrences in the knowledge of many of our preachers and members; they might do much good by writing an account thereof to be published.*

During the Conference year of 1802, Mr. Cooper visited three Annual Conferences, and sought to advance the interests of the Church in the sphere to which he was appointed. The spirit of opposition to his remaining in Philadelphia was still increasing, and within the year became so decided that the preachers of the Philadelphia Conference, as well as some of the laymen in Philadelphia, determined, if it were possible, to have him and the Book Concern removed. One of the grounds for the advocacy of such a course was, that he had now been stationed in Philadelphia five years, and as his brother ministers were subject to more frequent removals, according to the itinerant plan, he should stand in the same relation as they to the itinerant plan of appointment. The matter was laid before the Philadelphia Annual Conference, held at Smyrna, Delaware, May 19, 1803, and there it was resolved with great unanimity that the Book Concern should be removed to Baltimore, and there be carried forward under the supervision of Mr. Cooper. He declined at once to make the change, and by that action called forth the following letter from Bishop Asbury to him, which

* Minutes, 1802.

being now given to the reader, the reasons for his declining to consent both to the will of the Philadelphia Conference and the desire of the Bishop, will be set forth. The Bishop wrote:

MY DEAR BROTHER: As the Executive of the Conference, and your friend, I think it my duty to tell you that I think it your duty, in obedience to the Conference, to move to Baltimore about the first of October. You know there have been many changes among your brethren. I hope that you also will bear your part. It is my wish, if I cannot keep the people out of contention, to save the preachers. As to any reports that are false and groundless, you can easily combat them in Baltimore as well as in Philadelphia, by word or letter.

I think of any preacher that has been stationed in Philadelphia for six or seven years, I would conclude it was time for him to be removed if he was not local, and altogether out of my power. I wish every person that can be moved to be moved, and every thing that can be done for peace and union to be done.

You are not ignorant that other preachers have been called, suspended, and some removed at a word, to serve the wishes of some dissatisfied minds. You will take your turn with others, and as there was such unanimity in the vote of the Conference, it ought to have weight with you. As an individual your going or staying is nothing to me. I have no spleen against you. I only want peace in the Societies, by any good means. I wonder why you should wish to stay where you must have had great distress of mind, and I have thought it may be the cause of your ill health.

I am most sincerely, your friend,   F. ASBURY.

SOUDERSBURG, *July* 24, 1803.

MR. COOPER'S REASONS FOR OBJECTING TO GO TO BALTIMORE.

1. Because not for the interest of the Book Concern to incur the expense and risk of moving, etc.

2. The General Conference had fixed it in Philadelphia, and given no power to the Philadelphia Conference to remove it. George Roberts, though for removal, argued against the Philadelphia Conference's taking power on them, as in case of Chartered Fund, Trustees, etc.

3. The Baltimore Conference had not been consulted, etc. Why send it out of one district into another without discipline for it?

4. I purposed giving up the business, and concluded to leave it where I found it.

5. My workmen were engaged, and under way. They would have removed if I would have engaged to have kept the business and to keep them, or engage to them the work; neither of which I could do. I did not know who would succeed me, and I could make no engagement with or for them.

6. It would have been difficult to engage workmen at Baltimore to have entered our business, and put off their former customers, unless they could have had assurances of a continuation of the work, which I could not give them under the purpose of giving up the business; and I could not give assurances for what my successor would do. Hence it would have been difficult to have got the work done fast enough.

7. The removal, at all events, would cause a great stoppage and delay in the work. And as I apprehended another stoppage at and about Conference [General Conference, 1804—P.], which would have made two stoppages, etc., instead of one, so I concluded it would be better to let the work go on and have but one stoppage, and that at and about Conference.

8. After the vote of the Conference for removal, certain persons began to boast how they had prevailed in having the business removed, etc. *They!* Was it *they* that did it? and were all these difficulties, risks, expenses, and stoppages merely to please and oblige them? I concluded this must not be. I spoke to George Roberts about their triumph, and told him I would not go if this was the case and if they continued their triumphant boast. What did Cavender say to Sharpe? "*They* to get *me* out of town had got the business fixed," etc. *They,* indeed! This as evidence of boasting, etc.

9. Some one intimated that the vote was in consequence of my statement to Conference [informant, Sargent]. This appeared calculated to fix on me the blame, if there were any, and to take it on themselves if it suited their purpose.

It was clearly seen, during the year that intervened between the session of the Philadelphia Conference of 1803 and the General Conference of 1804, that Baltimore was not the most desirable place for locating the Book Concern; and during the session of the latter body New York was fixed upon as the place therefor. Here it has been established for eighty-two years, and is the chief depository of the Methodist Episcopal Church in America. Other important measures affecting the Book Concern were adopted. The direction of the affairs of the Concern was no longer put under the supervision of any of the Annual Conferences for the years between the General Conference sessions, but was intrusted to a "Committee on the Book Concern," appointed by the General Conference to hold office for four years. The Book Agents were assigned to charges in the churches of New York and Brooklyn, and were subjected to the rule of the Conference limiting the term of a pastoral charge to two years, though the rule did not apply to their term of office in the book business. Ezekiel Cooper was re-elected as General Book Agent; and John Wilson—not Daniel, as Dr. Stevens has it in his *History of the Methodist Episcopal Church*, nor Joshua, as stated in Simpson's *Cyclopedia of Methodism*, but *John* Wilson—was elected as Assistant Book Agent. These ministers were stationed: Mr. Cooper from 1805–1806 in Brooklyn, and from 1807–1808 in New York. Mr. Wilson, 1805–1806, New York; 1807–1808, Brooklyn. In 1804, the Book Concern not having been removed before all the Conferences had been held, they were simply set forth in the Minutes of that year as follows:

NEW YORK DISTRICT: William Thacher, presiding elder.
New York: Nich. Snethen, M. Coate, S. Merwin; Ezekiel Cooper, editor and general book steward; John Wilson, assistant editor and general book steward.

Having during the latter part of the year 1804 succeeded in establishing the Concern in New York, and engaged printers, binders, and office workers, the editing of books began to go forward with renewed vigor; and though Mr. Cooper had sought to be released from the responsibilities of the position to which the Church called him, he undertook them again, and found in his associate, Rev. John Wilson, an efficient, wise, discreet, and able counsellor. As the Church has from this date an accurate and detailed statement of the Book Concern, its managers and management, and as that institution is now known and acknowledged to be one of the most trustworthy and useful book establishments in the world, the writer will close this chapter with the introduction of the following letter from Bishop Asbury to Mr. Cooper:

NEW ROCHELLE, *Friday, July* 26, 1805.

MY VERY DEAR BROTHER: I have ridden rapidly two hundred and thirty miles in six days to redeem a day to write. I think that you might, with the assistance of Brother Wilson, attend five conferences out of the seven every year. You could take Virginia, Maryland, and Pennsylvania. Reasons for this, the critical state of the bills and banks; and that the preachers can be brought to a settlement better at Conference than at any other time.

Brother Crawford is appointed to ride with me. If he can render you any service at the Western or Southern Conferences you will give orders.

I should be exceedingly glad to see Mr. Wesley's Sermons published up to the ninth and last volume this year. Then I should be pleased to see a complete set of his Journals published in America, and a set of his Appeals. It's time, after thirty-five years—it is time these were done.

I have had a thought of buying a light Jersey wagon, that I may go at the rate of the mail-stage, and visit all the towns and cities in the winter, and go to the westward in the fall; but the greatness of the expense is one difficulty, the badness of the roads another.

I give up Dr. Coke, according to his own letter, unless he should come for good. I have no unjustifiable partiality for men of any nation under heaven; I love all; they have nothing to gain or lose from me.

I have no more to do with the Book Concern than another preacher, nor so much as some of them. If I was to keep a little stage the person in company, Brother Crawford or some other, would carry a choice selection of the books of the Connection.

When any one leaveth our Connection he leaves the Conference, not me; I would not have it thought I am any thing in the business. I am pleased to feel that we are not taught to look upon it as a calamity when any one leaves us, only we grieve they should lose their first love, and give the world cause to say the Methodist preachers may be bought with money as well as others. For my part, I am glad they are gone, and so the judicious part, preachers and people, will say: let them go, and welcome. Had we not been shorn, we might have added near an hundred this year.

Perhaps it has been a trial to your mind that Conference made the additional provision for Brother Wilson. They thought themselves justifiable; they did not think it right to require Brother Cooper to give up a part of his, yet they must know that to have a family in New York must make a difference. But then it is not known how soon you may have one.

Honor! Honor! Honorable men we are; but I conclude we have sunk in insolvency in the seven conferences, according to General Conference appropriation, about $15,000, if not $20,000; yet I never saw the Connection more united and cheerful, and determined to go on while liberty, equality, and order prevails; and the work of God goeth on with increasing rapidity in every conference, district, and circuit more or less.

I should be pleased with your company to Second River on Monday, at the new church near Newark. You can write me what you think the dividend will be; as the Western Conference and South, also, will go on for the next year, but will meet within this. You can write me, South, any commands you have for me as your organ, and the president of the Conferences.

I am, as ever, thy friend,   F. ASBURY.

CHAPTER XIV.

THE METHODIST EPISCOPAL CHURCH IN PHILADELPHIA,
1799–1804.

THE details embraced in the present chapter were not connected with the historical sketch given of the Church in Philadelphia in 1796, because Mr. Cooper's pastoral relation had ceased; and what is now furnished was held by him as secondary to the Book Concern management under his care. Yet it will be seen that the work of the ministry, in its ecclesiastical sense, was by no means neglected; on the contrary, he did all that he could to upbuild the Church and to increase the power and influence of Methodism.

Reference has been made, in several instances set forth in the last chapter, to a state of disorder in the Society in the city; and a true account thereof ought to be in hands of the Church of the present age, in order that the real condition may be set forth. It will be given herein.

During the three months of ministerial service rendered by Mr. Cooper he was called by Mr. Haskins to go about forty miles into New Jersey to join him in marriage to Eliza Richards, daughter of Esquire Richards, resident at Balsto. In making the tour he spent the night at Long-a-Coming, and thus accounts for the name of that village:

I find that Long-a-Coming took its name from the circumstance of a sick or wounded man, many years ago, who was brought from Egg Harbor through the wilderness of pines; and there being no houses or water on the road for a long distance, he often complained with thirst, and they told him he could not get any till they arrived at such a place; and he would cry out: "That place is long-a-coming."

The membership in the Philadelphia Society in 1799 was: whites, 411; blacks, 211. During the latter part of the summer the preachers stationed in the city with Mr. Cooper established a preaching service to be held every Sabbath afternoon at five o'clock in the State-house yard. The congregations were very large and orderly. It continued until interrupted by the breaking out again of the yellow fever.

In April, 1800, Dr. Coke made a visit to Philadelphia and spent a week with the churches. At that time St. George's was undergoing repairs, and the doctor's ministerial services were confined to the other three churches, namely: Ebenezer (white), and Bethel and Zoar (colored), and State-house yard. The conference year closed with a loss of four white members and an increase of forty-six colored. The preachers that were appointed to the Society in Philadelphia in 1799 were Philip Bruce, Lemuel Green, and Charles Cavender. In 1800 only one person, Lawrence McCombs, was stationed there. This made it necessary for Ezekiel Cooper and the "located" ministers to perform more ministerial service than formerly, and brought them into closer association with the growing interests of the charge. The statement of this fact is due to the multitudinous friends of Mr. Cooper and to the student of Methodist history, as otherwise he would be liable to the charge of intermeddling with the administration of him who had been placed by the Conference in charge of the Society. We will now give a report of the disorder of which we have made mention, in Mr. Cooper's own statement. He says:

This summer was a trying season to me on various occasions, but particularly on account of a most disagreeable variance existing among some of our leading and most respectable members of Society, which drew almost the whole Society into a party spirit on the one side or the other; and, unfortunately, Brother McCombs, the stationed preacher, entered deeply into a party spirit on one side of the subject of dispute, which drew the great displeasure of the others against him: consequently, his influence and usefulness was destroyed among the others. He struck in with those who were considered the most wealthy and respectable members, but who were opposed by the poor, who had the majority of members on their side. Thus the wealthy and respectable minority were on one side, and the poor majority on the other. It became a very serious question which should prevail: wealth and worldly respectability on the one side, or the majority on the other?

I for a long time endeavored to stand neutral, so that I might, if possible, contribute toward an accommodation or compromise. On sundry questions of moment I kept my judgment to myself, not letting either side know what was my opinion. In other questions I took a middle ground, agreeing partly with one and partly with the other; because I saw that each party was disposed to strain the questions altogether on their own side, and in their own favor, right or wrong; and, consequently, in my opinion, ran into errors on both sides; therefore, as I considered them partly wrong and partly right on those questions, I thought in conscience, prudence, and duty that I was bound to agree to the right and disagree to the wrong on either side; whether with respect to the merits of the question itself, or with respect to the spirit and manner of treating it, or with respect to the apparent design or end they had in view to accomplish. Thus in the same question I sometimes agreed as to the merits of the question, but disagreed with the spirit or manner of managing it; at other times disagreed as to the merits of the case, but thought favorable as to the intentions and designs. Other times, in complex and complicated cases, I could approve of one part: but, at the same time, disapprove of the other part of the case. However, I resolved to follow the dictates of my own judgment, and not suffer myself to be so led into the spirit of party, as to disapprove altogether on the one side, to approve altogether on the other, right or wrong. No! not if all the Society should be displeased with me. Thus I strove to keep the middle ground, which, I thought, was the right and impartial ground There appeared to me to be wrongs on both sides which I did not and could not approve. But in some points I believed the one side right, and in other points I believed the other side to be right.

I still, for a considerable time, lived in hopes that they might be prevailed on to come to an amicable settlement of their differences; but the further they went the less hope I had. At times I would almost despair of an agreement or union ever taking place; then, again, I would get a little hope. I resolved to try after union and peace, and to follow after it, so far as I could, with a clear judgment. But ah! at length many of the warm, fiery, and intemperate minds which had more zeal and prejudice than wisdom and prudence—more of self-will and passion than brotherly kindness and Christian moderation—more of self-importance than self-knowledge—became extremely offended with me, for no other cause that I know of than because I ventured to oppose them wherein I believed them to be wrong. They were astonished at me. The wealthy and respectable were surprised at me to take part with, what they called, the poor and ignorant part of the Society against them; and the others lamented and were surprised that I did not give them a more decided support in opposition to, what they considered, the overbearing measures of what they called "the great men." I told them it was but a small matter to be judged of man's judgment. I did not intend that any man or men should be the rule of my judgment, rich or poor; and that I did not mean to devote myself to the one side or the other on principles of party, and intended to know no party further than I believed the cause right.

At length. on some measures of Mr. McCombs, the stationed preacher, in breaking several class-leaders who differed with him in opinion, etc., which Mr. Everett, the presiding elder, thought a stretch of power, a difference took place with them ; and as the stationed preacher was stiff in his measures, and would not yield to the presiding elder in certain matters which he thought right, the elder resolved to move him to another station in the district, and to place Mr. Sneath in the city to take the charge and government of the Society. Mr. McCombs did not go to the circuit to which he was appointed, but Mr. Sneath came to the city and took the charge according to Mr. Everett's direction.

Now matters appeared to be less likely to be made up than ever. Some of the local preachers, of what was called the respectable party, refused to take appointments from, or to preach under, the administration of Mr. Sneath. They also, together with a number of other members, declined coming to the Church; some came not at all, and others came very seldom. My hopes of a compromise were now almost gone; yet I made a proposition that there should be a committee of an equal number on both sides appointed to devise a plan for the restoration of peace and unity, and that the terms and conditions agreed upon should not be in anywise contrary to the Discipline of the Church, and that, when agreed upon, it should be laid before the presiding eider for his approbation, which being given, all parties should agree and restore peace. But this proposition was not agreed to. It was particularly opposed by Mr. McCombs and his party. The presiding elder had assured me, that if the two parties would agree on terms of peace he would submit to them, provided the terms were agreeable to the Discipline of the Church.

However, it appeared plainly that no terms would do except the elder would reinstate Mr. McCombs to the charge and government of the Church, and that the preachers and members would agree to give up to certain views and wishes of what was called the respectable party. I now began to see that the dispute would end in a division. I could see no prospect of a compromise whatever, and lost all hope of a settlement. And, indeed, I more than ever disapproved of the temper and spirit of the party called the wealthy and respectable party. They appeared determined to submit to no terms whatever, excepting on certain conditions of their own proposing, and which the other party would not agree to; and it really appeared unreasonable that one party should be the sole arbiters, and exclusively point out and fix the certain terms of agreement. They also —numbers of them—gave way to such bitterness of spirit, and to such an abusive practice of evil-speaking and of persecution, that I, more than ever, was convinced that their motives were not pure and that their designs were not good. I further considered myself more than ever in duty bound to oppose them with respect to their leading measures, and particularly to oppose the principle and spirit which appeared to govern them, and I took measures and made arrangements accordingly. Not from a principle of party or passion, but, in my judgment, the good of the Church and the interest of religion required it of me. Of course, I was now considered by them as decidedly in favor of the poor, and, as they called them, the ignorant part of the Society.

I shall now consider myself as with the poor, and opposed to what was called the rich; and they were pleased to call me the leader, the counselor, and the mainspring or organ of those they were opposed to. Nevertheless, I do not know that I changed my opinion as to one point that I had before made up my judgment upon. But new measures and procedures among them, and the spirit and temper existing among them, compelled me to oppose them for the true interest of the Church. They set up opposite meetings in private houses, and held meetings in the jail, etc., and refused attending our regular meetings.

In the midst of this business a work of religion broke out among us, which the others opposed with much severity, and endeavored to make it be believed that it was a delusion, etc. This still appeared worse and worse in them. They found they could not prevail, having the presiding elder, Mr. Sneath, myself, the Quarterly Meeting Conference, and the majority of the Society against them; they resolved to carry their measures to the next Annual Conference, by way of protest against the presiding elder and the Quarterly Conference. They accordingly wrote off to the Bishops, who were in the South. The others wrote also, and the business lay in an unsettled way till Conference.

At Conference, in the spring of 1801, the business was brought forward, but the Conference revoked nothing that had been done. Mr. Everett, the elder, and Mr. McCombs made up, and the Conference requested the Bishops to write a letter to the members, recommending them on all sides to drop the dispute, and return to peace and quietude. The decision of the Conference and the letter of the Bishops gave additional offense to the dissatisfied party, and they in a body withdrew, and became a separate body from the Methodist Church. They now set up their worship in the old City Academy, having their separate preachers and members.

When those dissatisfied members withdrew they left the church in debt near $3,000, which themselves had principally contracted before they gave up, they having had the management of the temporal affairs of the Church. It was now supposed, and intimated by those who withdrew, that we should never be able to pay the debt, and that the church would be sold by the creditors, and that they would buy it, etc., etc. Nay, the stone-cutter told me that some of them had advised him to sue for his money. This was strange work; but I was more surprised when I was informed that some of them wished the church to be sold: then I thought it no wonder for them to advise the creditors to sue. However, there was no suit commenced against us, but in less than a year we made up the whole amount of the money, and paid off the whole debt against the church. Before the following Conference we raised more than $4,000, paid the old debt, and supported two preachers. The ground-rent had not been paid for two years. We also insured $6,000 on the church, from fire and loss by fire, for seven years, which had never been insured. We also proceeded and finished the Ebenezer Church, which had not been plastered, neither had galleries been put up, although it had been built for many years. So that we did more than used to be done when the rich and great were with us.

Whatever cause this was owing to I choose not at present to decide upon. But certainly we felt no disadvantage or loss as to temporal supplies. And as to the work of religion, it went on gloriously. There were about sixty withdrew from the church, and about four hundred joined us, so that we lost nothing in numbers. There never had been so great a revival in Philadelphia before. It was remarkable that the work broke out after the division took place in fact, and the dissatisfied people had refused to come to the church. This showed the goodness of God, and was, no doubt, owing in part to some secondary cause which I feel backward to decide upon.

At the Conference in the spring of 1802, it was agreed upon to give the separates a preacher upon such honorable terms as they and the Bishops might agree upon, as they now had purchased a part of the old Academy for their worship. I did not oppose this measure, though, I confess, I have very little faith that it will work well. However, I calmly wait to see the issue of the experiment, and sincerely wish it may terminate well. But it will be a long time before certain individuals can be brought to any degree of unity or fellowship. Nay, I doubt whether they ever will. I wish I had more ground to believe that there would be a good understanding between the two Societies. It is my intention not to obstruct, but try to promote, peace. O may the Lord bring good out of all these things!

The above extract from Mr. Cooper's Journal will serve to explain to the reader the numerous allusions made in letters heretofore given concerning the state of affairs in the Philadelphia Society, and also the reason for naming two charges as being in Philadelphia in the Conference Minutes of 1802. Under question 12, "What numbers are in Society?" the answer for Philadelphia is: "Philadelphia, whites, 721; colored, 456. Academy, whites, 102."* No such representation

* See Annual Conference Minutes, 1802, p. 11.

is made of any other city, though at that time New
York had a larger number of churches, and required
more pastors to supply them. The union of the two
Societies having been effected at that Conference, the
distinction does not appear in the Minutes for several
following years. This Academy Society—Whitefield's
Academy—having now laid aside their weapons of
warfare against the Methodist Episcopal Church,
founded, this year, the Union Church in Philadelphia,
which has since grown up to be one of the most important charges in that city. In 1804 the total membership
in the city was, whites, 821; colored, 647, an increase,
notwithstanding their difficulties, in four years of 804
members.

CHAPTER XV.

PRESIDING ELDERSHIP IN THE METHODIST EPISCOPAL CHURCH.

THIS office, which really was introduced with the establishment of the Methodist Episcopal Church in America, did not assume its distinctive feature of separation from any local pastoral charge, and supervision of a district including several pastoral charges, until after the session of the General Conference of 1792. Prior to that time, the elders of the Church for several years had, for the most part, no circuit or station, as had their brethren who had not attained to this office, but were supervisors over two or more circuits, mainly with a view to the administering of the sacraments to their congregations. The Annual Conference Minutes of 1785 reported twenty elders in the Church. In 1786 there were twenty-four elders; in 1787, twenty-five. In 1788 the districts were enlarged; so that the number of elders was decreased to twenty-two.

In 1789 the title of presiding elder was for the first time set forth in the Annual Conference Minutes, and was adopted, apparently, in order to designate the persons who should meet with the Bishops in Council, which it was agreed by the Conferences was to be held at Cokesbury, on the 1st of the following December. Be this as it may, the title was dropped the following year, and not used again until 1797. To state this matter clearly, it is deemed expedient to refer here to the action of the several Annual Conferences of 1789, as published in the Annual Minutes before the session of the Council. The plan laid before the Conferences, and adopted by a majority of the preachers, contained the following:

Quest. 16. Whereas, the holding of general conferences on this extensive continent would be attended with a variety of difficulties, and many inconveniences to the work of God; and whereas, we judge it expedient that a Council should be formed of chosen men out of the several districts, as representatives of the whole Connection, to meet at stated times: in what manner is this Council to be formed, what shall be its powers, and what further regulations shall be made concerning it? *

The answer to the first question was:

Ans. 1.   Our bishops and presiding elders shall be the members of this Council; provided that the members who form the Council be never fewer than nine.   And if any unavoidable circumstance prevent the attendance of a presiding elder at the Council, he shall have authority to send another elder out of his own district to represent him; but the elder so sent by the absenting presiding elder shall have no vote in the Council without the approbation of the bishop or bishops and presiding elders present.   And if, after the above-mentioned provisions are complied with, any unavoidable circumstance, or any contingency, reduce the number to less than nine, the bishop shall immediately summon [enough of] such elders as do not preside to complete the number.

Dr. Emory, in his valuable *History of the Discipline*, incorrectly said, "The title" (Presiding Elder) " does not occur in the Annual Minutes till 1797." The persons designated in 1789 as *Presiding Elders* were Richard Ivey, Reuben Ellis, Edward Morris, John Tunnell, James O'Kelly, Phillip Bruce, Nelson Reed, Richard Whatcoat, Henry Willis, Lemuel Green, James O. Cromwell, Freeborn Garrettson, Francis Poythress.

This is the only instance in the history of the Methodist Episcopal Church until 1797 when such a clas-

---

* The above is from the "Minutes" taken at the several Conferences of the Methodist Episcopal Church in America, for the year 1789. New York: Printed by William Ross, in Broad Street. MDCCLXXXIX.

sification of appointments was made, thus designating
the persons who were to compose the Council ordered.
The arrangement was carried out. The first Council,
that of 1789, was, besides Bishop Asbury, composed of
eleven members, all designated elders; but of that
number nine were *presiding* elders, one elder, Joseph
Everett, in place of Richard Whatcoat, *presiding* elder,
and John Dickins, also an elder and book steward, in
place of Henry Willis, *presiding* elder. Among the
measures adopted by that body, it was determined that
the members of the Council for 1790 should be composed of the most experienced elders in the Connection, who should be elected in the Annual Conferences
by ballot, and the title of the tract containing an account of the proceedings of that body was:

Minutes taken at a Council of the Bishops and delegated Elders of
the Methodist Episcopal Church, held at Baltimore, in the State of
Maryland, December 1, 1790.

The growing demands of the work in all the Conferences called loudly for a large supply of elders to ad-
minister the ordinances, and to exercise full clerical
supervision over the local Societies. The number was
soon increased. While in 1789 there were thirty—seventeen over the districts, thirteen on circuits and stations—in 1790 there were sixty-seven, twenty of whom
were presiding elders. In 1791, out of sixty-two elders,
eighteen were over districts. In 1792, out of seventy-
eight, eighteen.

At the General Conference of 1792, begun in Baltimore, November 1, the office of presiding elder was
distinctly and formally recognized and established,
and its duties defined. As some of the preachers
doubted whether the bishops had power to appoint
such an office or officer in the Church, the Confer-

ence determined, says Rev. Jesse Lee, that there should be presiding elders, and that they should be chosen, stationed, and changed by the bishop. However, a new rule was formed respecting them, as follows: "The bishop shall not allow' an elder to preside in the same district more than four years successively." His duty was to travel and preach through his district; to take charge of all the Methodist preachers therein; to change, receive, or suspend the traveling preachers within his jurisdiction in the absence of a bishop; to be present, as far as practicable, at all the quarterly meetings; and, in the absence of a bishop, to preside over the annual conference of his district, performing all the duties of the episcopal office save that of ordination.

The spirit of those who doubted the propriety of intrusting the appointment of presiding elders solely to the bishop was afterward manifested in the effort to establish a rule making it the duty of the Annual Conferences to elect their presiding elders by ballot. This was agitated, more or less, in the nine succeeding sessions of the General Conference, and at times created intense emotion. The subject was informally and privately discussed among the members of the General Conferences of 1796 and 1800, but in 1804 a motion was introduced into the Conference to make the office elective, and was warmly discussed. Allusion to the whole question is made in the following letter written to Ezekiel Cooper during the pendency of the motion :

MY BROTHER: He that ruleth over man should be just. I am deeply sensible of the difficulties that will always attend my speaking in, or entering into the debates of, either a General or Yearly Conference. If I have gained any thing by serving you in America for thirty-three years it is your confidence and affection.

I wish some person may, when the debate comes to elders, or [to] one that has the charge of circuits, changing class leaders, etc., that the characters and standing of these men may be considered. Then let it be [shown] that all the men upon that floor are presiding elders, as having charges of districts, circuits, towns, or stations.

The elders of stations say it is their right of office to rule. Who is lord over them? a few men a thousand miles distant may write to them. The presiding elders have given up their right of a station, or of a circuit, to be at the will of another. They hold their appointment four years, or during pleasure—the pleasure of the episcopacy—and great displeasure of the circuit eldership—at least of some of them. I conclude they have beaten these presiding elders, being Romans, untried, uncondemned. I hoped it was for correction, but I am now assured it was, in some, designed for destruction. These presiding elders have not asked this office; they have said: We are not fit for the office in our own estimation. The episcopacy say: Fit, perfectly fit! Who is fit? A sense of your own unfitness will make you diffident, humble, and diligent.

The elders of stations—what I would call local presiding elders—in towns, cities, and circuits, do not stand at the will or at the charge of another as to office, go where they may. In short, every deacon that has a charge—every elder that has the charge of a station or circuit—is a presiding elder in a sense; and there would be no help for the greatest abuses of power were it not for the interposition of presiding elders and quarterly meetings. I beg you will state the case of those ejected leaders; many will know whom you mean.

  I am,   F. ASBURY.

I think of all the men in the connection we ought to guard against these office-right men, these local presiding elders for three or four years in a town, or that can change or suspend leaders of twenty or thirty years' standing; but let it be known for what fault: are they erroneous or are they immoral? Then expel them.

Henry Willis is called a local preacher by some, but how many miles has he rode in the year, attending every other Sabbath at Fredericktown? Thirty miles a day; a man so afflicted as he is! Mark that!

In 1808 Ezekiel Cooper and Joshua Wells introduced a motion before the General Conference in its quadrennial session, to make " An elective presiding eldership."

After a free discussion it was defeated.* Again in 1812 it was discussed warmly for two days; but the advocates thereof were defeated by three votes. It came up again in the General Conference of 1816— was "elaborately debated, but lost." †

We shall now lay before the reader a thorough and more minute statement of this question, for the reasons that the Church ought to be in possession of these facts, and that our historians have not followed the investigation further than down to the year 1816.

The General Conference convened in Baltimore, Md., in May, 1820, had been in session only a few days before the Rev. Timothy Merritt offered a resolution that the presiding eldership be made elective. The writer has before him a paper prepared by the Rev. Ezekiel Cooper, and designed originally to be issued from the press, but withheld, probably to avoid an increase of the excitement which prevailed throughout the Church after the adjournment of the General Conference. Its publication now will exert no disturbing influence, as the question has been settled for sixty years or more. It is as follows:

'A brief narrative of the proceedings and occurrences at the General Conference of the Methodist Episcopal Church in the month of May, A.D., 1820, at Baltimore, relative to the question: "By whom are the presiding elders to be chosen?" and which incidentally involved the question of the resignation of the Rev. Joshua Soule, bishop elect, and consequently prevented his consecration or ordination to the office of superintendent; chiefly from notes taken down in writing at and during the time of the General Conference by one of the members, to prevent and to correct any misunderstandings or misrepresentations upon that subject.

Be it known, and well remembered, that at an early period of the General Conference the Rev. Timothy Merritt, a delegate from

---

* See Stevens's *History of the Methodist Episcopal Church*, vol. iv, p. 440.
† *Ibid.*, pp. 452, 454.

New England Conference, proposed in his place as a member of the General Conference a resolution, that in the answer to the question, "By whom are the presiding elders to be chosen?" it be inserted, "By the Annual Conferences." Whereupon one of the Bishops intimated to him a desire that the said motion or resolution should not then be acted upon, inasmuch as a compromise was contemplated to harmonize the views and to conciliate and meet the wishes of the brethren on that subject. Upon which the said T. Merritt consented to withhold his motion or resolution for a few days, to give time for accommodation, if any was seriously intended by those who differed with him on the question. After some days he received a note from the said Bishop, letting him know that there was no compromise to be expected. Whereupon the said T. Merritt, being informed that an accommodation was not to be expected, after some deliberation and consultation with some of his brethren brought his motion or resolution forward: that the Annual Conferences should choose or elect their own presiding elders, who were to rule and govern the brethren in their several districts. The question being under discussion for some time—and as many as eighteen members having spoken on the subject, nine on each side, for and against the resolution—and considerable excitement having been raised, which appeared unfavorable to the unity and peace of Christian brethren, it was moved by Ezekiel Cooper, and seconded by John Emory, to lay the resolution in debate on the table until next morning, to give time for cool and calm deliberation, and to afford an opportunity to propose another resolution, which had for its object a conciliatory course, to harmonize and accommodate the views of brethren. This being agreed to, then a resolution was moved by the said Ezekiel Cooper, and seconded by the said John Emory, that at each Annual Conference, after ascertaining the number of presiding elders wanted, the bishops should nominate three times the number wanted, and out of such nominations the Conferences should elect the presiding elders by ballot, without debate. This, as a middle course, was disapproved of by some of the friends of T. Merritt's resolution; but they agreed to submit to it for the sake of conciliation. It was, however, warmly and irritatingly opposed by some of the other side, who appeared determined to yield to no accommodation; nothing would do for them but that the Bishops, independent of any control by the Conferences, should have the absolute power to choose and appoint and remove the presiding elders at pleasure. After this resolution had been opposed by some and advocated by others for a considerable time, it apparently gained ground, and was in a way of probable success. At length it was laid on the table to make room for another resolution, to give the business a different direction, which was first proposed and read by Stephen G. Roszel, and then moved by N. Bangs and seconded by William Capers, and carried. [That motion was] to appoint a committee of six, three on each side of the question, to confer with the Bishops upon the subject, and to report the next day whether any, and if any what, alterations might be made to reconcile the wishes of the brethren upon this subject. The Bishops themselves appointed the committee, who were Ezekiel Cooper, Nathan Bangs, and John Emory on the one part, for the election of presiding elders by the Conferences, and Stephen G. Roszel, Joshua Wells, and William Capers on the other part, for the Bishops choosing them independently of the Conferences.

The said committee accordingly met in the evening and conferred with the three Bishops, William McKendree, E. George, and R. R. Roberts; but that evening they made up no report. The next day the committee met again, and made up a report, which was, in the afternoon, brought before the Conference by Ezekiel Cooper, the chairman of the said committee, and introduced in substance nearly as follows, namely: The committee appointed to confer with the Bishops upon the subject of electing the presiding elders, and directed to report this day "whether any, and if any what, alterations might be made to conciliate the wishes of the brethren," beg leave now to report: That they have had a free conversation with the three Bishops; one of whom expresses himself unfavorable to any change, but appeared desirous of conciliation and seemed unwilling to oppose accommodation, and did not specifically object to a compromise; however, he did not express any opinion or wish, for or against, any particular terms of accommodation, as if disposed to leave it with the other Bishops, the Committee, and the General Conference. Another of the Bishops expressly and frankly admitted and acknowledged that he was in favor of accommodation, and wished a compromise upon the general principles of the resolution offered by Ezekiel Cooper and John Emory, now lying on your table, for the Bishops to nominate three times the number wanted, and the Conferences to elect out of such nomination. The other Bishop as frankly acknowledged that he was decidedly in favor of the Conferences having a voice in the choice or election of the presiding elders, and believed that an alteration or change of the present rule was expedient and proper. On principles of accommodation, he inclined to the opinion that it would be better for the Conferences, by ballot, to nominate three times the number wanted, and the bishops to choose the presiding elders out of such nomination; but for conciliation he would agree to the opinion in favor of the nomination by the Bishops and the election by the Conference. So that it appears conclusively that two of the three bishops are decidedly in favor of the principle of the resolution on your table, for the sake of accommodation as a conciliatory course, and to promote peace, harmony, and unity; and the other Bishop expressed no direct opposition to the course.

Therefore, your committee have unanimously agreed, by and with the earnest advice especially of one of the bishops, (E. G.,) and the concurrent agreement of another, (R. R. R.,) to recommend the adoption of the following resolutions, signed with all our names, interchangeably, as knowing no party in the present stage of the question, as the mutual act and unanimous decision of us all jointly, namely:

" *Resolved.* 1. That whenever in any Annual Conference there shall be a vacancy or vacancies in the office of presiding elder, in consequence of his period of service of four years having expired, or the bishop wishing to remove any presiding elder, or by death, resignation. or otherwise, the bishop or president of the Conference having ascertained the number wanted from any of those causes, shall nominate three times the number; out of which the Conference shall elect by ballot, without debate, the number wanted. Provided, when there is more than one wanted, not more than three at a time shall be nominated, nor more than one at a time elected. Provided, also, that in case of any vacancy or vacancies in the office of presiding elder, in the interval of any Annual Conference, the bishop shall have authority to fill the said vacancy or vacancies, until the ensuing Annual Conference.

" *Resolved,* 2. The presiding elders be and are hereby made the advisory council of the bishop, or president of the Conference, in stationing the preachers.

E. COOPER,	J. WELLS,
S. G. ROSZEL,	J. EMORY,
N. BANGS,	W. CAPERS."

The above resolutions each of the committee pledged himself to support as the act and deed of them all jointly; and this was agreeably to the earnest request of Bishop George, who was present when the report was agreed upon and signed. The report was opposed by a few; but the resolutions, as reported, were adopted by a majority of sixty-one to twenty-five votes—considerably more than two thirds; and it was now supposed that the subject, by mutual agreement, in harmony and peace was put to rest. It was now apparent that more love, unity, and brotherly-kindness prevailed than at any other period during the sitting of the Conference. The writer of this narrative knows it to be a fact, that certain members who had been pointedly opposed to each other's views, and that to the wounding of each other's feelings very seriously, now held out the olive-branch of peace to one another in brotherly congratulations; that each had yielded to the other some points which they had wished to have been carried, but had given them up in order to meet their brethren on the middle ground—the happy medium—of condescending to one another, in order to strengthen the bonds of union.

But, unfortunately, this pleasing state of things continued only a few days, when the senior superintendent, Bishop McKendree, came into Conference, which he seldom attended on account of indisposition, and, with an apparent distress and painful displeasure in his appearance and in his speech, he addressed the Conference in a melancholy and alarming introduction, by observing he was the bearer of bad or sad tidings, and had a disagreeable communication to make, etc. After a number of preliminary observations verbally made, tending to excite surprise and alarm, as though some awful intelligence was about to be divulged, and which made some of the preachers, in emphatic whispers, ask each other, with much pathos and apparent solicitude, "What is the matter? What is it? What does he allude to?" He presented a paper addressed to the Episcopacy, from J. Soule, bishop elect, which was read in open Conference, signifying, in plain terms, that if he was consecrated and set apart to the office of superintendent or bishop in the Church, he would not hold himself bound to be governed by the decision and resolution of the General Conference relative to the nomination and election of presiding elders, and substantially protested against the resolution and rule passed by the Conference as, in his opinion, unconstitutional, and that he could not, in conscience, execute or comply with it. Thus as bishop elect only, and a delegate in the Conference, protesting, in fact, against the decision of considerably more than two thirds of the General Conference, and which had received the full approbation of two thirds of the bishops—that is, two out of three had approved the resolution, and the third had allowed the report of the committee to be signed without expressing positive opposition—and now the bishop elect, before his consecration, comes forward, supported by the senior bishop, to overthrow or put at defiance the authority of more than two thirds of the General Conference.

This produced a great sensation, much excitement, and surprise. The paper containing the protest, being addressed to the Episcopacy, though read to the Conference, was not suffered to remain in possession of the Conference, but was withdrawn by the senior bishop, who subjoined a number of remarks of his own in support of the doctrine advanced by the bishop elect: intimating, in plain terms, that he knew of no tribunal to test and determine the constitutionality of the proceedings of the General Conference, excepting the Episcopacy; and recommended the repeal or suspension of the rule for the election of presiding elders at least for four years, declaring it, in his opinion, unconstitutional, and not obligatory on the bishops to enforce or submit to it. This, in the estimation of many, was a high and unjustifiable ground for a bishop and bishop elect to take. But, even if the doctrine were correct, two out of three of the Episcopacy had admitted the act to be a constitutional one, and, therefore, settled. However, even the Pope, with all his great power, holds himself bound to yield to the decision of a General Council; and hence it was that Luther and others appealed from the Pope to a General Council.

It was, however, soon discovered that the opinion and influence of the senior bishop, in support of the doctrine advanced by the bishop elect, produced a change in the minds of a number who had voted on the conciliatory plan for the election of presiding elders, and that a purpose was formed to reconsider and overset, if possible, all that was done. Therefore, in the afternoon of the same day, a resolution was brought forward by Daniel Ostrander, seconded by James Smith, requesting the Superintendents to postpone the ordination or consecration of J. Soule, the bishop elect, until he had given satisfactory explanations to the Conference. The bishop elect declared he had no explanations to give, but had said what he meant, and meant what he said; and renewed his declaration, which went, as was conceived, to put the General Conference and their resolutions at defiance, if they did not comport with his opinion and constructions of the constitutionality of what was done. Some members expressed themselves dissatisfied at the pertinacious adherence of the bishop elect to his protest and declaration that he had no explanation to give, and the resolution requesting a postponement of his ordination until an explanation be given was withdrawn by the mover, in order to take some other course for redress and safety. Immediately a motion was made by John Collins to reconsider the resolutions of the Conference on the election of presiding elders, with the avowed intention to reverse or suspend what had been done; upon which a disagreeable debate ensued, in the course of which a number of inflammatory observations were made, which were considered unkind, ungenerous, and illiberal, bearing a threatening aspect, and somewhat insulting toward those who wished a reform, and thought it was proper to curtail the bishops' power in some degree. They declared they would try strength so long as one hair was left in the head, and were determined to do away what had been done, and return to the old plan, etc.; thereby setting at defiance the feelings of others, and the solemn pledge of conciliation mutually entered into, and that under the apparent dictate or influence of a bishop elect and the senior bishop. After a warm, confused debate, which produced great excitement, tending to sow the seeds of discord and to impair and destroy the peace and union of brethren, the question for reconsideration was taken by ballot, and lost. [Here let it be remarked, that at one time during the debate the question was attempted, but failed.] It was then hoped that the matter would rest, and not be agitated any more, and that peace would again be restored. But our hopes were disappointed.

The bishop elect and some others, as coadjutors to the senior bishop, in their great efforts to maintain an undue episcopal power appeared to have exerted all their ingenuity and influence in and out of the Conference; and it appeared they had gained over at least twenty members who had voted for the election of presiding elders on the compromise agreed upon; and now these very men, in opposition to their own votes and in opposition to the solemn pledge which some of them had entered into to support the measure, now turned round, under certain influences, and were determined to overset all that was done by the General Conference, even at the risk of producing a division in the Connection, and in violation of good faith in breaking the truce or covenant of peace virtually entered into. Under these circumstances two protests had been prepared and signed; the one, against the alarming doctrine set up in support of the episcopal power—that the bishops had authority to overthrow and put at defiance the decisions of a General Conference, under a pretense of unconstitutionality which they assumed the right of determining; the other, against the consecration of the bishop elect, provided he persisted in maintaining a doctrine so repugnant to the prerogatives, rights, and privileges of the Conferences, and so replete with evil and ruinous consequences to the ecclesiastical and evangelical rights and liberties of the Church in all its membership; which was insufferable, and not to be submitted to by a free people who intended to maintain their liberties in a free country and a free Church. These protests were signed by many, and ready to be used if occasion demanded it. E. Cooper and Martin Ruter gave two of the bishops information that such a protest was prepared and would, probably, be entered if they proceeded; and E. Hedding gave the bishop elect information of the protest against his consecration, and that, under the circumstances, it would be entered against him. The consecration was delayed a few days, and at length the bishops resolved not to ordain or consecrate him in the public congregation, but to perform the ceremony in the Conference; and they announced it in Conference and appointed the hour. Whereupon the bishop elect gave in his resignation, assigning as a reason that he was informed there was a protest prepared to be entered against his consecration. It was resolved by Conference that his resignation lie on the table, and not be acted on till the next day, to give time for cool reflection and calm deliberation. The succeeding day it was called up for consideration. By a small majority of the Conference it was voted that he be permitted, and is at liberty, to withdraw his resignation, if he chooses. But for sundry reasons, pretty well understood, he declined withdrawing it. It was then moved and resolved by the Conference that his resignation be accepted and received, and so entered on the Journals. Thus closed the business of the bishop elect by his own resignation; and with this the protests were of no further use, and they were laid aside and not presented at all. But, nevertheless, the trouble was not ended. Stephen G. Roszel, the zealous and active leader of the party so much determined on supporting the episcopal prerogatives, and so much resolved against the right of the Conferences to elect their own presiding elders, formed a combination to make one bold effort more to overthrow or suspend what the Conference had done on that subject. And although he had pledged himself, as a member of the Committee of Compromise, and engaged, in the presence of Bishop George, with every other member of the Committee, to support the resolutions; yet now he had turned round, with two others of the Committee, J. Wells and W. Capers, to do away or suspend what they had engaged to support. A paper being prepared among the party, in and out of Conference, under such various influences and considerations as they were capable of using and urging to produce an excitement to serve the purpose, they prevailed with forty-five members (taking their own words for it) to sign the paper, which may be considered, according to their own declaration, their solemn league and covenant to suspend the new rule which provided for the election of presiding elders. Having their forty-five pledged on their paper, obtained in a strange way and painful to detail, which was now a bare majority of the Conference and no more, a resolution was moved by Edward Cannon to suspend the Conciliatory Resolutions or law of the General Conference respecting the election of presiding elders, and advising or directing the bishops to act under the old rule until the next General Conference. This course was objected to as out of order, for it could not be suspended without reconsideration; and they had moved for a reconsideration and lost it; and, of course, it was out of order to reconsider and suspend what the Conference had previously done unless they first obtained a vote of Conference for reconsideration; and the Conference had decided by a vote against the reconsideration. But they had their forty-five names on paper who were pledged and bound to support the measure before it was moved in Conference; and having thus obtained their majority in covenant, they appeared determined to press and force it through, whether in or out of order, right or wrong. In vain was urged the unfairness and irregularity of the procedure in obtaining and procuring their boasted majority, as they had done, by prevailing on members of the Conference to give a written pledge, in a private way, to support a measure before it was publicly debated or even moved on the floor of Conference, and that in defiance of the decision of the Conference against the reconsideration; also, in vain was it urged that it was out of order and contrary to the established rules and general usages of deliberative bodies and of our own particular rules of order in General Conference. At every point they had their forty-five men to decide —for they had resolved to carry their purpose.

An indefinite postponement was called for, but rejected. A postponement for one day was requested, to give time for reflection and deliberation, that the Conference might not act in a case of so much importance under such excitement and apparent confusion and disorder; but their forty-five men, all marshaled at their post, would not allow a postponement at all; no, not for one night nor for an hour! The time for regular adjournment by the rules of the house arrived, and an adjournment was called for, which was "always in order;" but their forty-five members refused to adjourn; and they moved and carried a resolve that the Conference would not rise till the vote on the suspension was taken. When they discovered that several in the opposition wanted to speak and be heard against the suspension before the vote was taken, then they moved and called for the previous question. In vain did some of the members request and entreat to be heard in opposition to the suspension. They even were answered by being told it was useless to say any thing more; they would not be convinced, and wanted to hear no more, and exultingly proclaimed they had their forty-five — which they knew was a majority — and were determined to suspend the new rule, and resolved on closing all further debate or argument by the previous question; which they insisted on and carried, and thus exultingly "put the opposition to silence," in defiance of every plea and request to be heard. And then the main question was forced upon the minority and carried, in what was conceived to be an unjust and arbitrary manner, and an outrage upon order, rights, and privileges. Thus at all hazards, risking all consequences, and in violation of a mutual compromise entered into by parties to conciliate each other's views and wishes, the forty-five members, by strength and power, the evening only before the Conference rose, and in the absence of sundry members who were opposed to their proceedings, disregarding the arguments, the feelings, the rights, and the privileges of their brethren, forced upon the Conference their own pre-determined purposes, suspending the resolution, apparently under the influence, control, and direction of prelatical influence, and in subservient compliance with episcopal dictation or control, for the purpose of supporting and maintaining the power and authority of the bishops over their brethren.

Therefore, in the fear of God, we do most seriously, sincerely, and conscientiously protest against the arbitrary proceedings of those forty-five members as unjust, ungenerous, and unscriptural, and as not being obligatory or binding upon us or the Annual Conferences, or any other free and independent men. And we do also most solemnly protest against the high-toned doctrine set up and advanced: that the episcopacy are to judge of the constitutionality of the proceedings of a General Conference; and that their judgment or opinion is to overthrow, make void, suspend, and put at defiance the decisions and proceedings of a General Conference. And we do further most solemnly protest against the precedent or example of delegates of the Annual Conferences, in General Conference assembled, passively surrendering their own judgments, and implicitly yielding themselves to be controlled, governed, and directed into this or that particular course or measure by the mere dictate or mandate of a bishop or

21

bishops, as though such bishop or bishops were infallible, or as if such delegates had not sagacity, liberty, or independence sufficient to judge for themselves. And we do furthermore protest, in the most solemn and decided terms, against the servile surrender of our rights, liberties, and privileges to any ecclesiastical domination whatever; but that, on the contrary, it is our duty to God, to our brethren, to the Church of Christ, and to ourselves, by all lawful and righteous means, to maintain our rights, liberties, and privileges, civil and religious, as citizens and Christians, in *peace, union, and brotherly kindness, if we possibly can,* but otherwise if we must. And if necessity be forced upon us, "To your tents, O Israel ! "

The excitement occasioned by the rejection of the rule for the election of presiding elders was, in some parts of the Church, very great, notably within the bounds of the Philadelphia, New York, New England, and Genesee Annual Conferences. To gain some idea of the degree of agitation the following documents are inserted. The first is a letter from Bishop George to Rev. Ezekiel Cooper, after the close of the Philadelphia Annual Conference, held in Milford, Del., in May, 1821:

May 20, 1821.

MY DEAR BROTHER: Since we parted at Milford my mind has been frequently and solemnly impressed to ask you one favor in this way, that is, to write my request, that you may memorize it. The favor is this, that you would use your influence in the bounds and among the members of the Philadelphia Conference against a divisive spirit, constantly pleading against partisan doctrines or divisive decisions. For we must clearly see that a division in the Church on this old controverted subject would be like sawing a living man asunder; for it would be tearing the living body of Christ asunder, that is, if the Methodists be living Christians, and by this means separating firm friends and opening a door for endless disputations among those friends who have long labored together, mingling tears with tears, prayers with prayers, sacrifices with sacrifices, to build up the Societies that are now scattered through North America. These suffering, laborious veterans must not be separated: let them live in each other's affections, as did Jonathan and David, and let their mansions be near each other in the house not made with hands. My meaning is this: if the suspended resolution can as peaceably go into operation as it first came in'o existence, let us say Amen; but if a majority of our brethren should say otherwise, let us be ready to acquiesce, believing they have as much right to their opinion as we have.

I conclude with hoping you will comply with my request, and pray for your friend,   ENOCH GEORGE.

P. S. I am not disposed to ask you to disturb any who are at rest, but I am disposed to plead with you to make efforts, if you find them necessary; for there have been some unplesant things said on that subject since General Conference, namely, "that a divison was inevitable." I think there is nothing that demands it.   E. G.

The second is a letter addressed by Bishop McKendree to the several Conferences mentioned, a copy of which was taken by Ezekiel Cooper. It is as follows:

To the Philadelphia. New York, New England, and Genesee Annual Conferences for 1822.

DEAR BRETHREN: I believe the resolutions passed at the last General Conference, authorizing the respective Annual Conferences to elect the presiding elders, are an infringement on the constitution of the Methodist Episcopal Church, nor am I alone in this opinion. Many of the preachers believe the same. One of many reasons in support of this opinion is as follows: It is the duty of a bishop to travel through the work at large, to oversee the spiritual and temporal business of the Church. But to oversee implies power to overrule, or manage business officially; and, from the answer to the third question of the fourth section of the Form of Discipline, on the Duties of a Bishop, taken in connection with the other parts, it evidently follows that the overruling power by which the bishops are enabled to superintend the business of the Church consists in appointing and overruling the preachers, especially the presiding elders, who, on their respective districts are authorized to execute all the powers of the General Superintendents [ordination only excepted]; and, therefore, but for their being under the control of the bishops, they might counteract all their measures and render the General Superintendency a mere name. This power the presiding elder possesses by virtue of his appointment to that office.

The long established Discipline of the Church invests the bishops with the power of choosing the presiding elders; but the resolutions of the last General Conference would invest the Annual Conferences with this power. Admit this change, and no elder could do the du-

310   LIGH

ties of a presiding elder, although appointed by a bishop to a district, unless that appointment was conformable to those resolutions; therefore, the presiding elders evidently derive their executive authority from the Annual Conferences, and not from the bishops, which implies an essential change in our system of government—a change which affects the General Superintendency in its vital parts, and must, therefore, be an infringement on the constitution.

That the delegated General Conference (whose existence is inseparable from the constitution) has no legitimate authority to destroy the itinerant General Superintendency must be admitted; but to transfer the power of choosing presiding elders from the bishops to the Annual Conferences implies power to say the bishops shall neither nominate the presiding elders, station the preachers, nor make any change after they are stationed.

Small, therefore, as the change made by these resolutions is said to be, it includes an increase of power in favor of the delegated Conference, which will enable it to effect changes in our system of government which it does not now possess, and by which ruinous changes might be effected. Preachers of this opinion appear to be inclined to accommodate their brethren who contend for the resolutions, provided the change is constitutionally effected, and an increase of the power of the delegated Conference prevented.

To accommodate and settle this unhappy difference among us, some of the sister Conferences think they have gone far! You are invited to take up the subject, and adopt such measures as will harmonize the body.   Yours respectfully,   W. McKENDREE.

The bishops are hereby requested to lay this before the Conferences.
     Rev. R. R. Roberts, Bishop, M. E. C.   W. McK.

The above letter, directed to Bishop Roberts, was by him laid before the Conferences mentioned in the address, and they severally took action thereupon. That of the Philadelphia and New York Conferences, signed by the secretaries of those bodies, is here given. 1. The Philadelphia Conference:

Whereas, Bishop McKendree in his communication to this Conference has pronounced that the resolutions of the last General Conference relative to the election of presiding elders are, in his belief, an infringement on the constitution of the Methodist Episcopal Church; therefore:

...iction of this Confer-
... makes any infringe-
...tions of our Church.

2. That the Restrictive Regulations do not, in our opinion,
...restrict any changes, alterations, or new modification of
...Episcopal power, or duties; provided such changes or alterations
...do away Episcopacy, nor destroy the plan of our itinerant gen-
...superintendency. Carried unanimously.

True copy, given to N. Bangs. L. LAWRENSON, *Sect.*

The action of the New York Conference was:

Whereas, Bishop McKendree, in his observations addressed to this
Conference, expressed his belief or opinion that the resolutions rel-
ative to the election of presiding elders, passed at the last General
Conference, were unconstitutional, and considering it proper for this
Conference to express some sentiment on the said question thus
introduced by the bishop to our consideration; therefore,

Resolved, 1. That, in the opinion of this Conference, there is nothing in the said resolutions passed by the General Conference that in-
fringes any part of the Constitution of our Church, or that violates
any of the Restrictive Regulations in our Discipline.

Resolved, 2. That, in the opinion of this Conference, there is nothing
in the Restrictive Regulations in our Discipline to prevent any alterations or new modifications of the Episcopal powers and duties, provided such changes do not do away Episcopacy nor destroy the plan
of General Superintendency. L. CLARK.

Thus we have given the history of this subject
which for more than forty years agitated the Church.

ADDENDA.

EARLY METHODISM AND SLAVERY.

THE agency of the Methodist Episcopal Church in the abolishment of slavery in the United States of America has never been duly estimated and set forth, especially in her earlier history, either by our Church historians or by other writers on that subject. It is due to the fact, we think, that the records accessible to them were meagre.

The statements in the Discipline of the Church, and in the Minutes of the Conferences, both General and Annual, are necessarily brief; and, guided by them only, the reader would conclude that the early hostility of the Church to the system was gradually overcome, both among ministers and laymen, and retained in the Discipline and proceedings of the General Conferences more as a formal than a vital principle. We shall, therefore, present a more enlarged view of the great struggle for the emancipation of the colored people in the several States, as waged by our Church, and embracing therein both their spiritual and civil freedom. We begin with the rule passed by the Methodist Conference of 1780, referring the reader to Simpson's Cyclopedia, article "Slavery," for preliminary statements and other valuable information.

In 1780 the Conference Minutes, under the form of questions and answers, presents the following:

Quest. 16. Ought not this Conference to require those traveling preachers who hold slaves to give promises to set them free?
Ans. Yes.

Quest. 17. Does this Conference acknowledge that slavery is contrary to the laws of God, man, and nature, and hurtful to society, contrary to the dictates of conscience and pure religion, and doing that which we would not others should do to us and ours? Do we pass our disapprobation on all our friends who keep slaves, and advise their freedom?

Ans. Yes.

In 1783 appears the following:

Quest. 10. What shall be done with our local preachers who hold slaves contrary to the laws which authorize their freedom in any of the United States?

Ans. We will try them another year. In the meantime let every assistant deal faithfully and plainly with every one, and report to the next Conference. It may then be necessary to suspend them.

In 1784 three questions and answers are given:

Quest. 12. What shall we do with our friends that will buy and sell slaves?

Ans. If they buy with no other design than to hold them as slaves, and have been previously warned, they shall be expelled; and permited to sell on no consideration.

Quest. 13. What shall we do with our local preachers who will not emancipate their slaves in the States where the laws admit it?

Ans. Try those in Virginia another year, and suspend the preachers in Maryland, Delaware, Pennsylvania, and New Jersey.

Quest. 22. What shall be done with our traveling preachers that now are, or hereafter shall be, possessed of slaves, and refuse to manumit them where the law permits?

Ans. Employ them no more.

At the organization of the Methodist Episcopal Church at the close of the year 1784 the following was enacted relative to slavery:

Quest. 41. Are there any directions to be given concerning the negroes?

Ans. Let every preacher, as often as possible, meet them in class. Let the assistant always appoint a proper white person as their leader. Let the assistant also make a regular return to the Conference of the number of negroes in society in their respective circuits.

Quest. 42. What methods can we take to extirpate slavery?

Ans. We are deeply conscious of the impropriety of making new terms of communion for a religious society already established, except on the most pressing occasion; and such we esteem the practice of holding our fellow-creatures in slavery. We view it as contrary to the golden law of God, on which hang all the law and the prophets and the inalienable rights of mankind, as well as to every principle of the revolution, to hold in the deepest debasement, in a more abject slavery than is perhaps to be found in any part of the world except America, so many souls, all capable of the image of God. We, therefore think it our most bounden duty to take immediately some effectual methods to extirpate this abomination from among us; and for that purpose we add the following to the rules of our Society, to wit:

1. Every member of our society who has slaves in his possession shall, within twelve months after notice given to him by the assistant (which notice the assistants are required immediately and without delay to give in their respective circuits), legally execute and record an instrument whereby he emancipates and sets free every slave in his possession who is between the ages of forty and forty-five immediately, or at the furthest, when they arrive at the age of forty-five; and every slave who is between the ages of twenty-five and forty immediately, or at the furthest at the expiration of five years from the date of said instrument; and every slave who is between the ages of twenty and twenty-five immediately, or at furthest when they arrive at the age of thirty; and every slave under the age of twenty as soon as they arrive at the age of twenty-five at furthest; and every infant, born in slavery after the above-mentioned rules are complied with, immediately on its birth.

2. Every assistant shall keep a journal, in which he shall regularly minute down the names and ages of all the slaves belonging to the masters in his respective circuit, and also the date of every instrument executed and recorded for the manumission of the slaves, with the name of the court, book, and folio, in which said instruments respectively shall have been recorded, which journal shall be handed down in each circuit to the succeeding assistants.

3. In consideration that these rules form a new term of communion, every person concerned who will not comply with them shall have liberty quietly to withdraw himself from our society within the twelve months succeeding the notice given as aforesaid; otherwise the assistant shall exclude him in the society.

4. No person so voluntarily withdrawn or so excluded shall ever

partake of the Supper of the Lord with the Methodists till he complies with the above requisitions.

5. No person holding slaves shall in future be admitted into society, or to the Lord's Supper, till he previously complies with these rules concerning slavery.

N. B. These rules are to affect the members of our society no further than as they are consistent with the laws of the States in which they reside.   And respecting our brethren in Virginia that are concerned, and after due consideration of their peculiar circumstances, we will allow them two years from the notice given to consider the expediency of compliance or non-compliance with these rules.

Quest. 43. What shall be done with those who buy or sell slaves, or give them away?

Ans. They are immediately to be expelled, unless they buy them on purpose to free them.

In 1785 the Annual Conferences recommended the suspension of the execution of the above rules " till the deliberations of a future Conference; and that an equal space of time be allowed all our members for consideration, when the minute shall be put in force." But to show the feelings of the societies on the subject, they appended:

N. B. We do hold in the deepest abhorrence the practice of slavery, and shall not cease to seek its destruction by all wise and prudent means.

From this period the Annual Minutes contain no record of the action of those bodies in regard to the civil rights of the colored people, but give expression to their views in regard to their spiritual welfare. Thus we have, in 1787, the following in the Minutes of that year:

Quest. 17. What direction shall we give for the promotion of the spiritual welfare of the colored people?

Ans. We conjure all our ministers and preachers by the love of God and the salvation of souls, and do require them by all the authority that is invested in us, to leave nothing undone for the spiritual benefit and salvation of them within their respective circuits or districts; and for this purpose to embrace every opportunity of inquiring into the state of their souls, and to unite in society those who appear to have a real desire of fleeing from the wrath to come; to meet such in class, and to exercise the whole Methodist Discipline among them.

While in the Conferences, at this period, no additional rules were passed on the subject of slavery, the ministers themselves, for the most part, were active in disseminating the principles of freedom, and in showing from the pulpit and the press the wickedness of American slavery. To illustrate this, in addition to the detail given in this volume, the following extracts from Mr. Cooper's documents will show that he denounced slavery from the press, and boldly challenged the arguments of those who advocated the system of slavery then practiced. Read the following:

For the Maryland Gazette:

Is not liberty the grand American shrine? Freedom is the chief corner-stone of our excellent republic, constitution, and government. Behold upon this basis our flourishing empire fitly raised and united.

The inestimable value of human rights was duly considered in time of our subjection to a foreign power; Americans, free and independent in spirit, believing " freedom the just due of every man," laid claim to their inalienable rights, which no king or nation had right to deprive them of. This claim being denied, our countrymen boldly ventured both fortune and life—they fought, bled, and died—to recover that freedom which is by the law of nature granted to every man, the "just due of every man." We resolved to lose our lives or gain our liberty. And what is life when liberty is gone? 'Tis a servile state of ignominious existence which is little, if any, preferable to death. I marvel that our memories are so treacherous as to forget the noble sentiments and impressions of freedom which inspired our breasts with animated zeal in the time of Britanic oppression. Then, sir, we extended the right of freedom indiscriminately to " every man." Why do we now discriminate, and deny this right to a certain species of the human race? The argument that the " Negroes were providentially intended to be slaves " is a most groundless proposition, and I confess a surprise that any man should ever advance it. The Algerines, with equal propriety, might argue providence in their capturing Europeans and others and condemning them to slavery. I can find neither proof nor reason that a difference in color, features, or hair should distinguish any man as an unhappy subject of bondage. "There were slaves of old," 'tis true, but this no more proves the right of slavery now than the ancient monarchies and despotic powers prove that we should have a despotic monarch to rule with absolute power over us; the argument stands just as good, and defies a gainsaying. Such arguments will not suffice for the sons of liberty; we will leave them for an unenlightened or tyrannized people; neither the one nor the other corresponds with our ideal principles. I wish a consistency in and among all men, civil or religious; a correspondence between principle and practice; and candidly think without it the glory of any man or nation is proportionably eclipsed: incongruity is a disparagement in any case whatever. I blush at the conduct of many who are freemen in principle; have declared for and supported the cause of liberty; and still persist in holding their fellow-creatures in perpetual bondage. I agree that " slaves are a man's property; " his arbitrary but not his just property, and no human law will look upon them as such. The law of nature evidently allows every man his freedom; and certainly any law is inhuman and unjust that counteracts the law of God in nature; hence no just law can entail civil slavery on any part of the human species whatever. You "bought your slaves." True, "this is a hardship;" but on whom? More on the poor slaves than you; I had much rather lose my money than my liberty. He who sold you the slaves had no just right to sell the liberties of men, for he sold the rights which the law of God in nature and our country declare to be the due of those he sold. Is it any argument that I should not recover my property or rights because I have heretofore been unjustly kept out of them? Suppose my father before me was kept unjustly from his rights, and they were sold through various hands: if I can prove my rights, show my heirship and just claim, it would be arbitrary and unjust in any judge or jury not to give the verdict in my favor. And, pray, what rights under heaven are so interesting and desirable as liberty, which every body knows is the due of every man? Here is the poor slave under the despotic authority of his master; 'tis out of his power to get redress; he looks up with sorrow under oppression; dare not speak for himself under pain of many lashes from a merciless, cruel hand; and still we give judgment against the forlorn sufferer, that another shall hold his rights from him and his posterity; and this against the plainest remonstrances that equity and justice, joined with reason and humanity, can give upon the firm principles of inalienable rights in nature's law.

Were we in their predicament, what prayers could we lift to Heaven that our usurpers might only have human compassion! How should we wish some way for redress! We should view ourselves the most cruelly treated. How hard, we should think, the hearts of rulers not to feel for our situation of bondage and misery, and at least to mitigate, if not relieve, our sufferings. To see husbands and wives torn asunder forever; to behold parents and children parted, no more to see each other; transported to distant States or islands, there to languish out their days in sorrow—is enough to shock humanity. O avarice, full of all cruelty, when wilt thou let men feel for others as for themselves? We sing the songs of liberty, which sound to foreign lands. When shall America indeed be a free country? My dear sir, none are so blind as those blinded by the dust of interest, or who will not see. Let every man, if he can, lay his hand upon his heart and appeal to God, conscience, and his country, and say, "Freedom is not the just due of every man." If he does, he must shut his eyes or blush.   A FREEMAN.

ANNAPOLIS, *November* 8, 1790.

The controversy between Mr. Cooper and "A True Friend to the Union," after continuing for some time, was brought to a close by the withdrawal of the latter from the field. Another article will now be given, showing that Mr. Cooper had gained the victory:

For the Maryland Gazette.

TO MY CORRESPONDENT, A FRIEND TO THE UNION: Though you have taken your "leave of the subject," I must beg leave to make a few remarks in answer to your last.

I confess I think it high time for you to give up all appearance of opposition to liberty, and hope no friend to the Union will ever attempt to fasten the iron yoke of bondage on any human creature. He that strikes at liberty strikes at the Constitution and foundation of the Union.

Your apology, or reason for not answering my arguments, stands just for nothing, if I understand "right." Such a side-stroke might, with some propriety, be advanced in favor of the oppressed, who cannot come at their "right between individuals," or any other way, in a domestic or civil sense. Why is not some method "adopted in political government" to remedy this disgraceful evil? Is it the want of power or of will? I conceive they "could," if they "would," empower every man in the State who can show his lawful claim to come at and recover his right; and I am truly sorry that any American should be unwilling to allow every individual his just claim. An Indian or a Negro should have his due; nay! 'tis an old adage, "Give a dog his due." Justice demands it, deny it who can; freedom is the just due of every man, hence 'tis unjust and arbitrary not to grant it.

What do you mean by a "curse metaphorically?" Perhaps you mean it figures out a curse to come; this is more awful and dreadful than as I understood you. Let me, without any appearance of prejudice to or against color, features, or hair, ask: "What kind of freedom would it be, and what right have we to bring it about on exportation?" Sir, we have no right to banish any man unless he has previously violated some law which inflicts this punishment as due for his crime. A contrary sentiment cannot correspond with the idea that all men are born equally free, and stand upon equal ground in point of human rights to liberty. But where would you export them to? They are as much Americans now as we; and we are as much Europeans as they are Africans. Nothing but a mind biased by partiality or prejudice can countermand or contemn this idea or argument. Did you ever read Clarkson's *Essay on the Impolicy of the African Slave-trade, and on the Slavery and Commerce of the Human Species?* If it would have any influence, I would recommend it to you and every friend to his country and fellow-creatures. I think every reader of it must feel for the oppressed, and blush for the oppressor. Be advised by your friend to give that essay an attentive reading if you can procure it.

Probably, my thus writing gives disgust to numbers; but I must adhere to reason, truth, and equity. Any man who will refute my arguments already advanced, and those which I still have to advance, and also offer just reasons on the contrary question, very possibly will make me his proselyte; if I know myself, I am open to conviction upon this or any other subject whatever. Let me not be condemned by those who would wish advocates for freedom to be shot like a squirrel; but if any think me in an error, they should convince me by argument

Your observation, "the press is free," is matter of great pleasure to freemen; the liberties of the people depend in a great measure upon the freedom of the press. Old Guttenberg and Faustus, the inventors of printing in Mentz, should never be forgotten by those who wish the rights and privileges of the people pointed out to the public and defended. Through this medium justice and truth maintain their cause, and error gets the lash of reason and argument.

Gentlemen and free citizens, the greater part, far the greater part of you, cannot disapprove the friendly defense of liberty in favor of a helpless, abject, and almost friendless race. I am stunned with astonishment to think that any should fly in the face of the most equitable principles our country and humane feelings can advance in support of the rights of men. But there is an absurd prejudice which predominates over the minds of members, which will not acknowledge that an Indian or a negro should have justice done them; or that liberty or life is as dear to them as to us.

I cannot think such men ignorantly presume negroes are not men or human creatures; yet they say freedom is the due of all men. Why, then, in the name of common sense or reason, do they contradict themselves, and deny that right to the poor forlorn creatures?

But, to harp a little more on that despicable practice of transporting slaves as chattels to distant parts, making their merchandise of human flesh. I lately had the pleasure of being in company with a respectable gentleman from Charleston, S. C., who informs me that the humane citizens of feeling there are surprised and grieved at the numerous public sales of Negroes from Maryland and elsewhere. Must it not be a tyrannical heart that partakes in such a traffic? Who would not shudder to go on board a vessel where such a cargo was, and there see the streaming eyes, the breaking hearts, the dejected, unintelligent accents of lamentation among men, women, and children—the husband and the wife, the parent and the child, parted by tyranny and avarice, no more allowed to see or speak with their nearest connections forever? Shocking! shocking! And is Maryland guilty of this atrocious scene? Let every man of feeling use his influence to put a period to this shameful practice.

I shall not question my friend for taking his leave of the subject. But I do believe he is convinced of the propriety of my arguments and justice of my cause. Under this impression I shall conclude, hoping the cause of liberty will annually gain numerous friends and advocates.

Liberty is the first star of glory in our Commonwealth; it has much emerged from its total, yet remains under a considerable, eclipse. May Providence hasten the day when despotism and tyranny shall be done away, and this luminary, liberty, be no more obscured by arbitrary power or any other opaque body whatever. So, for the present, I drop anchor, wishing liberty to all, and great glory to America, where I hope ever to claim a title to citizenship as   A FREEMAN.

The bold utterances and unanswerable arguments advanced by Mr. Cooper in behalf of the colored slave in the United States provoked a spirit of wrath in some of those who could not set aside or confute his reasonings; and one of the number, under the signature of "Abaris," attempted by ridicule and low sentiment to express, in verse, the feeling that had been aroused among those opposed to the abolition of slavery. It was published in the *Maryland Gazette,* issued at Annapolis, Md., only a short time previous to Mr. Cooper's change of his ministerial field of labor to Alexandria, Va., which was in the early part of the year 1791. Mr. Cooper replied to the writer in the columns of the same paper; and in some respects struck a more decided blow upon the advocates of human slavery. His reply follows:

For the Maryland Gazette, Annapolis.

MESSRS. GREEN: In your last week's paper I discovered a piece of poetry, doggerel doubly distilled, directed to me, with the signature "A. B. A. R. I. S." Had the performance been any way genteel or considerable, I could consent to address to the author a reply; but as it is an opprobrious subterfuge, I shall only make a few cursory remarks upon his production, and offer them through your impartial press, if you please, to his and my readers.

I mean to make his great signature the text of my present strictures. Abaris signifies "a Scythian, and priest of Apollo," who was endued by that god with the gift of prophecy; and also, by virtue of an arrow or dart given him by Apollo, he traveled swiftly through the air without eating, and gave oracles in all parts." Probably he has prophesied in divining that my "schemes for liberty may be effected in a short time;" though I expect not too soon nor by the "decree of fate," but by the wisdom of civil government, under the providence of God. I am no heathen philosopher, ascribing results to fate, but a professor of the Christian religion.

His whole oracle seems to be delivered while he was flying through
the air, having no argument as a foundation to settle on. It most
certainly is a labyrinth, and a mazy flight; but the virtue of his
arrow or wings fail him before his oracles are spread in all parts. He
should take heed lest his fall proves to be in the "dirt" or "hog-
stye." As to fear of a "hungry belly," by-the-by, "Abaris," we are
told, flies without eating; probably he has engrossed the power of
hunger as he wishes to do the power of equity and reason. I think
would he take a little food of instruction it might add to his prudence,
and enable him to give wiser and better oracles. I have been con-
jecturing, Apollo gave him a crooked arrow or a very blunt dart, as I
see he goes on so slowly and awkwardly; it would take him an age at
his present rate of flying to spread his oracles through the continent
of equitable and reasonable minds. I don't know what success he
might meet in a despotic mind, or country of tyrannical power, where
avarice substitutes prejudice, ambition, and hypothesis for argument,
justice, truth, and reason. Americans should be better informed than
to adhere to such artifices.

He signifies, in his rhymes, that were slaves liberated they would
go in "rags, dirt, be lazy, steal, and court the gallows," but the greatest alarm appears to be the "black wives," which he has properly
thrown under a note of admiration. He ought to know that many
"who've been set free" are industrious, civil people in the circle where
they move. And of the same style of life I think he will find as
Bembo says: "White men be lazy, steal, and come to gallows too."
In a general way they would not steal so much in freedom as in
bondage; some masters press them to it by almost starving them, as
is frequently the case, though not so general as formerly, giving them
five or six ears of corn a day for their whole support, and no time
to grind and cook that but as taken from the hours allotted for sleep!
If one out of twenty should steal, they are all branded with the epithet
of "rogue;" and, poor creatures, if ever so honest or innocent, they
can get no redress nor have their character retrieved. In the greatest sufferings, and under the greatest reproaches, having no character
to gain or lose, I have wondered they were not worse than they are!
Had they liberty, the case would be different; they would have a
character to think of, and interest would stir them up to industry.
There is certainly a better principle in them than Abaris is aware of.
The laws of the land would rule and keep them in civil order equally
with the whites in the same sphere of life; and as they improved,
which they are capable of doing, would still shine in society more and

more respectably. I am very sure, Abaris himself is not half a match for Phillis Wheatley (a Negro girl) in poetry; her poems are published to the world, and are worth reading.

I am probably as much principled against the whites taking "black wives" or husbands as Abaris himself. My sons and daughters "shall be better taught;" I hope his will, also; then we need not fear from that quarter. If that is ever the case, which may be, the whites and not the blacks will be to blame; they will never be compelled to intermarry; it must be a low choice of their own. Let us not blame the innocent, but the guilty.

I think my friend Abaris had better never appear again till he has arguments to defend his opinions or refute those he comes forth against, unless he resolves to be slain by Perseus, which was the lot of old Abaris. Perseus also delivered Andromeda from a sea monster that would have devoured her. May Liberty, like that fair daughter of Cephas, be delivered from Tyranny, that huge sea-monster!

I have no desire of another poem from my correspondent, unless he first learns better how to compose it, and on some argument, too, that may be worth reading. Nevertheless, be assured I am not offended, but am ready to receive, at any time, a friendly letter from him (he may change his signature, if he pleases); but should he descend from gentility to groveling, I shall take but little notice of him, further than, even then, to be his friend and well-wisher in all equitable cases; and, were he in bondage, would as freely rescue him from unjust slavery if I could as I would liberty from tyranny, or as Perseus did Andromeda from the sea monster.

I am, still, A FREEMAN.

Mr. Cooper had been in his new charge in Alexandria, Va., but a few months before he felt called upon to use the public press in giving utterance to his sentiments against Negro slavery. We present the following letters, the first written for the *Maryland Journal,* the second, for the *Virginia Gazette:*

ALEXANDRIA, *April* 18, 1791.

MESSRS. GODDARD AND ANGELL: In your *Journal* of the 12th instant I discover a piece with the signature "Lawyer," in justification of slavery and opposition to liberty. I wish to make a few cursory remarks on that gentleman's essay, and if you please, to

22

offer them through the medium of your press to the candid consideration of those who are interestedly or consciously concerned upon the subject of slavery.

If Lawyer was in the predicament of a slave, no doubt his opinion would be as far from its present state as liberty is from bondage. The farmer's observation, that "opinions change with circumstances," is very just. Truth and justice compose the standard for a due judgment, and not our secular interest and prejudices. We seldom hear any but slaveholders, or those under their influence, oppose the equity of enfranchising the abject sufferers under bondage. This is a clear demonstration that they are more influenced by interest and prejudice than by reason, truth, and justice. Indifferent men are universally acknowledged to be the most eligible judges in all cases of equity, they not being biased by self-interest. Though, indeed, the cause of liberty is so plain that judicious, candid slaveholders generally acknowledge slavery to be a violation of human rights.

I am surprised at Lawyer that he should fly to the Holy Scriptures (the very book which teaches us the eternal rule of justice) in order to vindicate the violation of the law of God in nature, and thereby strive to justify men in their arbitrary despotism over the rights and liberties of their fellow-creatures. This is the very book, gentlemen, that teaches us to "do unto all men as we would wish they should do unto us." It teaches us to let the oppressed go free, and shows unto us the danger of oppression. See Eccles. iv, 1; Isa. i, 17; Prov. xxiv, 31.) Numerous texts could readily be brought in favor of this cause. But to return to Lawyer's arguments. He certainly did not reflect that, since bond-servants were allowed of as slaves in Scripture, the dispensation of God's people is changed. Those to whom he alludes were under the Mosaic, but we are under the Christian, dispensation. Christ, when he came, expounded the spirituality of the law, and clearly showed that many things which were vindicated by the letter were done away by the spirit. See his sermon upon the Mount, also various other parts of the New Testament, especially the gospels. Some things were allowed of, by reason of the hardness of their hearts and the wickedness of the people, which were not so intended from the beginning nor so intended to the end, the evil of which is fully manifested by the glorious light of the Gospel.

Would Lawyer presume to vindicate the customs of ancient times as justifiable now? Would he say that the laws or rules of the Jews, in the letter, should be enforced now? Then we must have a king as well as a slave. God allowed them to have monarchs—not that monarchy or slavery was providentially intended from the beginning. Had the people conducted themselves right, they would have been happy without a king or a slave. They took "the heathen round about," and "made them bondmen and bondmaids." But who were those heathen? Were they Negroes? I apprehend Negroes were not round about Palestine or Judea, but far off in distant parts of Africa. If Negroes were "the progeny of Canaan," it could hardly be the offspring of Canaan here made bondmen of; and if those bondmen were Canaan's posterity, which the Jews took round about them, then the Negroes must be another race. Probably the bondmen and bondmaids were in part the children of Abraham instead of Canaan. Esau's posterity served Jacob's. Where did Ishmael's descendants reside? Is Lawyer certain that those "slaves" were not from Abraham through Ishmael or Esau? If not, his argument is not worth a straw. How does he know but himself or many worthy citizens are the offspring of Ishmael or Esau? Upon conjecture the Algerines or others might plead the lawfulness of enslaving us; and how should we disprove their plea, but that no one part of the human race has a right to enslave another? Let the ancient customs be what they might, and occasioned by this or that circumstance, this is no plea of justification to us in the open rebellion against the law of God in nature. Now, we are to adhere to truth, justice, humanity, and reason. Our countrymen have long declared "freedom to be the just due of every man." All truly human laws agree with the law of nature in every thing consistent with society; both correspond with the divine law in the equitable principles of granting every man his just due, which includes "freedom." Unjust or inhuman laws, hypotheses, and despotism, should never influence our minds to consent that nature's just law is not to be regarded.

Had Lawyer the eloquence of a Demosthenes or Cicero he would even then find it a hard task to justify the injustice of slavery, and convince Americans that freedom is not their due equally with all human kind.

Gentlemen, upon what principles could Lawyer reconcile himself and posterity to be doomed to endless slavery? The thought of being led captive in hard bondage makes nature recoil. Our feelings shudder when we think of many who are toiling their lives away at the galleys in Algiers. But we lose sensation when we think of the poor blacks in the most cruel bondage. Have these poor creatures no friends to sympathize with their distresses? The same that wounds and pains us, wounds and pains them. All our feelings are in them. Behold them toiling, sweating, fainting, bleeding, and dying under the iron rod of oppression! Will no one speak a word for those who dare not and cannot speak for themselves? O compassion, awake in the breasts of men! O justice and mercy, plead the cause of the afflicted and oppressed! A STUDENT.

Mr. Cooper failed not to maintain the above principles, in advocacy of freedom for the colored people of the United States, both publicly and in private; and in so doing awakened in some a spirit of opposition, which at length was publicly manifested by one of the leaders of the opposition, who boasted that "he was able to defend slavery against any man."

Immediately Mr. Cooper challenged him to come forth to meet him in controversy, and, on the 17th of November, published an article in the *Virginia Gazette*, wherein he set forth "that it would be a difficult matter for any one to defend the principles of slavery upon reason or justice." To this a reply was made, in the same paper of the following week, under the signature of "Love Truth," which brought forth from Mr. Cooper the following answer:

For the Virginia Gazette.

TO MR. LOVE TRUTH:

SIR: You observed in the last *Gazette* that my "piece of the 15th inst., seemed to be aimed at somebody, yet thought it was Mr. Nobody's business to answer it." Then how came you to step into Mr. Nobody's shoes, and do his work? O! but you give me to understand that it is because the shoe fits you. Inasmuch as you "unfortunately differ with me on the subject of slavery," and are fearful that I, without an answer, "might get wise in my own conceit," you come forth, wondrously, to humble me. I am thankful to be kept humble; but I wanted wisdom also. I wished to have provoked the pen of "somebody" to have come forth and taught his countrymen the justice of slavery; to have shown us wherein it consists with equity, reason, human rights, philosophy, or religion. You have made a pompous stroke in your reply; but O, sir! you have not rent the veil of ignorance; you have not overset my mistake or supposed error in liberty; nor established somebody's self-confident truth in slavery; no, not by a single argument. Your address to me appears. principally, to be a composition of words darkening counsel without knowledge.

If you were apprehensive I "might be wise in my own conceit," why did not you, or Mr. Somebody to aid you, show the fallacy of my proposition: "Freedom the just due of every man!" I apprehend it would be a hard task for me to prevent, by many answers, your being wise in your own conceit, and as to Mr. Somebody, a Paine or a Newton cannot prevent his own conceited wisdom.

You have "heard it somewhere positively asserted, that if the effect be good, the cause that produced it must be good also." And do you affirm the contrary? Why did you not show us, or the person who advanced it, his error? I have heard it, as an indisputable truth, that a corrupt tree cannot bring forth good fruit; and that "all good effects spring from God as the productive cause;" and that "God is the author of all good. Now, can you prove that any moral good springs from an evil cause? If you can, or "Mr. Somebody" to aid you, I shall gladly see your proofs, reasonings, and arguments. But. sir, if you write again, let us have some kind of argument, either to prove that I am wrong or that you are right. Sarcastic warmth will never do honor to you, or your cause, neither stand in the place of argument. By so doing, you will never convince me that it is consistent with justice, charity, or reason to deprive a human being of his inalienable rights any more than to deprive you of your most lawful profession.

If you can prove clearly that civil and domestic slavery is right, then I am sure kings and bishops, in civil monarchy and ecclesiastical hierarchy, as well as the doctrine of passive obedience and nonresistance, may bring in their despotic claims.

Sir, I shall leave you at present. I assure you, I am your friend; and were you in Algiers, in Africa, under the toil of bondage, and were your children to be subject, after you, to perpetual slavery, to fatigue and labor under task-masters from day to day till death relieved your pain and set you free from such affliction. I would as warmly plead your right of liberty and wish the iron yoke broken off from your neck; I would as gladly see you free in the enjoyment of your natural rights as any others. And why should not Africans in America have their right as well as Americans in Africa? State the case closely, and do not all your feelings recoil at the thought?

Then we will close the subject. Do unto all as you would they should do unto you. This is the most infallible law or rule of equity.

    I am still, and hope to remain,   A FREEMAN.

    November 28, 1791.

As the legislation of the Methodist Episcopal Church on this grave subject has been fully set forth in her Discipline, and the action of her General Conferences been given by her historians, from time to time, the reader is referred to them for information on this branch of the subject; while it shall be our work to mark the facts connected with the internal developments of the opposition raised in certain quarters by the persistent cry of the faithful ministry of the Church, freedom is the right of every man.

It will be seen by reference to Stevens's *History of the Methodist Episcopal Church* * that Rev. Ezekiel Cooper proposed, in the General Conference of 1800, "that a committee be appointed to prepare an affectionate address to the Methodist Societies in the United States, stating the evils of the spirit and practice of slavery, and the necessity of doing away the evil as far as the laws of the respective States will allow; and that the said address be laid before the Conference for their consideration, and, if agreed to, be signed by the bishops in behalf of the Conference." The committee was appointed, the address prepared, adopted by the General Conference, and sent forth. It provoked great resentment in Charleston, S. C., leading to the following movements of the enemies of the Methodist Episcopal Church in that city, and of the defenders of her legislation against slavery. First appeared the rector of Trinity Protestant Episcopal Church in a note to the *Charles on Times:*

---

* *History of the Methodist Episcopal Church*, vol. iv, p. 176.

MESSRS. COX & SHEPPARD: You are requested to inform the public, through the medium of the *Times*, that Trinity Church, in Hazel Street, is not under the jurisdiction of Dr. Coke or Bishop Asbury, and is not nor ever was connected with the Methodist meeting in Cumberland Street. I deem this information necessary, in consequence of some recent transactions in that meeting-house, and which at present very properly interests the public mind, lest a similarity of names should confound the innocent with the guilty.

P. MATHEWS, *Minister of Trinity Church.*

October 28.

To this, one of the Methodist ministers immediately replied:

MESSRS. COX & SHEPPARD:

GENTLEMEN: I desire through the medium of your paper to join issue with the Rev. P. Mathews, in assuring the public at large that there is no connection between Trinity Church and the Methodist Episcopal Church in Cumberland Street, and must add, at the same time, that I should esteem the opinion of there being any connection between them as a more serious injury than the transient displeasure of a misinformed, but otherwise a generous, populace.

GEORGE DOUGHARTY.

CHARLESTON, *October* 29, 1800.

The Rev. Mr. Dougharty had prior to this suffered from the violence of a mob, and a more particular account thereof will soon be given in a letter from the Rev. John Harper, the colleague of Mr. Dougharty, to Ezekiel Cooper. Such was the excitement that Mr. Harper was constrained to make a sworn deposition in regard to the whole affair, in so far as he was connected with it. We give it entire, together with his annotations thereon.

To the Public.

In order to do away the prejudices of the public, the following statement of facts is humbly submitted to their perusal:

That late in the month of June last, or early in July, to the best of my knowledge, on being informed that his honor the intendant of this City was in possession of an address, sent out by the General Conference of the ministers of the Methodist Episcopal Church, assembled in the city of Baltimore in May last, I forthwith went to the intendant, accompanied by a friend, and desired to see the said address, which he, the intendant, showed me. That this was the first time I knew that such an address was composed or circulated. That soon after I asked Mr. Timothy, printer, if he had seen such an address, who told me that he had; that some weeks before it had been in many of the newspapers which he had received from the northward, and, having found one of the papers which contained the address, he gave it to me. That I did not know that I should ever have seen the address in any other way than in newspapers, until about the 8th of September, when I received several boxes of new books from Philadelphia, and on opening some of them I found a few printed copies of the above-mentioned address. That as I had seen one copy of it (the address) in a newspaper in possession of the intendant, and another in a newspaper which Mr. Timothy gave me, and as Mr. Timothy told me that many of them had come in newspapers from the northward, and as I supposed that many of the inhabitants of this city were subscribers for the Northern newspapers, who would, of course, see the address, I did not think it criminal or wrong to give away a few copies of it to persons whom I believed to be persons of prudence and respectability. That on the 22d instant the intendant asked me whether I had any more copies of the address in my possession. I told him I did not know; that there were some boxes of books which I had not opened, and that there might be some copies of the address in them. The intendant then proposed waiting upon me at a convenient time, when I might open the boxes in his presence. I told him if he would come in I would open them immediately. He came in, and I opened the boxes in his presence and found, I suppose, six or eight sheets of the above-mentioned address. I did not count them. The intendant said he thought they ought to be destroyed. I replied: Sir, if you think proper, we will walk back and burn them. He (the intendant) then went with me into the kitchen, carrying the said addresses in his hand, and cast them into the fire, reserving only one or two copies for his own use. That I never showed or read the above-mentioned address to any black or colored person whatsoever, nor do I know of any member of the Methodist Episcopal Church who has showed or read it to any black or colored persons.

That whatever my sentiments may be on the subject of the address,

I have ever thought it my duty in my intercourse with slaves to inculcate humility, submission, diligence, and faithfulness, as duties becoming their station, and calculated to render them safe and happy; nor have I ever desired to see that which the address recommends carried into effect by any other than lawful, honorable, and innocent means, and not by mobs, tumults, insurrections, or any means of so unhappy a tendency.   JOHN HARPER.

Sworn before me, this 30th of October, 1800.

CHARLES TEW, J. P.

Following the deposition above given, Mr. Harper says:

The public will observe from the above statement of facts, 1. That I was not present at the framing of this address. 2. That it was in circulation in this city in public newspapers before I knew that any such address existed. 3. That it is more than probable that as the address was circulated in the Northern newspapers, they were received by sundry persons in this city, besides his honor the intendant, and Mr. Timothy. I add, 4thly, that I am authorized to say, and I shall name my authority when lawfully required so to do, that a gentleman in this city received a number of the addresses from the northward and distributed them, and that they were in circulation during the week of the election; and further, that a number of them were carried to a public coffee-house in this city and distributed among a number of gentlemen who were assembled there.

Now, I ask the candid and discerning citizens of Charleston if these addresses have been received by so many persons from the north-ward, beside myself, and put into the hands of so many of the citizens, what assurance have these citizens given that they have made no imprudent use of them? and whether any such assurance has been demanded of them? I ask, further, what justice or mercy is there in singling out one individual and holding him up as the object of public indignation and popular rage, when others who have done the same thing are suffered to pass unnoticed?

I would entreat those who have manifested the greatest zeal against me to put themselves for a moment in my place, and consider what would be their feelings if they were circumstanced as I am. I am almost a stranger in this city, although not in the city of Baltimore; I have a wife and six children, the eldest of whom is not yet eleven years, and the youngest not five weeks old. In this city are the means of our sustenance. I must be destitute of all the feelings of a man if I am not interested in its tranquillity and happiness; nor can I consider an attempt to rob me of the good will of its inhabitants (on which, under God, I am dependent for my peace and safety, and in a great measure for the necessaries and comforts of life) in any other light than as one of the greatest acts of cruelty that can possibly be exercised upon one. The prayer of my heart is, that God may forgive those who have attempted it; and if ever they are strangers in a strange land, may they meet with those who know the heart of a stranger and not with the sons of cruelty and violence.

October 25.   JOHN HARPER.

We now give Mr. Harper's letter to Mr. Cooper:

DEAR BROTHER: The five boxes of books by Captain Wheland and three by Captain Sweetzer came safe to hand, but still we are in great want of hymn books. I believe you cannot send us too many of them. You will have a good remittance from Brother Blanton after our Conference.

We have lately had a good deal of trouble on account of the address from the General Conference on the subject of emancipation. My house was beset on the 22d of last month by, I suppose, two hundred angry men, with a lawyer of note at their head, who uttered great threats. The Sunday night following, after preaching, and after I had come out of the church and was on my way home, I was encompassed with a numerous band of the "Champions of Liberty," but was defended from the effects of their rage by some friends, who now bear the marks of hard blows as the effect of their interposition. The next evening, Monday, there was a public prayer-meeting. I was not present, and but few of our friends attended. After it was over the mob got hold of Brother Dougharty, struck him, threw him down, dragged him to a pump and pumped water on him. The two following days appearances grew more and more threatening. False reports were industriously propagated which induced me to publish in the papers of last Friday a vindication of my conduct, which I enclose to you with Mr. Mathews's attack and Brother Dougharty's repulse, which is all the newspaper work we have had. Before I published my vindication, it was the general opinion of my friends that I ought to remove from this place in order to preserve my life. I had made up my mind to do so, and expected to have my affairs arranged so as to have taken a passage for myself and family with

Captain Sweetzer, so that if the Lord had not stilled the madness of the people, instead of seeing this paper you would have seen me with a very numerous train. However, I know not how it will be with us. I believe the storm is not yet over. Although my enemies are partly silenced on the subject of the address, yet their attention is turned to that part of the Discipline which respects slavery, and to Mr. Rice's address to the Convention of Kentucky.

These books have been read in the City Council, and it is known that I have circulated them. They are said by the highest authority to be highly inimical to the tranquillity of the country. Some magistrates of the highest respectability have given it as their opinion that we need not expect peace in this State unless we abjure our principles respecting slavery contained in the form of Discipline. There is one striking peculiarity in this contest. I have done something very bad, yet my bitterest enemies dare not lay it before the public, to let them see how bad it is, nor dare I, in my defense—so that lookers-on know not what we are fighting about.

It is the general opinion that if Mr. Asbury comes here it will be at the peril of his life; and I think so, too, unless the mountain is covered with horses of fire and chariots of fire. I thank you for the kind offer you made of your services, and I expect I will before long make use of it. My kind love to sister Dickins and family. I remain, dear brother,

Yours affectionately,   J. HARPER.

The address referred to in the above letter contained the action of the General Conference of 1800, and was issued from the Methodist Book Concern in Philadelphia in tract form, and was circulated through the Societies in all the States. The enemies of the Church in the South also circulated these tracts, and provoked opposition to the spiritual as well as civil welfare of the colored people. An illustration of this is given in the action of the civil authority of the city of Richmond, Virginia, in 1802, whereby the blacks were denied the privilege of attending the Sabbath evening services held by the Methodists. The account is taken from a letter written by the Rev. Alexander McCaine, the pastor of the Methodist Episcopal Church in Richmond for that year, addressed to the Rev. George Roberts, then stationed in Philadelphia. He says:

To my dear Brother Roberts: When we were about parting last spring, I remember there was something said about writing on both sides. Hitherto I have postponed it, as I had nothing agreeable to relate. When I came here I found a small, disorderly Society—a small congregation of a Sunday, and at night not more than four or five whites to begin with. It was not long before I was obliged to stop some and expel others. This brought on me the lash of tongues, and from within and without I had not peace, I may say, for one day. Methodism was despised by the great, complained against to the civil magistrates by the middle, and persecuted and stoned by the lower classes. They have striven by every method to stop our night meetings, but in vain; and after repeated complaints to the mayor of the city, he came, and to Brother Coulling spoke against it, calling it "abominable enthusiasm," etc. But when he found he could not scare us to desist, nor legally prevent it, he said he would stop the blacks, and if there were five people of color after dark in our meeting he would fine me and the rest three dollars per head, or I must receive thirty lashes on the bare back. Being invited, the next Sunday afternoon he came to hear me, and before him I forbade the blacks from coming, as there was a law against it. Such a place I never was in before; the collections, public and private, for a long time would not near pay my board. However, I hope to scuffle along, and sometimes I think I will see better days. I am encouraged the more as these disturbances in and out of Society have, I trust, come to a head. Many have been turned out, and now I hope their places will be filled up by those who by a steady continuance in well-doing will put to silence the ignorance of foolish men.

I have, thank God, enjoyed health since I came here. I hope you and yours have been equally blessed in the midst of sickness. I think I feel nothing but a desire to live and die for God. O, brother, pray for me; I need the prayers of all. Give my love to Sister Roberts. Write to me, if you please.

I remain, yours affectionately,   Alexander McCaine.

September 29, 1802.

We shall close this chapter with an Ode on Slavery, designed for publication, and sent to Ezekiel Cooper with that intent. Though written by J. P. more than

eighty years ago, and therefore neither new nor polished, it deserves a place in the historic annals of the
Church. We give a portion of the poem, withholding
the full name of the author. He says:

> When first I crossed the wide Atlantic main
> And sought Columbia's happy shore to gain,
> A land of peace and freedom I expected,
> Where none of Adam's race would be neglected;
> For on Britannia's plains I heard the sound,
> Through all the Eastern climes it echoed round,
> That in America all men were free:
> Thus stood the firm Congressional decree.
>
> But soon I saw the truth which Homer sings,
> That principle and practice are two things;
> For tho' the maxim stands, All men are free,
> In practice they declare, It shall not be.
>
> A race of men who lived in peace before,
> By cruel hands are dragged from Afric's shore,
> And in America are doomed to dwell
> In chains, by old Apollyon forged in hell.
> Nor is this all. Their children (yet unborn)
> Are doomed to cruel bondage in their turn;
> The whip, the scourge, the scanty pittance meet;
> And cringe beneath an overseer's feet!
>
> With grief I saw how they were bought and sold:
> The wife, the child, the husband, young and old,
> Without distinction they are doomed to pain,
> And drag through life the horrid, slavish chain!
> 'Twould far surpass the wisdom of a man
> The full extent of all their grief to scan;
> Their bitter anguish, pain, and deep distress
> The powers of eloquence cannot express!
>
> Suppose thyself reduced to such a state,
> And bound through life to drudge both soon and late;
> Suppose thy loving wife torn from thy side,
> Thy children sold to feed another's pride!
> With hunger, cold, and nakedness to spend
> Their wretched lives, till life itself should end—

Say, would not such a scene be worse than death,
And make you wish you ne'er had drawn your breath?
And are they men?   Like us the very same!
For from one stock the different branches came;
Alike susceptible of joy and grief,
Of ease and pain, of misery and relief!
Why then should kindred dust be so abused?
Of all the sweets of social life refused,
Why should a part of Adam's fallen race
Reduce their brethren under such disgrace?
Is it because their color is not white
That they're deprived of every human right?
Or do their sable numbers so increase
That policy prohibits their release?

'Twas thus the Israelites in Pharaoh's land
Were made to groan beneath the tyrant's hand,
Till Moses, at Jehovah's word, arose,
Divinely taught to vindicate their cause!
See how the venerable man of God
Approaches Egypt's monarch with his rod;
Behold him stand! and numerous signs are given
To prove his mission is derived from heaven!

But hardened Pharaoh, with his hostile band,
Will neither hear, nor own Jehovah's hand;
They cry, " We don't the God of Israel know,
And, therefore, will not let the people go."
(Now, as there's nothing new beneath the sun,
So slavery prevails as it begun;
For sure, if men the God of Israel knew,
They'd render unto every man his due.)
But stand and see the terrors of the Lord,
When once he takes and whets his glittering sword!
Their streams and stagnant pools are turned to blood,
And all the land in deep confusion stood!
The fly, the pestilence, the fire, and hail,
With horror through the land of Ham prevail;
His tenfold judgments spread the dread alarm,
And Israel 's freed by an Almighty arm!

Now God is good, the true eternal Pan !
Alike benevolent to every man ;
He sees distress with pity's softest eye,
And with compassion hears the mourner cry.

And shall the men who fought in freedom's cause
So basely violate her sacred laws ?
And shall not God, the holy, just, and wise,
To plead the cause of innocence arise ?
He hath a controversy with the land ;
His armies stand arranged at his command ;
The fly, the pestilence, the brandished sword,
Proclaim the awful terrors of the Lord !
Afflictions rise not merely from the dust,
But plagues are sent to punish the unjust ;
Who will not own their day of visitation
Must meet his anger in their desolation !

America ! be wise ; revere the rod ;
Break off thy sins, and turn to Jacob's God.
Who knows but he, whose anger seems to burn,
May from the fierceness of his anger turn.
Arise betimes, and break off every yoke,
Let go the oppressed before you feel his stroke ;
For he who captive leads must captive be,
And he who freedom gives shall be made free.

You who profess to love the Lord indeed,
Who are from sin and Satan's bondage freed,
Will you refuse to let the captive go,
As if you did not Israel's Saviour know ?
The man who did ten thousand talents owe
His lord forgave, and let the debtor go ;
But when his fellow-servant he abused
His lord was wroth, and further grace refused.

So will the sovereign Lord of earth and skies
Deal by the men who mercy's rules despise ;
For judgment without mercy they shall know
Who to their fellow-dust no mercy show !

CPSIA information can be obtained at www.ICGtesting.com
Printed in the USA
LVOW132103220412

278410LV00004B/13/A